UNCERTAIN MANDATE

Politics of the U.N. Congo Operation

REPUBLIC OF THE CONGO
The Six Provinces as of July, 1960

UNCERTAIN MANDATE

Politics of the U.N. Congo Operation

Ernest W. Lefever

The Johns Hopkins Press, Baltimore, Maryland

To Margaret, David, and Bryce

Contents

Table of Appendixes

Preface

Since World War II, international peace has been threatened or breached a hundred times by brush fire conflict in the Third World. But only once has the United Nations intervened with a militarily significant force—in the Congo in 1960. The U.N. Command in Korea was essentially a U.S. operation with the sanction of the Security Council and the General Assembly. In Kashmir, the Gaza Strip, and Cyprus, a small number of U.N. military personnel were sent to patrol an existing truce. In the Congo there was no truce to police and no line to patrol. It was not even clear who the adversaries were.

Precipitated by the abrupt and premature withdrawal of Belgian authority, the Congo's turbulence was almost wholly internal. Though the crisis did not present a self-evident threat to international peace, the Security Council, with unprecedented haste, authorized Dag Hammarskjold to dispatch a multinational force to the heart of Africa. This was made possible by a massive U.S. airlift. For the first four years of its independence, the Congo was the grudging host to this foreign legion of 15,000 men and officers from thirty countries.

The U.N. Mission to the Congo was by far the largest, most complex, most costly, and most controversial operation ever managed by the secretariat of an international organization. As such, it is rich in irony and paradox. Sent to contain a local crisis, the mission magnified the crisis and compounded the political conflict by internationalizing the Congo. At the same time, the U.N. presence muted the violence of the adversaries. Designed to insulate the Congo from the Cold War, the mission insured that the Cold War would be waged there, but under constraints that furthered the interests of the United States and frustrated the interests of the Soviet Union.

The Security Council simultaneously instructed the Force to be neutral in the internal Congolese struggle and to take sides against Moise Tshombe, Katanga's secessionist leader. It repeatedly called for the expulsion of the small number of Belgian military personnel who were assisting Katanga, and authorized the use of force for this purpose. But the same Council never condemned or took action against the tangible military assistance provided by the Soviet bloc and Red China to the Stanleyville rebels in 1964 who were a greater threat to the political integrity of the Congo than secessionist Katanga.

The present political analysis of the U.N. Congo peacekeeping mission is based on the premise that the multinational effort did not suspend internal or international politics, but rather provided an additional instrument to be used, manipulated, or ignored by the governments who had, or imagined they had, a stake in the outcome of the Congo crisis. As a supplement to and not a substitute for traditional efforts by states to influence events in the Congo, the U.N. Mission did not preclude diplomatic representation or covert political activity. The normal struggle of power and interest, pressure and persuasion, assistance and advice, persisted and was only slightly inhibited by the legal constraints imposed by the Security Council and the actual presence of the large and obvious U.N. establishment in the Congo.

The behavior of the great powers, Belgium, the Afro-Asian states, and other governments, as well as of factions within the Congo, toward the U.N. Mission, is examined in terms of their political interests and objectives. The accomplishments and failures of the mission are assessed in terms of the Security Council mandate, the expectations of the supporting states, and the political cost of the effort, all in light of possible alternative ways of managing the Congo crisis. While the major focus is on political analysis, considerable attention is given to the legal, administrative, and military aspects of U.N. intervention.

This book draws heavily upon information and insights gained in three research projects directed by the author during the past six years. The first (Study DAIS conducted at the Institute for Defense Analyses for the Department of Defense and completed in 1963) deals broadly with the role of international military forces and only incidentally with the Congo. The second is a book, *Crisis in the Congo*, published by the Brookings Institution in 1965; it emphasizes the U.S. contribution to the peacekeeping mission. The third is a report, *United Nations Peace-keeping in the Congo: 1960–1964: An Analysis of Political, Executive, and Military Control*, prepared at Brookings for the U.S. Arms Control and Disarmament Agency (ACDA) and submitted in 1966.

Among those whose help I would like to acknowledge at the Institute for Defense Analyses are James E. King, Jr., Major General John B. Cary, USAF, Ret., Robert A. Gessert, Lester G. Hawkins, and Eric Stevenson. At the Brookings Institution, I am indebted to H. Field Haviland, Jr., Robert E. Asher, Ruth B. Russell, and Wynfred Joshua who was my research associate on the ACDA project. Miss Joshua worked mainly on the role of Britain, France, and Belgium. Lieutenant Colonel Austin W. Bach, USA, Ret., the military consultant on the ACDA study, also deserves mention. A special word of appreciation is due Robert E. Osgood, director of the Washington Center of Foreign Policy Research of The Johns Hopkins University, who was a consultant on the three preceding projects, and who encouraged me to undertake this book.

Outside of scholarly circles, I am indebted to perhaps three hundred men of practical affairs in the United States, and in two dozen countries of Europe, Asia, and Africa who talked with me—some more freely than others—about their role in the Congo drama and their views on its larger significance. These include U.N. officials, past and present; diplomats; statesmen; and military officers. I can mention only a few here. First, are three former U.S. ambassadors to the Congo: Clare H. Timberlake, Edmund A. Gullion, and G. McMurtrie Godley, and three former U.S. consuls in Elisabethville, now Lumumbashi:[1] Lewis Hoffacker, Jonathan Dean, and Arthur Tienken. Four American military officers have been especially helpful: Colonel Knut Raudstein, USA, Lieutenant Colonel Harold D. Asbury, USA, former military attaché and assistant attaché in Leopoldville, now Kinshasa; and Colonel Clarence Nelson, USA, and Colonel Arthur B. Swan, USAF, formerly with the U.S. Mission to the United Nations. Since this book depends in part on interviews, most of which were on a nonattribution basis, the precise source is not given in certain footnotes.

---

[1] On July 1, 1966, the names of major cities in the Congo were Africanized. Leopoldville became Kinshasa, Elisabethville became Lubumbashi, Stanleyville became Kisangani, etc. In this book, which covers the period to mid-1964, only the original names are used.

As a modest gesture of appreciation, I have dedicated this book to my wife and two young sons who have accepted with commendable patience my absence during three field trips to the Congo and elsewhere, as well as my long hours at the office while I was at home.

The views expressed in this book are mine and do not purport to be those of my present or former colleagues, or of other persons consulted in this or earlier projects.

Ernest W. Lefever

September, 1967
The Brookings Institution
Washington, D.C.

UNCERTAIN MANDATE

Politics of the U.N. Congo Operation

1.

Internationalizing the Congo Crisis

On July 4, 1960, the Congo's fifth day of independence from Belgium, a handful of Congolese soldiers in Leopoldville mutinied. This largely local and isolated disturbance in the barracks of Camp Leopold II, unlike the similar unrest in Tanganyika three-and-one-half years later, was not contained. Unchecked, it became the prelude to a tragicomic drama of chaos and conflict that involved the great powers and a score of other states for four turbulent years.

Under the impact of rapidly unfolding events, the rich and strategically located Congo became the uncertain stage of the largest field operation ever authorized and managed by the United Nations or any other international organization.[1] From July, 1960 through June, 1964, the U.N. Peacekeeping Force in the Congo (UNF) drew upon 93,000 men and officers from 34 states who provided 675,000 man-months of service. At its height, the Force numbered almost 20,000. The total cost was $411 million. The recruiting, supplying, and commanding of an improvised and multinational force of this size in the heart of Africa was for four years the chief preoccupation of the U.N. Secretariat, and placed a severe strain on the administrative structure and financial resources of the organization.

If the Congo operation was unprecedented in size and scope, it was also unsurpassed in the controversy it precipitated in the press, the chambers of the United Nations, and in the chancelleries of the world.

---

[1] The Korean operation, nominally under the U.N. command, and involving military assistance from twenty-two governments, was initiated, planned, managed, and largely financed by the United States. When President Harry S Truman's initiative was endorsed in the Security Council on June 27, 1950, due to the absence of the Soviet delegate, the operation gained the moral approval of that body. In legal terms, the United States could be called the executive agent of the United Nations in Korea. See Ruth B. Russell, *United Nations Experience With Military Forces: Political and Legal Aspects* (Washington: Brookings Institution Staff Paper, 1964), pp. 24–43.

Many questions of consequence can be asked about this hotly debated peacekeeping experiment. Was the operation legally authorized
and conducted? Did the Secretary-General exceed his Security Council
mandate? How effectively did the mission serve its multiple objectives?
How efficient was the operation? The present book is not addressed
primarily to these questions, though each of them will be treated in
passing.

This study focuses rather on the politics of the U.N. operation—the
dynamic interplay of factions within the Congo and governments outside as these actors attempted to use and influence the Secretary-
General, the Security Council, and the General Assembly to advance
their objectives in Central Africa and in the larger world. The methods
used by political leaders to support, modify, capture, or destroy the
UNF included the traditional diplomatic instruments of persuasion
and threat, the giving or withholding of manpower or financial support, direct pressure on U.N. officials in the Congo, and occasionally
specific measures designed to obstruct the operation.

Caught in the crossfire of domestic and international political conflict was the Secretary-General. As Commander in Chief of the UNF,
was he able to maintain the integrity of the operation? This is a
fundamental political question. (An even more basic question is
whether the Security Council acted wisely in view of other political
alternatives for dealing with the crisis.) In terms of integrity, did any
Congolese faction, any government, or any international bloc, succeed in capturing, even temporarily, the UNF for its own purposes or
in forcing the Secretary-General to depart from what he regarded as
the proper course?

Anticipating a principal conclusion of this inquiry, it can be said
that the UNF was never captured or subverted by a Congolese faction,
a government, or a bloc. Nor did the Secretary-General ever become a
captive of political forces operating contrary to the Security Council
mandate. It is equally true, however, that the entire peacekeeping
mission was authorized, sustained, and strongly influenced by an informal and shifting coalition of governments under the leadership of the
United States. The Secretary-General was in a real sense the instrument
of this supporting coalition, but he was by no means simply its tool.
He had a leverage of his own, rooted partly in the authority conferred
upon him by the Security Council, and partly in the failure of members of the supporting coalition to agree either on specific objectives for
the Congo mission or on specific permissible means for pursuing the
general objectives.

It may also be said that the UNF, and the U.N. presence in the Congo generally, were not wholly neutral or nonpartisan toward the internal conflict between factions and regions. Though the UNF was pledged not to be "a party to or in any way intervene in or be used to influence the outcome of any internal conflict, constitutional or other-wise,"[2] it was impossible for the Secretary-General to remain aloof and it would have been irresponsible of him to have done so even if it were possible. This does not mean that Dag Hammarskjold or U Thant quickly or easily took sides. It does mean that their actions had the effect of assisting some internal forces over others, an effect generally in accord with the implicit and explicit intention of the Council resolutions.

In spite of the heavy political and financial cost of the U.N. opera-tion, and contrary to certain hopes expressed in its behalf, the inter-nationalization of the crisis did not "keep the cold war out of the Congo,"[3] did not prevent Big Power rivalry on Congolese soil, and did not stop the interference of outside governments in the Congo's in-ternal affairs. The U. N. Mission did not preclude normal diplomatic representation or covert activity in the Congo by interested govern-ments. In short, the active operations of this large, internationally au-thorized, multinational military establishment on the territory of a legally sovereign state did not suspend either internal or international politics. But it did provide a legal-political-military presence which frustrated some political interests and furthered others. An ever-present factor in the Congo drama, the UNF was both an instrument and an actor. As an instrument of the multistate system it was supported or opposed, used or ignored by governments. Many states and several Congolese factions sought to alter the U.N. operation so it would better serve their objectives.

In this sense, the U.N. intervention in the Congo was profoundly and inescapably political. The United Nations is not an independent entity above world politics and international conflict. It is rather a barometer of conflict and an instrument ready to serve the common interests of a working coalition of states when such a coalition can find legal expression under the U.N. Charter. Such a common interest, how-

[2] Security Council Resolution (August 9, 1960).
[3] In 1961, Adlai E. Stevenson said "the only way to keep the cold war out of the Congo is to keep the U.N. in the Congo." *U.N. Security Council, Official Records,* S/PV 943 (Feb. 15, 1961), p. 9. (Hereafter this document will be referred to as U.N., *SCOR.*)

ever vaguely expressed, was registered by the Security Council in July, 1960, in response to the Congo crisis.

CAUSES OF THE CRISIS

In mid-1960 the Congo quickly became the world's most dramatic example of instant independence. After a half-century of paternalistic rule, Brussels cut loose its colony on five months' notice.[4] As Crawford Young observed, "total colonialism was replaced by total independence virtually overnight," and after the Army mutiny, "Africa's most revolutionary decolonization was followed by its most radical Africanization."[5] When externally imposed authority, the only element of order and cohesion in the vast expanse of a territory as large as Western Europe, was abruptly withdrawn, the endemic centrifugal forces of tribalism, regionalism, and conflicting political ambitions asserted themselves. Chaos and violence followed.

Why did Brussels give in to pressures for immediate independence when every Belgian colonial official knew that the Congolese were not able to manage their own affairs without substantial and continued assistance from Belgian administrative, military, and technical personnel? Why was not a three-year or five-year transitional plan adopted? Most observers believe that Brussels, under novel and diverse domestic and external pressures, acted in a mood of panic. Some Belgian politicians wanted to avoid a "Belgian Algeria."[6] Others, emphasizing the extent of Congolese dependence upon Belgian personnel, believed that the Belgian presence and influence could continue after independence day much as it had before. In spite of such a fundamental shift in political authority, they felt that most Belgian administrators, civil servants, and Army officers could continue serving the new government as they had the colonial administration. Another factor was the virtual absence of a "colonial mentality" among the Belgian people—they were happy to be freed of responsibility for the Congo.

[4] For a description of Belgian colonial policy see Catherine Hoskyns, *The Congo Since Independence: January, 1960–December, 1961* (London: Oxford University Press for the Royal Institute of International Affairs, 1965), pp. 1–41; Crawford Young, *Politics in the Congo* (Princeton: Princeton University Press, 1965), pp. 10–161; René Lemarchand, *Political Awakening in the Belgian Congo* (Berkeley: University of California Press, 1964), pp. 55–163.

[5] Young, *Politics in the Congo,* pp. 572 and 575.

[6] Robert Murphy, *Diplomat Among Warriors* (New York: Doubleday, 1964), pp. 332–33.

On June 30, 1960, the Congo received its independence amid the mingled emotions of hope and anxiety. As the drama unfolded, the hopes were dashed and the anxieties were confirmed.

The fundamental cause of the crisis was the incapacity of the Congolese political leaders to govern the new state, and the absence of effective arrangements on the part of the Belgian government or any other outside authority to compensate for this internal weakness. The immediate cause for the crisis was the July 4 mutiny among Congolese soldiers of the *Force publique* in Leopoldville and at Thysville (95 miles away) the following day, and the failure of the Belgian officers or the Congolese authorities alone or in co-operation to stop these disorders before they got out of hand.[7]

The *Force publique* in 1960 was a 25,000-man national security force, combining the functions of an army and a police establishment. Its entire officer corps of 1,100 was Belgian. Even after independence, its commander was Belgian Lieutenant General Emil Janssens, who made no plans for accelerating the training and promotion of Congolese. He assumed that his white officers would continue to serve until equally qualified Congolese could replace them. Prime Minister Patrice Lumumba had publicly taken the same position. The mission of the Force was to maintain law and order, protect property, and secure the border. It had a good reputation for discipline and effectiveness.[8]

The Belgian officers at Leopoldville and Thysville were probably capable of restoring order, but they were hesitant to act decisively because of their uncertain authority and role under an independent Congolese government. This uncertainty was the product of premature independence and lack of planning for the transitional period. Had they acted quickly and firmly, they might well have been able to pacify the situation. Such forthright action also might have deterred similar disorder at other *Force publique* camps, or provided a precedent for dealing with such disturbances should they occur. In the very first hours of the mutiny, the Belgians probably could have restored order without the actual use of violence. Had they found it necessary to discipline or even shoot a few ringleaders (and thereby had been able to stop the mutiny), the Congo crisis as we know it would not have developed. The United Nations would not have entered the picture.

[7] For a brief account of the early days of the crisis, see Hoskyns, *Congo Since Independence*, pp. 85–104. An over-all view is presented in the Chronology (Appendix A).

[8] U.S. Army, *Area Handbook for the Republic of the Congo (Leopoldville)*, Special Operations Research Office, American University (Washington: U.S. Government Printing Office, 1962), pp. 622–23.

The object of this speculation is to emphasize the small scale of the initial trouble. Ineptitude, inexperience, the absence of contingency plans, and panic on the part of the Belgians and the Congolese and a general atmosphere of anxiety enflamed by rumor and mutual suspicion, permitted the situation to get out of hand. The failure to employ effectively minimum coercion for a brief period at the early stage of civil disorder, compelled the use of greater and more prolonged coercion at later stages.

In the first hours and days of the crisis, the Belgian government did not use its metropolitan troops then stationed in the Congo because it could not get permission to do so from Prime Minister Lumumba, who was also Defense Minister.[9]

After the mutiny spread and many Europeans fled in panic, Brussels flew in paratroopers to reinforce their two Congo bases. From July 10 through July 18, Belgian troops were peaceably deployed in twenty-six places (ten in Katanga and sixteen elsewhere), where they restored order and helped in the evacuation of Europeans who wanted to leave. Among the places assisted were Leopoldville, Elisabethville, Coquilhatville, Luluabourg, Jadotville, Kongolo, and Albertville.[10]

In sharp contrast to this peaceful and effective deployment of troops, often at the urgent request of Congolese authorities, Belgian intervention in the port city of Matadi on July 11 resulted in a fight in which 12 to 20 Congolese were killed and 13 Belgians wounded.[11] The Matadi incident,[12] exaggerated reports of which were broadcast throughout the Congo, was a crucial turning point in Belgian-Congolese relations. This event precipitated the declaration of Katangan independence by President Moise Tshombe that same day. These two developments made co-operation virtually impossible between the Lumumba government and Belgian authorities in the security field.

[9] The Belgian troops were located in two Belgian bases, one at Kitona at the mouth of the Congo River, and the other at Kamina in Katanga. These bases were held by Brussels under the Treaty of Friendship signed with the Congolese on the eve of Independence Day, but not approved by either parliament. Under the treaty: "All military intervention by Belgian forces stationed in Congo bases can take place only on the express command of the Congolese Minister of Defense."

[10] W. J. Ganshof van der Meersch, *Fin de la Souveraineté au Congo* (Brussels: Institut Royal des Relations Internationales, 1963), p. 460.

[11] Belgian troops were also involved in hostilities on July 2, 1960, at Kolwezi in Katanga. In a clash between Belgian paratroopers and 250 Congolese soldiers, "a dozen or more Congolese and two Belgians were killed." Hoskyns, *Congo Since Independence*, p. 142.

[12] This and several other key military incidents and developments are briefly summarized in Appendix H.

By this time, the *Force publique* was torn by internal conflict and had ceased to exist as a cohesive and disciplined army. Lieutenant-General Janssens and the great majority of the Belgian officers had been summarily dismissed and replaced by inexperienced Congolese noncommissioned officers. On July 8, the name of the force was changed to *Armée Nationale Congolaise* (ANC).[13] On the same day President Joseph Kasavubu, as commander in chief of the Army and Prime Minister Lumumba, as minister of national defense, promoted a former sergeant, Victor Lundula, to the rank of major general, and placed him in command of the ANC. Joseph Mobutu was named chief of staff.

Charges at the time that the *Force publique* mutiny was plotted by the Communists, or the Belgians, or Lumumba, cannot be sustained by the record. It was a tragedy of errors on all sides. Neither the Congolese nor the Belgians sought to destroy the unity or the reliability of the Force.[14]

In the beginning the soldiers simply wanted better pay and the hope of modest promotion. They were envious of the material benefits received by the new political elite and were understandably more hostile toward Lumumba than toward their Belgian officers. They were prepared to serve under Belgian officers above the NCO rank until Congolese could be trained to take their places. But after the Matadi incident, rational cooperation between Lumumba and the Belgians became impossible.

The abrupt Africanization of the ANC officer corps was a disaster which has plagued the Congo ever since. The new Congolese officers were seldom respected or obeyed by their troops. Many of the junior officers did not take orders from their superiors. The Army headquarters in Leopoldville had little control beyond the capital city. The division, disunity, and demoralization within the ANC was both a cause and a symptom of the political and tribal disunity and chaos in the Congo. Rather than being an instrument of stability and security, most ANC units during the four years of U.N. peacekeeping were a source of disorder and violence. The indiscipline and irresponsibility of Congolese soldiers was a major, if not *the* major, threat to internal law and order throughout the entire period.

[13] Centre de Recherche et d'Information Socio-Politique, *Congo: 1960*, I, prepared by J. J. Gérard-Libois and Benoit Verhaegen (Brussels: Les Dossiers du CRISP, n.d.), 408. (Hereafter cited as CRISP, *Congo: 1960* or *Congo: 1961*, etc.)

[14] The evidence to support this conclusion is summarized in Hoskyns, *Congo Since Independence*, pp. 101–04.

HOW THE UNITED NATIONS INTERVENED

When the Lumumba government realized it was incapable of controlling the ANC and of maintaining civil order, it sought outside military assistance. Belgium, which was soon to be accused of aggression by Lumumba, was ruled out. During a hectic four-day period, various Congolese leaders requested military assistance from the United States, the Soviet Union, Ghana, and the United Nations.

On July 10, 1960, one day before the Matadi incident and the declaration of Katanga's independence, Kasavubu and Lumumba made an oral request for U.N. assistance on the advice of U.S. Ambassador-designate Clare H. Timberlake, who had been in the Congo since June 28. They requested aid to restore discipline in the ANC and to shore up the administration which was thrown into chaos by the exodus of Belgian administrators, civil servants, and technicians. The appeal, vaguely limited to technical military assistance, was addressed to Undersecretary Ralph J. Bunche, who was representing the Secretary-General Dag Hammarskjold in Leopoldville at the time. Bunche immediately cabled the appeal to Hammarskjold, who called together on July 12 the U.N. delegates from Ethiopia, Ghana, Guinea, Liberia, Libya, Morocco, Sudan, Tunisia, and the United Arab Republic, to discuss possible African contributions to a program of "technical assistance in the security field" for the Congo.

On the same day, July 12, in Leopoldville, Timberlake was invited to a Congolese cabinet meeting, along with several Belgian diplomats. Kasavubu and Lumumba were absent, traveling around the country trying to calm the soldiers and helping to supervise the selection of Congolese officers for the ANC. During the meeting, Deputy Prime Minister Antoine Gizenga and Foreign Minister Justin Bomboko asked Timberlake to request 3,000 American troops to restore law and order.[15] They formalized the request in writing. Before forwarding it to Washington, Timberlake told them that direct U.S. aid was unlikely, and that in any event the matter was already before the Secretary-General because of the oral request by Kasavubu and Lumumba to Bunche. Almost immediately after the receipt of the Congolese appeal for American military assistance, President Dwight D. Eisenhower advised Leopoldville to seek help through the United Nations.

A delegation from Ghana,[16] which had just arrived in Leopoldville

---

[15] Hoskyns, *Congo Since Independence,* p. 114.

[16] It included Andrew Djin, President Kwame Nkrumah's special representative to the Congo; Brigadier General S. J. A. Otu; and John Elliot, the Ghanian Ambassador in Moscow.

to assist the Lumumba government, advised the Congolese against accepting American military aid and suggested they address their appeal to the United Nations.

Also on July 12, Kasavubu and Lumumba, on the basis of exaggerated reports of the Matadi incident, demanded that Belgian troops withdraw from the Congo within two days. From Luluabourg they sent their first cable, via Bunche, to the Secretary-General. This message solicited urgent U.N. "military assistance" because of the "external aggression" and "colonialist machinations" of Belgium which were described as "a threat to international peace" and a violation of the Treaty of Friendship. They also protested Belgian military support of Katanga's secession. This written message differed significantly in tone and substance from the original oral appeal which had focused on the restoration of internal law and order.

On the following day, July 13, when Kasavubu and Lumumba heard about the Gizenga-Bomboko plea for American aid, they sent a second telegram to the Secretary-General stating that "the purpose of the aid requested is not to restore the internal situation in the Congo, but rather to protect the national territory against acts of aggression committed by Belgian metropolitan troops." They also insisted upon a U.N. force from neutral nations, and not from the United States.[17]

Also on July 13, Gizenga, apparently acting on his own, requested troops from Ghana as a stopgap until U.N. authorized troops could be sent.

Still greatly disturbed by the Gizenga-Bomboko request for U.S. aid, Lumumba sought the advice of Soviet representatives in Leopoldville. On July 14 he persuaded Kasavubu to join him in a cable to Soviet Premier Nikita S. Khrushchev stating that the Congo "is occupied by Belgian troops and the lives of the Republic's President and Prime Minister are in danger," and begging the Soviet Union "to watch hourly over the situation." This was generally interpreted as a veiled request for military assistance.[18] Khrushchev replied that Moscow would provide "any assistance that might be necessary for the victory" of the Congo's "just cause."

The significant difference between the original oral request to the Secretary-General from Kasavubu and Lumumba and their subsequent written requests was prompted primarily by the Matadi incident and Katanga secession. This difference reflected two basic ways of looking

[17] See Appendix B for the text of the two cables from Kasavubu and Lumumba.
[18] Ganshof van der Meersch, *Fin de la Souverainité*, p. 447.

at the Congo crisis. One emphasized the Congo's internal weakness, and the other external interference. These diverging viewpoints were expressed by various delegates in the Security Council debates, and attempts to bridge them accounted for some of the vagueness and ambiguity in the resulting resolutions.

It was in this confusing atmosphere, exacerbated by rumors and confused reporting of Congo developments, that Hammarskjold acted, and acted quickly. Invoking Article 99 of the U.N. Charter which gives the Secretary-General the authority to "bring to the Security Council any matter which in his opinion may threaten the maintenance of international peace and security," Hammarskjold called an urgent meeting on July 13 and gave his interpretation of what ought to be done about the crisis.

Hammarskjold's initiative on the Congo question was a logical extension of his deep commitment to decolonization in Africa, his desire to protect the new states and isolate them from the Cold War, his interest in making the United Nations a more effective peacekeeping instrument, and his readiness to strengthen the executive capacity of the Secretary-General. His special interest in the Congo grew out of his six-week African tour in early 1960, and reflected the importance he attached to this potentially influential country.[19]

On July 14, the Security Council adopted a compromise resolution presented by Tunisia and in harmony with Hammarskjold's interpretation of the problem. Citing no specific article of the U.N. Charter, the resolution called upon "Belgium to remove its troops" from the Congo and authorized the Secretary-General "to take the necessary steps, in consultation with the Government of the Republic of the Congo, to provide the Government with such military assistance as may be necessary" until the "national security forces may be able, in the opinion of the Government, to meet fully their tasks." The U.S.S.R. and the Afro-Asian states failed to get the Council to brand Belgium as an aggressor or to specify how and when the Belgian troops should be withdrawn. Washington and other moderate states felt the resolution placed sufficient emphasis on the necessity to restore law and order. It was adopted (by eight votes to zero), with Nationalist China, France, and the United Kingdom abstaining. Washington and Moscow were the only two permanent members of the Security Council to vote for an operation which was to become the most controversial in the history of the United Nations.

[19] The role of the Secretary-General is dealt with in Chap. 2.

WHY THE UNITED NATIONS INTERVENED

Of the dozens of civil wars and other armed conflicts since the United Nations was created, why was this particular crisis internationalized? The most important fact was that the United States and the Soviet Union preferred U.N. intervention to any plausible alternative in July, 1960. This was also true of the majority of the Security Council members. Neither France nor Britain, each unenthusiastic about authorizing a UNF, felt strongly enough to veto U.N. intervention.

Though it was the only government to receive a formal Congolese invitation for military assistance, Washington wanted to avoid direct military involvement from the outset, and preferred to channel its aid through the United Nations. In the absence of Western involvement, the United States feared the Soviet Union would exploit the chaos, threaten stability in the area, and jeopardize Congolese interests. Moscow, not Brussels, was regarded as the major threat to the Congo's independence. Washington wanted the new state to succeed and sought a moderate central government representing all major factions and capable of sustaining mutually beneficial relations with Western states.

For several reasons, Washington quickly ruled out direct military assistance to the Congo. Such aid, it was held, might be used as a pretext for more substantial Soviet intervention. The State Department also wanted to avoid charges of neo-colonialism that would inevitably follow bilateral assistance. In 1960 Washington thought it could best discharge its responsibility in independent Africa by quietly supporting constructive assistance from the former metropoles. Further, as the most consistent supporters of U.N. peacekeeping in principle, and having a positive appraisal of the U.N. Emergency Force (UNEF) in the Gaza Strip, the United States was predisposed to turn to the United Nations in certain types of crises where bilateral or alliance action was held to involve uncertain or unacceptable political costs. For these reasons, Washington provided the strongest initial support for U.N. action in the Congo. It remained the strongest and most consistent backer of the four-year effort.[20]

The chief aims of Moscow in the Congo were to strengthen the Lumumba government, transform it into a regime closely allied with the Soviet bloc, and thus to establish a base for extending Russian influence in tropical Africa. Posing as the true proponent of "national liberation," the U.S.S.R. was eager to demonstrate its zeal by support-

[20] The United States' role is discussed in Chap. 4.

ing efforts to expel the "Belgian colonialists," especially from Katanga. For tactical and pragmatic reasons, Moscow decided its objectives could be accomplished at less risk by a U.N. peacekeeping presence, which it saw as no serious barrier to Soviet diplomatic or covert operations. It appears that Moscow's immediate reason for supporting the July 14 Resolution was to prevent direct U.S. military aid. It may be that Moscow also thought that the U.N. multinational military presence (which at that time was expected to be largely African) would result in enough confusion to provide a cover for pursuing its covert policies with greater impunity. The Soviet leaders doubtless expected some of the more militant African or Asian states to support their purposes in the Congo. Moscow's hopes were soon dashed, but she was politically unable to veto subsequent Congo resolutions because they were broadly supported by the Afro-Asian neutralists whose aims the Soviet Union claimed to champion.[21]

Tunisia became the unofficial spokesman for the unaligned world in the Council. The support of the Afro-Asian states was based primarily on their interest in successful decolonization in the Congo and in avoiding a Big Power confrontation there. Though internal stability was a professed concern at the time, subsequent events demonstrate that this objective had a much lower priority than the expelling of the Belgian military and "colonial" presence. Tunisian Foreign Minister Mongi Slim, a moderate among the nonaligned leaders, characterized Belgian action in the Congo as aggression, but he did not insist that Brussels be so condemned in his resolution.[22]

Britain and France shared a common interest with the United States in containing the Congo's chaos and in maintaining stability in Central Africa, but they both had serious misgivings about internationalizing the crisis. London was concerned about Hammarskjold's probable interpretation and implementation of the resolution in the light of his strong advocacy of speedy decolonization, and feared the U.N. presence might interfere in internal Congolese affairs, thus establishing a disquieting precedent for possible U.N. intervention in the Rhodesian Federation and elsewhere in Africa. Britain abstained from voting on the July 14 Resolution.[23]

France abstained for the same reasons, but carried its position considerably further. Paris was opposed to U.N. intervention in principle.

---

[21] The Soviet role is discussed in Chap. 5.

[22] The roles of the Afro-Asian states that contributed troops to the UNF are discussed in Chap. 9.

[23] The British and French roles are discussed in Chap. 6.

President Charles de Gaulle preferred and later recommended that the Congo crisis be settled by a troika composed of France, Britain, and the United States.

The working consensus supporting U.N. intervention, symbolized by the eight affirmative votes in the Security Council, was the product of mixed motivations which reflected both the compatible and the conflicting interests of the states involved. As such, the decision of the Council can be seen as a temporary and uneasy consensus, not based upon a common understanding of the crisis or of what the United Nations should do, but rather upon a minimal agreement that the crisis in one way or another threatened the interests of each, and that the U.N. channel was the least risky way of dealing with it. There was no agreement on precisely what the Secretary-General should do; there was agreement only that he should do something.

The two basically different ways of looking at the crisis that divided the governments supporting the original resolution persisted throughout the peacekeeping effort. The Soviet Union and the militant African states continued to insist that Belgium (and sometimes the United States) was the main threat to the integrity and independence of the Congo. Tshombe, whom they regarded as a "puppet" of European financial interests, was the chief object of their attack. The United States, other Western countries, and some of the moderate Afro-Asian governments placed more emphasis on the internal weaknesses of the Congo. The Western states generally regarded direct or indirect Russian intervention in Congolese internal affairs as a serious danger.

LEGAL BASIS FOR THE U.N. ACTION

In spite of, and in part because of, the political confusion and the unprecedented aspects of the Congo crisis, questions of legality assumed an important place in the thinking of Hammarskjold, the deliberations of the Security Council, and the decisions of the governments involved. The present study is not primarily concerned with the protracted debate over the legality of the UNF or any of its more controversial operations, but it is essential to say a word about the legal basis for U.N. intervention and the nature of the obligation of member states. Any legal judgment is, of course, based on the assumption that actions of the Security Council or General Assembly in harmony with the Charter are legitimate and enjoy the status of legality in the international arena.

The Congo crisis was placed before the Council by Hammarskjold under Article 99, in full accord with the Charter. He reflected the minimal consensus of the supporters of the July 14 Resolution when he said that internal chaos "had created a situation which, through its consequences, imposed a threat to peace and security justifying United Nations' intervention," and that the finding of "a conflict between two parties" (presumably meaning two states) was "legally not essential for the justification" of U.N. action.[24]

In adopting the first and subsequent resolutions, the Council was operating within the Charter's terms of reference which provide two major ways to authorize the dispatch of military personnel to a trouble-spot.[25] Under Chapter VI, the Council may "at any stage of a dispute" that is "likely to endanger the maintenance of international peace and security" recommend "appropriate procedures or methods of adjustment" with a view to "a pacific settlement of the dispute."[26]

Under Chapter VII, the Council may "decide what measures shall be taken" in response to any situation it determines to be a "threat to the peace, breach of the peace, or act of aggression." The measures may include a wide range from the creation of a conciliation mission to "action by air, sea, or land forces as may be necessary to maintain or restore international peace and security." (Article 42.) U.N. enforcement action under Article 42 has never been expressly invoked by the Council, which even in the case of Korea only *recommended* that member states provide assistance to the Republic of Korea.

The first two Congo resolutions make no reference to the specific Charter articles under which the UNF was authorized, but the August 9, 1960 Resolution invoked Article 49 of Chapter VII. It can be said that the peacekeeping effort was based on Chapter VI, and the non-enforcement parts of Chapter VII. A U.N. peaceful settlement presence dispatched under this broad authority may be military or civilian, may range in size from one man to a force of 20,000 or more troops, and must have the consent of the host state. Its troops are voluntarily con-

---

24 U.N. *SCOR*, Supplement for July, Aug., Sept., 1960, S/4389 (July 18, 1960), p. 17.

25 Under certain circumstances, the General Assembly may also act. This authority, made explicit in the Uniting for Peace Resolution, illustrates the flexibility of the Charter. For an early study which anticipated the evolving role of the General Assembly, see H. Field Haviland, Jr., *The Political Role of the General Assembly* (New York: Carnegie Endowment for International Peace, 1951), esp. pp. 168–80. On several occasions, a stalemate in the Security Council on the Congo question resulted in its being transferred to the General Assembly, which also, because of its control over financial matters, determined the duration of the UNF.

26 The quotations are from Articles 33–38 of Chap. VI.

tributed by member governments. It is not a sanctions force, i.e., it may not take enforcement action against any state.

There was no need at any point for the Council to establish a finding of "aggression" by any state as a basis for acting in the Congo. No such finding was ever made in spite of attempts by the Soviet Union and some Afro-Asian states to have Belgium so condemned. The Council's determination that the crisis constituted a danger to international peace was sufficient legal grounds for authorizing the UNF.

An analysis of the first three Council resolutions and the debate preceding them leads to the conclusion that member states had a legal obligation to support, at least passively, the U.N. peacekeeping operation.[27]

Belgium was clearly a special case, since it was the only state other than the Congo mentioned in the resolutions. Further, Belgium was by implication acting illegally within the territory of another state. Brussels was, therefore, obligated to comply with the repeated requests of the Security Council to withdraw its troops, though the resolutions only "called upon" and never *ordered* Belgium to do so. The invocation of Articles 25 and 49 in the August 9 Resolution resolved this ambiguity. Article 25 calls upon U.N. members to "accept and carry out the decisions" of the Council. Article 49 says the same thing in different words.

The nature of the obligation of states other than Belgium to the U.N. Mission is more difficult to determine. Authorities are not agreed, partly because Articles 41 and 42 (the enforcement provisions) were never invoked, and partly because it was possible for member governments to hold that the Secretary-General was not properly implementing the "decisions of the Security Council." Nevertheless, the explicit invocation of Articles 25 and 49 by the Council apparently placed upon all member states a legal obligation to "accept" the decisions of the Council, and a similar, if imprecisely defined, obligation to assist "in carrying out measures decided upon" by the Council. Further, the February 21, 1961 Resolution reminded "all states of their obligation under" the previous Congo resolutions.

---

[27] Arguments supporting this conclusion have been advanced by various legal authorities, including Oscar Schachter, Director of the U.N. General Legal Division, and D. W. Bowett of Cambridge University. See Oscar Schachter's views presented in E. M. Miller, "Legal Aspects of the United Nations Action in the Congo," *American Journal of International Law,* Vol. 55, No. 1 (January, 1961), pp. 1–28. For a slightly different line of argument, see D. W. Bowett, *United Nations Forces: A Legal Study* (New York: Frederick A. Praeger, 1964), pp. 174–82.

This common-sense interpretation was not challenged by most member states which actively assisted, or passively accepted, the U.N. effort. The Soviet Union later challenged the validity of the Council resolutions on other grounds. France acknowledged the right of the Council to act, but did not feel bound to co-operate actively with the mission, though she voted for the July 22 Resolution.

The states accepting in principle an obligation to co-operate had ample room for debate and maneuver. Was a government obligated to comply with every request of the Secretary-General, to assist in some ways, or simply to refrain from obstructing the U.N. effort? Clearly, a state was not obligated to comply with every request, since troop contributions were voluntary. The provision of equipment and logistical support were also voluntary. Later, part of the financial support for the U.N. Force was made obligatory.[28] In practical terms, Belgium was obligated to withdraw its troops and other prohibited personnel under its jurisdiction. Other states, including the Congo, were obligated to co-operate with and not to obstruct the effort. While no government was required to provide planes for the United Nations, certain states were presumably obligated to grant over-flight and landing rights for planes on U.N. business traveling to and from the Congo. In any event, interested governments developed their basic policy toward the U.N. effort in accordance with their interests, and these policies were defended in legal terms when deemed necessary.

BROAD OBJECTIVES OF THE FORCE

The UNF in the Congo had the external appearance of a foreign army on occupation duty. But it was not an occupation force or a regular army at all. Its enemy was chaos and disorder. Its object was peace, not victory. Its purpose was broad, but its authority was severely limited.

In sharp contrast to the comparatively calm post-cease-fire situation in the Middle East which UNEF had been policing since 1956, the Congo crisis was complex, ever-changing, and compounded by a profound internal conflict. Unlike the Congo, Egypt, the host state for UNEF troops, had an effective government and no internal conflict. UNEF had a clear-cut mandate to patrol a specified area from which Egyptian forces were excluded. Its unchanging objectives were to deter border violations by both sides, to report violations by either, and to

[28] The financial issue is discussed in Chap. 11.

serve as an international plate-glass window should Egypt or Israel suddenly attack the other. Its mandate was never revised.[29]

In the Congo, there were two unsettled and interrelated problems. The simpler one was the continued Belgian military presence (and later the presence of other prohibited foreign nationals), particularly in Katanga. The much more difficult and persistent problem was the breakdown of law and order. The Congo's chaos was exacerbated by a naked power struggle among ill-disciplined Congolese political factions and a fragmented and irresponsible Congolese Army without a reliable officer corps.

To deal with these two basic problems, the Security Council identified two major objectives for the UNF—to facilitate the withdrawal of prohibited foreign personnel, and to maintain law and order. Because of the chaotic situation, the lack of an adequate precedent, and diverging views among Council members on the relative importance of the two objectives, the original July 14, 1960 Resolution was necessarily vague. Subsequent resolutions, which supplemented but never superseded the first one, were little better for the same reasons. They were less vague on the withdrawal of the Belgian military presence than on the restoration and maintenance of internal order. The precise objectives to be achieved by U.N. assistance, which included also U.N. civilian activities, were unspecified and left to the determination of the Secretary-General. There was no specific reference to the duration of the mission.

The more immediate and tangible objective was the withdrawal of the Belgian metropolitan troops who were in the Congo against the wishes of President Kasavubu and Prime Minister Lumumba. As it turned out, this objective was far easier to accomplish than the restoration of law and order.

The July 14 Resolution called upon "the Government of Belgium to withdraw" its troops from the Congo. The July 22 Resolution urged Belgium to withdraw its troops "speedily" and authorized "the Secretary-General to take all necessary action to this effect." The August 9 Resolution reaffirmed the first two and called upon Belgium to "withdraw immediately its troops from the Province of Katanga under

[29] UNEF was authorized by the General Assembly on November 4, 1956, and operated quietly until May, 1967, when it was withdrawn by Secretary-General U Thant at the request of President Gamal Abdul Nasser. For the constitutional bases of UNEF see Russell, *U.N. Experience with Military Forces*, pp. 50–71, and Bowett, *U.N. Forces: A Legal Study*, pp. 90–151. For a longer analysis, see Gabriella Rosner, *The United Nations Emergency Force* (New York: Columbia University Press, 1963).

speedy modalities determined by the Secretary-General." Nowhere did the resolutions specify the "modalities" to be employed.

By September, 1960, all Belgian troops had been voluntarily withdrawn in compliance with the resolutions, except for those in Katanga. Even there the troops were officially withdrawn, though 114 Belgian officers and 117 soldiers of other ranks remained and were seconded to Tshombe's government to direct his gendarmerie.[30]

The Council Resolution of February 21, 1961, called for "the immediate withdrawal and evacuation from the Congo of all Belgian and other foreign military and paramilitary personnel and political advisers not under the United Nations Command, and mercenaries." The first of three resolutions adopted by the General Assembly on April 15, 1961, reaffirmed the February Resolution and called the continued presence of prohibited foreigners "the central factor" in the Congo situation. Washington joined London and Paris in abstaining on this vote.

The final Council Resolution of November 24, 1961, adopted after the first clash between U.N. troops and Katangan gendarmes the previous September and known as Round One,[31] did not mention Belgium, but deplored the "armed action" of Katanga "with the aid of external resources and foreign mercenaries." It authorized the Secretary-General "to take vigorous action, including the use of a requisite measure of force, if necessary for the immediate apprehension, detention pending legal action and/or deportation of all foreign military and paramilitary personnel and political advisers not under the United Nations Command, and mercenaries." The United States voted for this resolution; Britain and France abstained.

The restoration and maintenance of law and order in the Congo was a comprehensive objective, beyond the capacity of any invited external agency fully to achieve. The greater portion of the seven Congo resolutions was devoted to this problem. The July 14 Resolution authorized "necessary steps" to provide "such military assistance as may be necessary" until Congolese "national security forces may be able, in the opinion of the Government, to meet fully their tasks." The July 22 Resolution stated that "the complete restoration of law and order . . .

---

[30] In the "Second Progress Report to the Secretary-General from his Special Representative in the Congo," Rajeshwar Dayal wrote: "As of October 31 [1960], there remained . . . 231 Belgian nationals (114 officers and 117 of other ranks) in the Katangese gendarmerie, and 58 Belgian officers in the police." *United Nations Review,* Vol. 7 (December, 1960), p. 27.

[31] The three armed clashes between the UNF and Katanga forces are referred to in this study as Rounds One, Two, and Three.

would effectively contribute to the maintenance of international peace and security," and requested "all States to refrain from any action which might tend to impede" progress toward this objective. Reflecting the deteriorating political situation dramatized by the Mobutu coup of September 14, 1960, and the announcement of Lumumba's violent death on February 13, 1961, the February 21 Resolution noted "a serious civil war situation" and urged immediate "appropriate measures," including "the use of force, if necessary" to "prevent the occurrence of civil war."

The same resolution also addressed itself to the Congo constitutional crisis, and belatedly to the disruptive role of ANC units. It urged that the Parliament be convened and that "Congolese armed units and personnel should be reorganized and brought under discipline and control" so the possibility of their interference "in the political life of the Congo" would be eliminated. The resolution did not specify who should discipline and control the ANC. Subsequent resolutions added no new elements.

Taken as a whole, the Council resolutions identified five objectives for the U.N. peacekeeping mission, the first three directed toward the internal situation, and the latter two toward external problems:

1. To restore and maintain law and order throughout the Congo.
2. To prevent civil war and curb tribal conflict.
3. To transform the ANC into a reliable internal security force.
4. To restore and to maintain the territorial integrity and political independence of the Congo.
5. To eliminate interference in the Congo's internal affairs, particularly the foreign military officers and advisors assisting secessionist Katanga.

AUTHORITY AND CONSTRAINTS

These far-reaching security objectives were virtually tantamount to those of a government, but the U.N. effort was endowed with none of the fundamental legal, political, or military attributes of a state. The UNF was not given the authority of an occupying power, nor was it granted the powers of a substitute government. It required the consent of the host government and its active or passive co-operation for the achievement of its goals.[32] In addition to the necessity for host-state consent, the UNF operated under two other severe legal constraints—

[32] Host-state consent is discussed in Chap. 3.

strict limitation on its authority to employ force, and the outright prohibition against interfering in internal affairs.

As the instrument of a nonenforcement, peaceful settlement operation, the UNF was restricted largely to the use of force in self-defense. In the beginning, Hammarskjold held that U.N. troops may use force "only in self-defense" and may not exercise "any *initiative* in the use of armed force."[33] This interpretation held until the February 21 Resolution authorized "the use of force, if necessary, in the last resort" to "prevent the occurrence of civil war." This resolution changed neither the legal basis of U.N. action nor "the basic self-defense posture of the Force," according to Oscar Schachter. He adds:

What it did was to authorize the Force, for the first time, to take up positions for the purpose of preventing civil war clashes (as in support of cease-fire arrangements and neutralized zones); if the troops were attacked while holding such positions, they could use force in defense, but this did not mean they were entitled to "take the initiative in an armed attack on an organized army group in the Congo."[34]

After Round One in Katanga in September, 1961, the permissible use of force was extended to that necessary to apprehend and detain prohibited foreigners (November 24, 1961 Resolution). Even with this broadened mandate to use force, the UNF was still essentially on a self-defense basis. It was never given the authority to perform many of the duties of a normal police establishment within a state, such as the right to inspect border crossing points for prohibited persons or military supplies.

These strict limitations on the use of force should be considered along with the right of the UNF to "freedom of movement" within the Congo. This right was "ensured" by the Congo government in the July 29, 1960 agreement with Hammarskjold, and reconfirmed in the Status Agreement of November 27, 1961. Paragraph 30 of the latter states:

The Government shall afford the members of the Force and officials serving under the United Nations in the Congo full freedom of movement throughout Congolese territory and to and from points of access to Congolese terri-

---

[33] U.N. *SCOR*, Supplement for July, Aug., Sept., 1960, S/4389 (July 18, 1960), pp. 16–24.

[34] Oscar Schachter, "Preventing the Internationalization of Internal Conflict: A Legal Analysis of the U.N. Congo Experience," *Proceedings of the American Society of International Law* (1963), p. 218.

tory. This freedom shall extend to the operation of vehicles, aircraft, vessels and equipment in the service of the United Nations.[35]

Neither the Secretary-General nor any of his Force commanders ever interpreted "freedom of movement" in a broad and unrestricted sense. From the outset it meant, as in UNEF, that the UNF had the right to establish certain positions essential to its functions, and the right to defend these positions, with force if necessary against attack. Freedom of movement did not, however, give the UNF the right to establish such positions by the initiation of military action. Given the turbulence in the Congo, the presence of undisciplined armed groups, and the incapacity of the Central Government or local authorities in Katanga or elsewhere to control the situation, the UNF under the law-and-order mandate felt compelled to establish roadblocks, checkpoints, and other positions. When these positions were attacked with the intention to dislodge the UNF, it had a legal right to fight back in self-defense. Freedom of movement, so defined, was essential to the UNF precisely because it lacked the authority to initiate the use of military force.

The principle of noninterference also limited the UNF and was far more difficult to observe than the restrictions on the use of force. Drawing largely from the UNEF experience, where there was no internal struggle in the host state, Hammarskjold insisted on strict noninterference in Congolese internal affairs. This point was made explicit in the August 9, 1960 Resolution, and was never abandoned by the Secretary-General nor seriously challenged by any Council member. The trouble arose in the application of the principle in a situation of turmoil where it was impossible to remain aloof from contending factions.[36]

INTERNATIONAL CHARACTER OF THE FORCE

To achieve the security objectives of the United Nations, Hammarskjold established a multinational peacekeeping force. Neither the July 14 Resolution nor any subsequent resolution ever mentioned a force or explicitly authorized the Secretary-General to create one. The Council members knew, however, that Hammarskjold planned to dis-

[35] The Status Agreement was circulated as *U.N. Document S/5004*. See also Appendix C for the text of the July 29, 1960 agreement between the Secretary-General and the Congo government.

[36] The practical application of the noninterference principle is discussed in Chap. 3.

patch a U.N. force if the draft resolution were adopted, so its establishment and deployment were in full harmony with the intentioɪ of the Council.

The basic character of the UNF for the Congo differed substantially from that of the U.N. Force in Korea and UNEF. In the Korean case, the "Council adopted a recommendation which entrusted a particular country, the United States, with the responsibility of providing independently for a multinational force . . . the command was entirely the responsibility of the United States and the personnel in the national contingents were not subject to the obligations or discipline of an international military service."[37]

UNEF was established by the General Assembly "as a subsidiary organ with a U.N. commander appointed by the Assembly, who acted under the instructions and guidance of the Secretary-General. Moreover, unlike the military operation in Korea, the expenses of UNEF were borne by the United Nations."[38]

Though much like UNEF in its basic conception, the Congo Force was established by the Secretary-General under the authority of the Security Council, and may be considered a "subsidiary organ" of the Council under Article 29, operating under the exclusive command and control of the Secretary-General. This placed great responsibility upon Hammarskjold which he sought conscientiously to discharged by clarifying the objectives of the Force and the ground rules for its composition and operations, and by reporting fully and frequently his views to the Council.

From the outset, Hammarskjold insisted on the international status of the UNF which was composed of voluntarily contributed national contingents and administered by a multinational headquarters staff. The Force, according to his view, had to be under his "exclusive command" and could not take orders from the host government or from governments contributing troops or other military personnel.[39] U.N. operations had to be "separate and distinct from activities of any national authorities." Specifically, troops in the Congo should neither seek nor follow instructions from their governments and should refrain

[37] Miller, *Am. Jo. Int. Law* (January, 1961), p. 10.
[38] *Ibid.*
[39] Hammarskjold's major operating principles were made clear to the Council on several occasions. A summary appears in his "First Report on the Congo Problem": U.N. *SCOR*, Supplement for July, Aug., Sept., 1960, S/4389 (July 18, 1960), pp. 16–20.

from any act or statement which would jeopardize the international or impartial status of the Force.[40]

In selecting the national contingents for the UNF, Hammarskjold insisted that he alone should decide its composition, although he would take the views of the host state into account. He believed in the principle of geographical universality, but qualified it in three ways to meet the special needs of the Congo: (1) as in the case of UNEF, units from permanent members of the Security Council should be excluded; (2) assistance should be sought first from "sister African nations, as an act of African solidarity;" (3) contingents from any state "possibly having a special interest in the situation" should be excluded. This was directed against the Belgians.

The actual composition of the Force was also affected by the availability of politically acceptable and militarily qualified contingents. No government seriously challenged Hammarskjold's selection principles, although France protested his emphasis on African troops. When the Soviet Union objected to Hammarskjold's use of a Canadian signals unit because Canada was a member of NATO, he said he did not feel compelled to exclude a state simply because it was a member of NATO or the Warsaw Pact "or any other grouping of that kind."[41]

Immediately after the adoption of the July 14 Resolution Hammarskjold requested certain African and European governments, with which he had already been in contact, to provide troop contingents and specialized military units in accordance with his principles of selection and his understanding of the international character of the Force. Within twenty-four hours the first troops for the UNF arrived in the Congo. These included 770 Ghanians transported by British planes, and 593 Tunisians brought in by U.S. Air Force C–130 aircraft. A month later, the Force totaled more than 14,000 men from twenty-four states. By August 10, the United States had airlifted 9,213 troops and 2,334 tons of equipment to the Congo. On September 2, the UNF numbered 16,082.[42]

---

[40] See Article 100 of the U.N. Charter. The actual performance of the UNF is discussed in Chap. 10.

[41] U.N., *SCOR*, S/PV 888 (August 21, 1960), pp. 26 and 52.

[42] The origin of troops is indicated in Appendix E.

2.

The Secretary-General: Instrument and Actor

Secretary-General Dag Hammarskjold was a complex man. His deep, almost agonizing involvement in the Congo crisis has left an indelible and controversial imprint. U Thant, suddenly thrust into his place by Hammarskjold's death at Ndola, was inclined to be more passive and hence less controversial. Hammarskjold had the greater impact on the United Nations Congo Mission because it was he who established the Force and set the pattern of precedents during the first hectic months. Thant had little choice but to follow his lead.

TWO MEN: ONE MANDATE

Hammarskjold played a leading role in bringing the Congo crisis before the Security Council. He drafted the first resolution that authorized him to "take the necessary steps" and requested him to report back "as appropriate." It was Hammarskjold who interpreted the Council resolutions, defined the specific objectives of the mission, established the rules of the operation, and chose the civilian and military subordinates to carry out his orders.

This broad authority was wholly consistent with the Council resolutions. The Secretary-General was the executive agent of the Council and the commander in chief of the peacekeeping Force. He was responsible for the executive and military control of the entire operation. The Council was responsible for the political control of the UNF. The Council authorized the mission, identified its major objectives, and provided general guidelines on permissible means. It was the responsibility of the Council to see that the Secretary-General adhered to its political-legal mandate. If he exceeded or misused his authority, or if he acted contrary to the mandate, it was the duty of the Council to call him to account. The Council in turn was an instrument of a coalition of supporting governments led by the United States.

The Secretary-General was also responsible to the General Assembly under the Congo resolutions adopted in the fall of 1960 and on April 15, 1961, and as far as UNF financing was concerned.

Though the Secretary-General was formally accountable only to the Council and Assembly, there were many informal constraints on his interpretation and implementation of the mandate. Both Hammarskjold and Thant were responsive to the balance of political forces in the world as they were reflected within the U.N. system.

To a great extent the Congo operation was directed by persons rather than by precedents, rules, or laws, With the vague and sometimes contradictory aims and limitations in the resolutions, a heavy dependence upon the Secretary-General was inevitable. Lacking specific directives, he was compelled to exercise initiative on a wide range of questions. The incapacity of the Council to be more specific was a consequence of divided counsel among its members, and the varying degrees of confidence in the Secretary-General among the great powers. The United States trusted Hammarskjold and his policies more than did France or Britain. The Soviet Union had little confidence in him.

Hammarskjold was a skilled, artful, and ambitious diplomat. He combined qualities not usually found in one man. Something of a brooding mystic in his private life (as his posthumously published *Markings* reveals), he was also an idealist and a humanitarian. He had a crusading, if not messianic, zeal.

Hammarskjold was far from naïve, and capable of shrewd, realistic assessments. Through his sensitive antenna, he calculated what could, and what could not be done. His expectations were tempered by an intuitive grasp of political reality, and his initiative was disciplined by caution. He knew that the real decisions in international politics were made by states, particularly the Big Powers. He knew that the office of Secretary-General was essentially an instrument, not an actor.

Hammarskjold's considerable initiative and alacrity in the Congo situation can be explained in part by three major interests he had developed since his election to office in 1953—a conviction that the United Nations had a positive role to play in dampening down brushfire conflict, a commitment to speedy decolonization and economic development in Africa, and a desire to serve both of these objectives by strengthening the executive powers of the Secretary-General.

The success of UNEF encouraged him to believe that the Organization could and should play a larger role in peacekeeping in the Third World outside of the Cold War orbit.

Hammarskjold's increasing interest in Africa, whetted by his 1960 trip to twenty-four African states and territories, coincided with the influx of the new and weak states from that continent into the United Nations. He welcomed the growing voice of the Afro-Asian bloc, and regarded the United Nations as a special guardian of the rights and interests of the fledgling states. He was a strong advocate of decolonizing the remaining areas governed by whites south of the Sahara, and of keeping the Cold War out of Africa. With his liberal Western orientation, he was wary of neo-colonial economic interests which continued to exercise what he regarded as excessive influence in states that had recently received their political independence.[1] Some observers considered Hammarskjold "anti-Belgian."[2]

Hammarskjold believed the executive arm of the United Nations could best be strengthened not by amending the Charter, but by extending a U.N. presence into trouble spots, particularly in Third World conflict situations. He looked upon the Congo as precisely this type of opportunity, though at the outset he thought only in terms of traditional economic aid, and a new form of technical-military assistance to shore up the lower levels of the ANC's officer corps. The military aid was to come primarily from other African states. The situation changed drastically when he received the Kasavubu-Lumumba cable of July 12, 1960, which referred to Belgian intervention as "external aggression" and called for urgent "military assistance." Hammarskjold quickly adjusted to the new and larger challenge, and continued to exercise his characteristic initiative on the Congo question until his death in September, 1961.

From the beginning, there was considerable criticism of the way Hammarskjold used his broad authority. The severest critic was the Soviet Union which proposed the troika arrangement of a three-man office of Secretary-General, designed to make the Communist veto effective over all significant executive action. Other governments felt that the Council evaded its responsibility by entrusting too much to the Secretary-General. The phrase, "leave it to Dag!" was sometimes used in a mood of frustrated resignation.[3] It must be said, however, that

---

[1] For an elaboration of Hammarskjold's views, see Joseph P. Lash, *Dag Hammarskjold: Custodian of the Brushfire Peace* (New York: Doubleday, 1961), pp. 203–12 and 223–28. See also Hoskyns, *Congo Since Independence*, pp. 106–13.

[2] See Chap. 7.

[3] This statement was used by the U.A.R. Representative on December 9, 1960. U.N., *SCOR*, S/PV 960 (December 20, 1960), p. 1497. He added: "This escapism on the part of the United Nations bodies was hardly fair, either to the Secretariat or to the United Nations as a whole."

Hammarskjold attempted conscientiously to pursue the objectives and to observe the constraints of the Council.

One of Hammarskjold's diplomatic skills was that of deliberate ambiguity. His interpretations of the already vague Council mandate were often couched in language which meant different things to different people. This was not duplicity on his part. He regarded such abstruseness as essential to give him sufficient latitude to act effectively when there was agreement only that something should be done. The British and the French criticized him for this quality. A French representative once called him a "master of the calculated imprecision."[4]

Thant had the same authority for administering the UNF as his predecessor, but he was a different man operating in a different situation. He inherited a complex task, aggravated by Big Power disagreement over the role of the Secretary-General and disappointment among the Afro-Asian states over the course of events in the Congo. Though he was less bold in some respects than Hammarskjold and though he was obviously eager to escape the wrath of the Soviet Union, he followed the Hammarskjold pattern. Perhaps the most controversial decision he took was to authorize Round Three, in which the UNF ended the secession of Katanga by force. But this was one of the few U.N. actions that found favor in Moscow. Another major decision, his refusal to permit the U.N. presence in the Congo to serve as an umbrella for several bilateral military assistance programs, was also supported by the Soviet Union. Unlike Hammarskjold, Thant never found himself in a position where he felt he had to make a decision strongly opposed by the U.S.S.R.

One can speculate that the Congo drama might have turned out quite differently if Hammarskjold had not died during the first clash between the UNF and Katanga, but evidence suggests that the outcome depended less on the personality of the Secretary-General than on the interplay of external and Congolese interests.

RELATION TO MEMBER STATES

Both Hammarskjold and Thant were sustained and guided, formally and informally, by a moderately stable coalition of states which stood behind the peacekeeping effort throughout its four years. The most important member was the United States, without whose political, financial, and logistical support the UNF would have collapsed. Gov-

---

[4] Lash, *Dag Hammarskjold*, p. 6.

ernments such as India, Ethiopia, and Nigeria, each of which provided more than 50,000 man-months to the Force, were also important.

The Secretary-General was the constant target of conflicting pressures and interests in the Congo and the larger world. Hammarskjold, who was under more severe pressure than Thant, modified his course of action somewhat in response to criticism from the Soviet Union, Belgium, France, and Britain.[5]

The views of the Congolese government and various competing internal factions were frequently pressed upon Hammarskjold, particularly on the Katanga problem. He engaged in correspondence with a half-dozen Congolese leaders, and often conferred with them. Their overtures were taken into account, but as in the case of outside pressures, both men successfully resisted efforts to alter substantially the original course.[6]

Hammarskjold also successfully resisted the effort of the U.A.R., Mali, Guinea, Yugoslavia, and Indonesia to change his policies, by first threatening to withdraw their troops from the UNF and then actually withdrawing them.[7]

At the outset Hammarskjold confined his formal consultation to the Security Council, which was never able to give him either the guidance he wanted or the legitimacy he felt he needed for his executive decisions. He told the Council he had a right to expect specific guidance, but in its absence "I have no other choice than to follow my conviction . . . implementation obviously means interpretation."[8] In December, 1960, he complained that for five months he and his "collaborators" in the Secretariat were forced to make "daily decisions, involving interpretations in detail," without adequate guidance from the Council or the Assembly. These organs, he said, were evading their clear responsibility.[9]

Because of the failure of the Security Council to give the advice he wanted and the criticism of some of the Afro-Asian states, on August 23, 1960, Hammarskjold established the Congo Advisory Committee, made up of representatives of states contributing troops to the UNF. He did this in part as a response to an urgent request from Deputy Prime Minister Gizenga that the Secretary-General "share his responsi-

---

[5] The impact of these governments is discussed below. See, *Soviet Union,* Chap. 5; *Belgium,* Chap. 7; *France and Britain,* Chap. 6.

[6] See Chap. 3.

[7] See Chap. 9.

[8] U.N., *SCOR,* S/P 888 (August 21, 1960), p. 21.

[9] U.N., *SCOR,* S/P 920 (December 13, 1960), p. 24.

bilities" with a group of Afro-Asian neutralist representatives. Hammarskjold rightly never shared responsibility, because it was entrusted to him alone. The Committee followed the pattern of a similar consultative group in UNEF, and functioned until the UNF left the Congo.

Though it was called an advisory committee, Hammarskjold also used it as a means of promoting his views and policies and as a buffer against criticism. He often referred to the advice of the Committee to support his decisions, but made it clear that he acted on his own authority. It is difficult to know how much he relied on the Committee or how he used its advice, since no records of its meetings have been published. Even if these records were available, the assessment would be difficult because advice was also received from many other sources. The Committee was an especially useful political instrument to Hammarskjold in dealing with sensitive issues such as the implementation of the February 21, 1961 Resolution, and the investigation of Lumumba's death.[10]

RELATION TO THE SECRETARIAT

The failure of the member states acting through the Council and the Assembly to provide adequate guidance forced Hammarskjold to rely on his own resources, including the advice of his chief aides in the Secretariat.

As U.N. civil servants, the Secretariat staff are pledged to be nonpolitical and to formulate plans and execute orders of the Secretary-General without regard to the interests of or pressures from the states to which they owe allegiance as citizens, or from any other states. According to Article 100 of the Charter, "the Secretary-General and his staff shall not seek or receive instructions from any government or from any other authority external to the Organization." Conversely, each member state shall "respect the exclusively international character" of the Secretariat and shall "not seek to influence them in the discharge of their responsibilities." Article 101 states that the staff shall be recruited "on as wide a geographical basis as possible."

Deeply committed to the proposition that the United Nations could manage the Congo situation successfully, Hammarskjold and his closest colleagues quickly generated ideas and plans which they discussed with

[10] On the February 21 Resolution, see U.N. *SCOR*, Jan., Feb., March, 1961, S/4752 (February 27, 1961), p. 176. On the Lumumba investigation, see U.N. *SCOR*, Supplement for Jan., Feb., March, 1961 S/4771 (March 20, 1961), p. 259.

members of the Security Council, the Congo Advisory Committee, and directly with interested states. From the very beginning, the Secretary-General relied heavily upon a small group of men in the Secretariat who came to be known as the *Congo Club*. The nucleus of this intimate advisory and action group included:[11]

> Ralph J. Bunche (U.S.), Undersecretary for Special Political Affairs
> Andrew W. Cordier (U.S.), Undersecretary for General Assembly Affairs
> C. V. Narasimhan (India), Staff Aide to the Secretary-General
> Brigadier I. J. Rikhye (India), Military Adviser to the Secretary-General
> Sir Alexander MacFarquhar (U.K.), Special Adviser on Civilian Operations in the Congo
> Heinz Wieschhoff (U.S.), Deputy to the Undersecretary for Special Political Affairs.

Other staff aides who joined the Club from time to time included Robert Gardiner (Ghana), who later became the Officer in Charge in Leopoldville; Francis C. Nwokedi (Nigeria); and Taieb Sahbani (Tunisia).[12]

The inner group of the Congo Club, which directed the day by day operations under Hammarskjold's guidance, consisted of three Americans, two Indians, and one Britisher. Later, when Africans were included they were from the notably moderate governments of Tunisia and Nigeria. Gardiner did not reflect the prevailing political views of the Nkrumah government. By design, Hammarskjold selected the members of the Congo Club from states supporting the Congo effort. This policy explicitly excluded Soviet citizens in the Secretariat.

According to one high official of the Secretariat, tight controls were placed over communications to and from the Congo, primarily to prevent messages from falling into the hands of unauthorized members of the staff, particularly Russians and citizens of other states pursuing policies similar to those of the Soviet Union in the Congo. One code system was reportedly restricted to Hammarskjold, Bunche, and Rikhye. Hammarskjold's exclusion of Soviet staff could be justified in practical operational terms, even though the primary motivation for the policy may have been political. In any event, the Soviet representative in the Security Council had full access to the official documents and the oral statements of the Secretary-General, and it was in the

[11] *New York Times,* October 19, 1961.
[12] Lash, *Dag Hammarskjold,* p. 259.

Council that the basic political decisions were made, or should have been made, not in the Secretariat whose function it was to implement the decisions.

The problem of dual loyalty is ever-present in the U.N. Secretariat. Staff are not required to, and do not, renounce their state citizenship nor their love of country. Some governments nominated persons for high Secretariat posts who were expected to report back to their capitals on the confidential operations of the Organization. Communist states are more inclined to use their nationals on the U.N. staff in this way than Western states because official Communist dogma insists that there are no neutral or disinterested men. Khrushchev's troika proposal was based on this proposition. He believed it was impossible for a Secretary-General to be genuinely neutral, so he wanted a politically balanced triumvirate which could act only when there was unanimity.

As far as the Congo operation is concerned, there was no evidence of serious dual or conflicting loyalties on the part of key persons in the Secretariat. Nor was there evidence that hidden loyalties substantially altered the Secretariat's interpretation, or implementation of, the Council mandate. Hammarskjold and Thant sought diligently to be impartial, and to a great extent succeeded. Their own political philosophy as well as the political pressures upon them doubtless had some effect on the decisions they made. The effect of the pressure on the man was doubtless related more to his prior disposition than to its source. Hammarskjold, for example, probably was more receptive to the "advice" of a moderate African state than to "advice" from Stockholm.

Turning to Hammarskjold's formal relations with the Secretariat, it should be noted that the magnitude and complexity of the Congo operation placed a heavy strain upon the total resources of the U.N. bureaucracy in New York and overseas. Most directly involved were seven subordinate offices of the Secretary-General, and various subdivisions of the Office of General Services, as follows:[13]

> *Offices of the Secretary-General*
>> Executive Office
>>> Undersecretary for General Assembly Affairs
>>> Military advisor to the Secretary-General

[13] The titles of the offices and services were taken from the *U.N. Telephone Directory* issued by the Office of General Services, April, 1965. Some offices changed their names during the Congo operation, and some new subdivisions were created in part to deal with the additional work occasioned by that effort.

> Undersecretary for Special Political Affairs
> Office of Legal Affairs
> Office of the Controller
>> Special Assistant for Peacekeeping
>> Office of Personnel
> *Office of General Services*
>> Communications, Archives and Records Service
>>> Telecommunications Section[14]
>> Purchase and Transportation Service
>> Field Operations Service

These and other supporting offices and services had both consultative and operational functions. The Military Adviser's Office and the Field Operations Service are of special significance.

MILITARY ADVISER TO THE SECRETARY-GENERAL

Shortly after the July, 14, 1960 Resolution, Hammarskjold named Brigadier Indar Jit Rikhye of India as his military adviser for the Congo effort. Three years later the position was made permanent under the title Military Adviser to the Secretary-General, though Rikhye had been giving advice on non-Congo questions for some time before this formal change. From April, 1958 to February, 1960, Rikhye had been the Chief of Staff for UNEF. Hammarskjold provided Rikhye with a small staff of one colonel and two majors, whose function was to advise the Secretary-General on strictly military matters.

Rikhye had no command responsibilities, but there were two major developments which confused and probably compromised his role as a staff adviser. The first occurred in August and September, 1960, when Rikhye was in the Congo to help organize the military effort. During this time he moved into the widely recognized command vacuum caused by the failure of Major General Carl von Horm of Sweden, the U.N. Force Commander, and his quickly recruited staff to cope with the complex and demanding Congo operation. Evidence indicates that Rikhye's assertion of authority, apparently with the approval of

[14] By 1963 there were "eight major U.N. transmitters, located in New York, Geneva, Pisa, Gaza, Jerusalem, Karachi, Bangkok, and Seoul; the establishment of each transmitter required the consent of the host government. Messages are relayed by cable to points not covered in the system—for instance, from Seoul to Tokyo. The network is used primarily by the field missions and peacekeeping missions." Edward H. Bowman and James E. Fanning, "The Logistics Problems of a U.N. Military Force," *International Organization*, Vol. 17, No. 2 (Spring, 1963), p. 356.

Hammarskjold, was made to ensure the effectiveness and integrity of the UNF. Nevertheless, his exercise of command functions clearly exceeded his terms of reference as an adviser.[15]

The second development was Hammarskjold's appointment of Rikhye as Acting Officer in Charge of the entire U.N. presence in the Congo (a civilian position), for a brief period during November, 1960. This also confused Rikhye's role as military adviser to the Secretary-General.

In addition, Rikhye made about thirty "trouble-shooting" trips to the Congo at the request of Hammarskjold.[16] Several ranking U.N. officers in the Congo complained that during these visits he interfered in their affairs. Further, he did not get on well with the ANC Commander, General Joseph Mobutu. While the unusual role of Rikhye doubtless caused friction and misunderstanding within the U.N. command, there is no substantial evidence to indicate that it seriously undercut the integrity of the mission. On the contrary, it may have helped to ensure effective executive and military control under difficult circumstances. This is not to say that there were not more acceptable ways to accomplish the same result. On balance, it was unwise to have Rikhye become so deeply involved in command.

In New York, Rikhye performed most useful work in helping the Secretary-General determine his Force requirements, and in recruiting contingents and specialized military personnel. He was a key member of the Congo Club. He also gave advice on the transportation of men and materiel to the Congo. In this latter function he, along with officials of the Field Operations Service, was greatly assisted by the U.S. government, which provided the bulk of the airlift to the Congo. The U.S. Air Force was designated by Washington as the executive agent for the materiel support of the operation. During the four-year effort, the Defense Department transported 118,091 troops and 18,569 tons of cargo into or out of the Congo, and airlifted 1,991 troops and 3,642 tons of cargo inside the Congo.[17] Washington also provided large quantities of arms, equipment, and food. Rikhye and Field Operations Service staff were virtually in daily contact with American military officers in the U.S. delegation to the United Nations in Washington, and overseas. Other governments supporting the effort were also, though not so deeply, in touch with the office of the military adviser.

---

[15] This and the following development involving Rikhye are discussed in Chap. 10.

[16] Interview with Major General Rikhye in New York (April 7, 1965).

[17] Data from Capt. William Alexander, USN, J–3, Joint Chiefs of Staff, Department of Defense (September 16, 1964).

FIELD OPERATIONS SERVICE

Established by the General Assembly in 1949 to provide technical support for the overseas activities of the United Nations, particularly UNEF, the Field Operations Service played a key role in fielding and maintaining the Congo operation. This service, along with other U.N. technical support operations, functioned under the Office of General Services. While the Field Operations Service did a fair job under novel and extenuating circumstances, its support of the UNF was not as efficient as a similar operation carried out by a competent national military establishment. It lacked both the experience and facilities for handling an operation as large and complex as the Congo effort.[18] This inexperience added to the *ad hoc* character of the UNF and led to strained relations between the Field Operations Service, on the one hand, and the Office of the Military Adviser and the U.N. Command on the other. One high U.N. official described this relationship as "atrocious," and said it resulted in inefficiency, waste, and confusion. The problem was largely inherent in the situation. Normally, military establishments operate their own procurement, supply, transportation, and communications systems at all levels. In the Congo, the U.N. Command had to depend entirely upon an external civilian agency for all forms of technical support outside the Congo, and for most supporting services in the Congo. The U.N. Command did have its own separate communications system. This unfamiliar dependence upon a civilian agency, and a relatively inexperienced one at that, led to complaints of inefficiency from both sides. The military officers tended to blame General Services for unnecessary duplication, delays, and interference, while officers in General Services tended to blame the U.N. Command for failing to estimate its materiel and manpower needs accurately and sufficiently in advance. The inherent problem was exacerbated by administrative and planning weaknesses on both sides, due in part to personnel not fully qualified for their assignments. The result was higher cost, delay, and even some bungling. But the Secretary-General did not lose control of the operation, nor were his orders disobeyed or seriously held up because of inefficiency.

THE CHAIN OF COMMAND

The command structure of the Congo operation embodied the principle of civilian supremacy. As Commander in Chief, the Secretary-

[18] See Bowman and Fanning, "*The Logistics Problems of a U.N. Military Force,*" pp. 356–57.

General had "full command authority over the Force." The Force Commander was "operationally responsible to the Secretary-General through the [civilian] Officer in Charge for the performance of all functions assigned to the Force by the United Nations, and for the deployment and assignment of troops at the disposal of the Force."[19]

Further, the Secretary-General had authority over "all administrative, executive, and financial matters affecting the Force" and was "responsible for the negotiation and conclusion of agreements with governments concerning the Force."[20] The chain of command can thus be diagrammed:

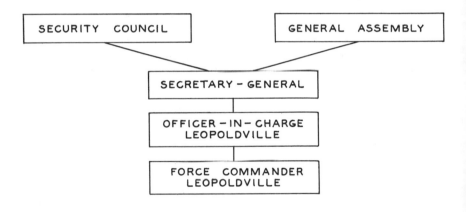

The Secretary-General was controlled only by the Council or the Assembly. He was advised formally by the Congo Advisory Committee, and informally by interested governments. He was both advised and assisted by his staff. His chief formal staff aides on the Congo were his

19 *The Regulations* (July 15, 1963), circulated as U.N. Document ST/SGB/ONUC/1, para. 11.
20 *Ibid.*, para. 16.

Military Adviser and his Adviser on Civilian Operations, but he actually received his day by day advice from the informal Congo Club.

In Leopoldville, the Officer in Charge, a civilian except for the brief period when Brigadier Rikhye filled the post, was the Secretary-General's top representative in the Congo. The Force Commander took his orders from the Secretary-General through the Officer in Charge. The Commander was advised by his multinational Headquarters Staff.

The same pattern was duplicated in Elisabethville, where there was a Sector Commander for Katanga, and a Chief Civilian Representative. In practice, the role of the Civilian Representative in Elisabethville was less clear than that of the Officer in Charge in Leopoldville. The Representative could not order the Katanga commander to act; such orders had to come from, or be endorsed by, the Force Commander in Leopoldville. It would appear that the Representative was an adviser rather than a link in the chain of command.[21]

The Force Commander had "full and exclusive authority" over his Headquarters Staff and all other members of the Force, except in the area of discipline, where serious cases were handed over to the jurisdiction of the national contingent commanders.

In this simple administrative structure, the straight line of command was occasionally breached by the intrusion of the Secretary-General's military adviser, blurred by inefficiency, or temporarily violated by unusual developments in the field. In three notable military incidents in the Congo, the Secretary-General's authority was, at least temporarily, challenged.[22] *First,* in July, 1960, Major General H. T. Alexander, the British commander of the Ghanian contingent, assumed a degree of control over U.N. troops, and peacefully disarmed some ANC units in Leopoldville. He was strongly reprimanded by Undersecretary Ralph J. Bunche for the "unauthorized" disarming of Congolese soldiers. *Second,* Conor Cruise O'Brien, the Civilian Representative in Elisabethville, on September 13, 1961, launched a U.N. military operation designed to capture key positions in Katanga and to arrest Katangan ministers, in an effort to end the secession of the province.

---

21 In an interview in Elisabethville (September 26, 1962), Eliu Mathu (Kenya), the U.N. Civilian Representative, said that he was sometimes bypassed in the communications between the Force Commander in Leopoldville and the Katanga commander. This may have been a matter of personalities. During the four years, there were in Elisabethville eleven different Civilian Representatives of ten different nationalities. On the military side, the operation was commanded most of the time by Indians, who were in charge during each of the three armed clashes between the UNF and Katanga forces.

22 These three incidents are discussed in Chap. 10.

O'Brien was widely criticized by U.N. officials and others for exceeding his authority. *Third,* during Round Three in Katanga (December, 1962–January, 1963), Brigadier Reginald S. Noronha, the commander of the Indian Brigade, crossed the Lufira River against explicit instructions of the New York headquarters not to do so. Bunche who was sent out to investigate the situation, concluded that there had been no insubordination.

Even in these three incidents which tested the executive control of the Secretary-General most severely and directly, it can be said (anticipating the analysis in Chapter 10), that the loss of control was only temporary and local, and as such had no serious impact on the fundamental character of the U.N. peacekeeping operation.

CONCLUSIONS

Throughout the four years, the Secretary-General maintained reasonably effective executive control of the Congo operation. The integrity of this control was challenged by political pressures, administrative inefficiency, unqualified personnel, and several specific incidents, but it was never seriously eroded.[23]

The Secretary-General was operating under a broad political-legal mandate, and had to be sensitive to the shifting balance of political forces. Hammarskjold and Thant recognized this, but they both made a distinction between political advice in general harmony with the Security Council mandate and political pressures contrary to the letter or spirit of the resolutions. It was precisely this distinction which enabled them to profit from the former and resist the latter.

The considerable degree of administrative inefficiency in the operation can be attributed largely to inherent factors such as the vague mandate, the multinational character of the Force, and the fact that the Secretariat was not equipped to handle a field operation of that size and complexity. This inefficiency led to waste, delay, and unnecessary expense, but it did not seriously compromise executive control.

The few top-ranking civilian and military officers who exceeded their authority or otherwise failed to perform their functions to the satisfaction of the Secretary-General constituted perhaps the most serious threat to the integrity of the operation. The O'Brien incident and the

[23] This conclusion is drawn in part from the analysis in Chaps. 3–10.

"Dayal problem"[24] are clearly linked to personalities. In important respects, these men did not measure up to the demands of their sensitive positions. The same might be said of General von Horn, Sture Linner, and Mahmoud Khiary (the latter two were involved in the O'Brien incident), who were not qualified by training or experience to handle their responsibilities. These men created difficulties—or permitted them to develop—which their replacements, confronting virtually the same problems, were able to avoid. Ironically, all of these men were personally appointed by Hammarskjold. Though Hammarskjold was not always the best judge of character and competence, it should be recalled that some of his appointments were made under the pressure of time and that he did select several very good men, notably Robert Gardiner of Ghana, the highly respected Officer in Charge of the Congo operation from February, 1962, to May, 1963. Further, the need for geographical and political spread in appointments and the restriction of top positions largely to nonaligned countries narrowed the field of choice. Nevertheless, Hammarskjold had an acknowledged weakness at this point, a weakness also illustrated by asking or permitting his Military Adviser, Brigadier Rikhye, to intrude into the line of command.[25]

While his unfortunate personnel choices certainly added some confusion, demoralization, and inefficiency, they did not (except in the case of the O'Brien incident), actually rupture executive control. And that rupture was quickly repaired. Control was temporarily lost also in the Alexander affair, occasioned by the concurrence of a command vacuum and a vigorous general, but again control was quickly restored.

The factor of dual loyalty was apparently not present in the cases of Dayal, O'Brien, or Alexander. Evidence suggests that each man was doing what he believed he should be doing on behalf of the United Nations. O'Brien and Dayal claimed they were following Hammarskjold's instructions. In the Alexander affair, the General acted in the absence of U.N. instructions for dealing with a specific problem. There is no evidence that these men were taking instructions from their own, or any other, government.

Moving to the larger problem of the Secretary-General's responsibility under the Security Council's political-legal mandate, many of the

---

[24] Rajeshwar Dayal of India was the U.N. Officer in Charge in the Congo from September, 1960, to May, 1961. He had severe difficulties in getting along with Congolese authorities, and Hammarskjold was criticized for not dismissing him sooner than he did. (This matter is discussed in Chap. 4.)

[25] This problem is discussed in Chap. 10.

charges of illegality made against Hammarskjold, and to a lesser extent Thant, appear to be rooted in criticism of their political judgments, or the substance of the Security Council mandate itself. The collective intent of the supporting coalition underwent modifications in response to a changing situation in the Congo. The Secretary-General was obligated to serve this political consensus, which was the parent of the legal mandate, as long as it did not violate the Charter.

Neither Hammarskjold nor Thant was ever censured by the Security Council or the General Assembly. When Hammarskjold interpreted the nature of the mandate, defined the constraints, or outlined his future plans for the UNF, he was never opposed and was repeatedly commended by the Council. His authority was reaffirmed, and on several occasions he was directed to take stronger measures. This suggests that charges that the Secretary-General exceeded his legal authority should be directed not toward him, but toward the Security Council. If the Secretary-General was overstepping his mandate or otherwise misusing his authority, he should have been censured by the Council. If the resolutions were so ambiguous that he could take action under one paragraph that was apparently prohibited by another, the Council should have cleared up the confusion by adopting new resolutions, or by other means.

In spite of the vague mandate, the lack of adequate legal precedents, and continuous political pressures, both Hammarskjold and Thant largely succeeded in their attempt to adhere to the legal principles of the Charter and to observe the fundamental intent of the successive resolutions. They may have made errors of analysis or judgment, but they sought to serve the purposes of the mandate rather than the interests of particular governments, blocs, or Congo factions. The role of the UNF in Katanga may be criticized on political grounds, but the actions authorized by Hammarskjold and Thant as a whole fell well within the objectives and constraints of the resolutions.

3.

The Congo: Stage and Actor

The Congo drama was played on many stages. Important acts took place in Washington, London, Paris, Brussels, and Casablanca, as well as in the chambers, corridors, and offices of the United Nations headquarters in New York.

The most intense and tragic drama unfolded in the Congo itself. That tortured country provided some of the major actors as well as the principal stage for intrigue and statesmanship.

From the outset, the relationship between the U.N. effort and the host-state was destined to be stormy. How could it be otherwise? The Congo was a legally sovereign state, but it was weak and torn by internal dissension. The foreign presence was large, painfully obstrusive to the Congolese, and obvious to the world. The U.N. presence was endowed with authority, prestige, and physical force, but it was neither a substitute government nor an occupying power. It was there with at least the nominal consent of the Congolese government, because that government was desperate for help.

Tension and conflict between the Secretary-General and his subordinates and the Congolese leaders was inevitable. Matters were seriously aggravated by the deepening chaos and confusion. At times, two competing factions claimed to be the legitimate government. At other times, there was virtually no government at all.

In four years there were four different central governments, two of which were regarded as illegal by the Secretary-General—the Council of Commissioners and the Ileo government. The first government, that of Lumumba, lasted only two months. Cyrille Adoula was Prime Minister for almost three years. Throughout the four years, Joseph Kasavubu served as President.[1]

---

[1] A concise Chronology of Congo events appears in Appendix A.

There were three different major rebel movements challenging the authority of Leopoldville—Katanga, Stanleyville, and South Kasai. The two most serious early challenges to the Central Government were secessionist Katanga and rebellious Stanleyville. For two-and-one-half years, Leopoldville was preoccupied with the problem of getting Katanga to recognize its authority. From the end of 1960, Stanleyville was an intermittent headache for the Central Government because Lumumba's heirs had established there a rival leftist regime which received political and some military support from the Communist bloc and associate states. The rebel movements of 1964, partly based in Stanleyville, seriously threatened the authority of Leopoldville.

THREE UNITED NATIONS–HOST-STATE RULES

It was in this turbulent Congo that the Secretary-General and the UNF sought to fulfill the mandate of the Security Council. Hammarskjold formulated three rules to govern the relations between the U.N. presence and the Congo government:

1. The U.N. Force requires the consent of the host state for its entry and presence, but as long as the Force is authorized by the Security Council, the Congolese government has an obligation to co-operate with it.

2. The U.N. Force should co-operate with the host government, but it should not become an instrument of the government.

3. The U.N. presence, including the Force, should not "be a party to or in any way intervene in or be used to influence the outcome of any internal conflict, constitutional or otherwise" (August 9, 1960 Resolution).

These rules, or principles, were not entirely consistent with one another, and were subject to varying interpretations. But they provided a norm, rooted in the authority of the Council and agreed to by the Secretary-General and the Central Government.

Rule One—Host-State Consent

The principle of host-state consent applied in part to the composition of the UNF as well as to its original entry. In choosing military units for the Congo, Hammarskjold said he would "take fully into account the viewpoint of the host government" and that "serious objections" against the participation of a specific state would usually "determine the action of the Organization."[2] On a number of occasions Hammarskjold was criticized by Congolese leaders for his use of non-African troops, but he refused to capitulate to this pressure. Several Council members supported his stand.[3] He avoided serious conflict by taking into account not only the political views of Leopoldville, but those of secessionist Katanga as well. Hammarskjold established the U.N. presence in Katanga when he arrived on August 12, 1960, with two companies of Swedish troops. He did not use troops from Guinea and Ghana, African states highly critical of Tshombe, though they were already in the Congo. In this he appears to have taken into account one of the conditions for entry which Tshombe had stipulated three days before.[4]

The initial entry of the UNF into the Congo was no problem because it had a clear invitation from the Lumumba-Kasabuvu government, but the duration of the Force presented a theoretically more serious problem. The July 14 Resolution stated that "military assistance" would continue until "the national security forces may be able, in the opinion of the government, to meet fully their tasks." Taken literally, this meant that Leopoldville could terminate the UNF unilaterally and at will. Matters were not that simple. From the start, the "good faith" of both parties was stressed. Further, the July 22 Resolution tied the "complete restoration of law and order" to the prospects for "international peace," and requested all states to co-operate with the effort. By implication the duration of the mission was to be determined by the Council. By invoking Articles 25 and 49, the August 9 Resolution placed an unspecified obligation on all member states to support the UNF as long as it was authorized by the Council. As matters developed, it was neither the Security Council nor the Leopoldville government which fixed the termination date but the General Assembly, because the duration of the UNF became closely linked to the problem of financing peacekeeping operations over which that body has jurisdiction.

[2] U.N., *GAOR*, A/3943 (October 9, 1958), Annexes, Agenda Item 65. This document is known as the Secretary-General's "Summary Study" derived from the UNEF experience. Many of the "Rules," including the language, for the Congo were taken directly from this study.

[3] U.N., *SCOR*, S/PV 889 (August 21–22, 1960), pp. 8, 16, 31, 36, and 56.

[4] For details of Tshombe's conditions and of Hammarskjold's entry, see Pierre Davister, *Katanga: enjeu du monde* (Brussels: Editions Europe–Afrique, 1960), pp. 146–55.

Rule Two—Co-operation Without Identification

The UNF needed the consent and co-operation of the host government if it was to be effective. At the same time, Hammarskjold insisted that the U.N. presence, including the Force, had to remain independent of the government and could not act as its instrument or agent. Likewise, it could not identify itself with any faction in the Congo. This role was elaborated on August 12, 1960, when Hammarskjold was under pressure from Lumumba to take military action against Katanga:

1. The United Nations Force cannot be used on behalf of the Central Government to subdue or to force the provincial government to a specific line of action;
2. United Nations facilities cannot be used to transport civilian or military representatives, under the authority of the Central Government, to Katanga against the desire of the Katanga Provincial Government;
3. The United Nations Force has no duty, or right, to protect civilian or military personnel, representing the Central Government arriving in Katanga beyond what follows from its general duty to maintain law and order;
4. The United Nations has no right to prevent the Central Government from taking any action which by its own means, in accordance with the purposes and principles of the Charter, it can carry through in relation to Katanga.[5]

As the drama unfolded the United Nations–host-state relationship was frequently characterized by friction and mutual distrust, especially on the Katanga question.

Rule Three—Noninterference and Nonintervention

The principle of noninterference by the UNF is closely related to the principle of nonidentification with the government. The former implies a denial of active support for any existing faction or interest, while the latter implies co-operation with the central government without identification. The categorical prohibition against U.N. intervention was greatly complicated by the positive mandate of the UNF to maintain order, prevent civil war, and protect the territorial integrity of a state which was torn apart by civil disorder, secession, and even rebellion. In this chaotic situation, it was obviously impossible for the UNF to fulfill its objectives even partially without violating the rule of

---

[5] Quoted from E. M. Miller, *Am. Jo. Int. Law* (January, 1961) p. 16, and based on U.N., *SCOR*, Fifteenth Year, Supplement for July, Aug., Sept., 1960, Document S/4417 (August 12, 1960), Add. 6, p. 70.

nonintervention. It could not remain wholly aloof and at the same time co-operate with the government.

Several major political developments are examined below to illustrate the relationship between the UNF and the Leopoldville government in the light of these three somewhat contradictory rules.

KASAVUBU'S DISMISSAL OF LUMUMBA

The natural rivalry between President Kasavubu and Prime Minister Lumumba began long before Independence Day. Lumumba's conniving with the Soviet bloc during the first two months of independence, his growing lack of self-control, and his unwillingness to accept an independent role for the UNF led the more moderate and calculating Kasavubu to lose whatever confidence he may have had in Lumumba. Charging that the Prime Minister was plunging the "nation into fratricidal war," Kasavubu dismissed him on September 5, and appointed Joseph Ileo, president of the Senate of the Congo, as Prime Minister.

That same day, in angry retaliation, Lumumba in three fiery speeches over Radio Leopoldville denounced Kasavubu, "dismissed" him as President, and called upon the workers and the Congolese army to rally to his cause.

Andrew W. Cordier, a U.S. citizen and the U.N. Undersecretary for General Assembly Affairs (then serving as Hammarskjold's temporary Special Representative in the Congo),[6] was confronted with the task of dealing with mounting disorder without interfering illegally in Congolese internal affairs. He acted quickly. On the evening of September 5, he closed all major airports in the country to non-U.N. traffic "in the interests of the maintenance of peace." The following day, he closed temporarily the Leopoldville radio station. Five years after the event, Cordier said:

> One move I made was to close the airports. Thus we checked the influx of reinforcements to those centers of gravest danger, particularly Leopoldville and South Kasai. It was also essential to turn off the transmitter of the Leopoldville radio station, since highly charged emotional appeals inciting the people were on the verge of producing a totally uncontrollable situation . . . these steps had to be taken as temporary measures to preserve law and order.

6 A list of the chief U.N. civilian and military representatives in the Congo, 1960–64, is found in Appendix D.

The various actions taken did contain the conflict, and respect for the United Nations Force and its individual members was greatly increased.[7]

Cordier's action also had a significant impact on the struggle for control of the Leopoldville government. Closing the airports blocked unilateral Soviet military action in behalf of Lumumba. (Direct Soviet aid, incidentally, was a violation of the Council resolutions.) Specifically, it prevented Soviet IL–14 planes from transporting Lumumbist troops to Leopoldville and elsewhere.

The closing of the radio station was a more serious deprivation for Lumumba than for Kasavubu because Lumumba was the more persuasive orator and Kasavubu had access to Radio Brazzaville across the river. After vigorous protests from both men, the Leopoldville radio was returned to the Central Government on September 12. The airports were retained under U.N. control.

The net political effect of Cordier's actions, whatever their intention, was to frustrate the ambitions of Lumumba and his outside supporters, and to advance the fortunes of Kasavubu and other moderate leaders. Under the circumstances, it was virtually impossible for U.N. officials or the UNF to take any significant initiative in the Congo without affecting its internal affairs. Further, many domestic matters had such immediate international implications that the two could not be separated in the real world of political decision, even if they could be in the world of legal abstractions.

The conclusion seems warranted that Cordier's closing of the airports to ground Soviet planes and his closing of the radio station can be justified under the law-and-order mandate, even though both actions substantially affected the internal political struggle. If Cordier had *not* acted in this way, the result of his failure to act may have influenced the internal situation even more, and in quite another direction.

GOVERNMENT REQUESTS FOR UNF AID

The greatest point of strain between the Secretary-General and the host state occurred during the Lumumba regime in 1960, when the Prime Minister insisted that the UNF become an instrument of his government in subduing secessionist Katanga by force. Lumumba was irritated by Hammarskjold's refusal to employ U.N. troops against

[7] Andrew W. Cordier, "Challenge in the Congo," *Think*, Vol. 31 (July–August, 1965), p. 28.

Katanga, his peaceful escorting of two companies of Swedish troops into Elisabethville on August 12, his refusal to permit an official Congolese government delegation to accompany the U.N. party to Katanga, and his alleged failure to consult closely with Lumumba.

In a sharply worded letter to Hammarskjold on August 14—two days after the introduction of the token U.N. force to Katanga, and five days after the August 9 Resolution which declared that the entry of the UNF into Katanga was "necessary"—Lumumba insisted that his government had a legal right to "call upon" the United Nations "to transport civilian and military representatives of the Central Government to Katanga in opposition to the provincial government."[8] In the same letter, he accused Hammarskjold of conniving with Tshombe and the Belgians, and of acting as though his government "did not exist." He concluded with four demands:

1. That UNF guard units be withdrawn from all airfields and be replaced by Congolese soldiers and police.

2. That all non-African UNF troops in Katanga be replaced immediately by Congolese and other African troops.

3. That U.N. aircraft be placed at Lumumba's disposal "for the transportation of Congolese troops and civilians engaged in restoring order throughout the country" (meaning Katanga).

4. That the UNF immediately "seize all arms and ammunition distributed by the Belgians in Katanga" and hand them over to the Leopoldville government.

Hammarskjold promptly rejected these demands and the interpretation behind them. In the remarkably frank exchange of letters that folowed, Lumumba asserted that "the government and people of the Congo have lost confidence in the Secretary-General of the United Nations."[9] Lumumba's emotional state was illustrated by an unusual request to Hammarskjold contained in the same note. He asked Hammarskjold, who was then visiting in Leopoldville, to delay his scheduled departure to New York for twenty-four hours to permit Lumumba's delegation to the Security Council to "travel on the same aircraft." Finally on August 20, Lumumba sent a telegram to the president of the Council, reiterating his earlier demand that the troops and facilities of the UNF be placed at his disposal.[10]

---

[8] U.N., *SCOR*, Supplement for July, Aug., and Sept., 1960, S/4417, Add. 7 (August 15, 1960), p. 72.

[9] *Ibid.*, p. 76.

[10] U.N., *SCOR*, Supplement for July, Aug., and Sept., 1960, S/4448 (August 20, 1960), p. 107.

In his reply, the Secretary-General said that the UNF must operate under his exclusive control and that, while he wanted to co-operate with the Congolese government, he had no legal obligation to become its instrument. His refusal to permit U.N. troops and facilities to become an adjunct to Lumumba's government did not preclude consultation between them. Nor did his position preclude co-operation with the government in joint or parallel action that was in accord with the Council mandate. The increasingly abusive posture of the Prime Minister, however, made consultation less and less frequent and co-operation virtually impossible.

Hammarskjold's forthright dealing with Lumumba reinforced the rule that the UNF should be independent of the Central Government. There was no significant attempt during the Council of Commissioners' and Ileo governments to make the United Nations an instrument of Leopoldville.

Eighteen months after Lumumba's blatant attempt to use the UNF, Prime Minister Adoula requested U.N. assistance for the specific purpose of occupying Stanleyville and arresting Gizenga. In this case, the Secretary-General complied and provided military assistance to the satisfaction of the host government because he believed that the request was in harmony with the Council mandate.

Certain details of this incident are instructive. On October 4, 1961, Deputy Prime Minister Gizenga, with the explicit permission of the Central Government, left for an eight-day visit to Stanleyville. Ignoring his promise to return, he stayed on, organized a Lumumbist political party, established a 300-man militia loyal only to him, and openly criticized the Leopoldville government. On January 8, 1962, the Chamber of Representatives voted 66–10 to order his return within forty-eight hours to face charges of secessionism. Gizenga refused.

On January 12, forty-one Representatives supported a motion of censure in the Chamber against Gizenga. Thereupon, he mobilized his militia, which took a position around his residence and erected roadblocks. General Victor Lundula, the provincial ANC commander who had sworn allegiance to Leopoldville on November 13, 1961, took counter-measures to maintain order. In a clash between Gizenga's militia and General Lundula's soldiers on January 13, eight of the former and six of the latter were killed.

On the same day, Adoula requested UNF assistance to maintain order in Stanleyville. Acting Secretary-General Thant authorized the assistance, and his order was conveyed to Colonel Teshome, commander of the 980-man Ethiopian Battalion in Stanleyville. Teshome conferred with General Lundula and provided assistance. By the evening of January 14, all of Gizenga's militia except 50 men had been disarmed. During the entire operation, only one UNF platoon had been engaged, and it "had not fired a shot."[11] In the afternoon of January 15, the Parliament removed Gizenga from his ministerial post by a vote of 67–1. On January 20, at the request of Adoula, Gizenga was flown in a U.N. plane to Leopoldville where he was subsequently placed under detention by the Prime Minister.

By assisting Leopoldville in this limited and essentially law-and-order operation, the UNF aided Adoula in bringing down the secessionist pretensions of Lumumba's heir. But it did not become the instrument of the Adoula government. Was this illegal U.N. intervention in internal affairs? It certainly favored Adoula over Gizenga, but the latter was a rebel whose activities posed a treat of civil war. The U.N. action, therefore, was an appropriate implementation of the February 21, 1961 Resolution, which authorized the use of force to prevent civil war. Even without this resolution, the Stanleyville operation which did not involve the UNF in hostilities could probably be legally justified under the original law-and-order mandate.

ORDINANCE 70 AND RUMPUNCH

A major source of tension between the United Nations and the host state was how to deal with secessionist Katanga, particularly how to eliminate foreign personnel who were assisting Tshombe. These foreigners in Katanga, often characterized by the undifferentiated term "mercenaries," fell into three categories. First were the 114 Belgian army officers and 117 other ranks officially lent to Tshombe by Brussels to train and command his gendarmerie, along with 58 Belgian officers in the service of the Katanga police.[12]

The second two categories were volunteers who worked for pay. Anticipating the repatriation of the seconded Belgians, which was completed in September, 1961, Tshombe in January started to recruit European mercenaries. By June, some 300 men from Belgium, France, South Africa, and the Rhodesias had enlisted in Katanga's service.

---

[11] Report by the Officer in Charge, *ONUC (Opération des Nations Unies au Congo* —United Nations Operation in the Congo), January 20, 1962, *United Nations Review*, Vol. 9 (February, 1962), p. 27.

[12] These figures as of October 8, 1960 were reported in Dayal's *Second Progress Report*. U.N., *SCOR*, Supplement for Oct., Nov., Dec., 1960, S/4557 (October 8, 1960), Pt. B, pp. 44–45.

About one-third were given training and command assignments. The larger group was organized into an all-white "International Company" under the command of a Britisher, Captain Richard William Browne. The unit's strength was about 200 officers and men, most of whom came from South Africa.[13]

Armed with the February 21 Resolution calling for the "immediate withdrawal . . . of all Belgian and other foreign military and paramilitary personnel and political advisers . . . and mercenaries" from the Congo Hammarskjold was determined to move energetically against Tshombe's foreign aides in co-operation with the Central Government. This determination was reinforced when the Parliament endorsed Cyrille Adoula as Prime Minister on August 2. Hammarskjold regarded him as the first legitimate prime minister since Lumumba. He welcomed the new "constitutional government," and said all U.N. aid "should be rendered exclusively to your government." The UNF, he added, "has only one goal, to aid your government in the maintenance of public order."[14]

Hammarskjold shared Adoula's overriding desire to end secession in Katanga, but the Secretary-General recognized the UNF had no authority to seek this objective by initiating military action. They were agreed, however, that direct action should be taken against Tshombe's mercenaries. To get the strongest possible legal basis for such action, Hammarskjold, through Mahmoud Khiary, his Chief of U.N. Civilian Operations in Leopoldville, requested the Adoula government immediately to issue an order threatening the mercenaries with expulsion and then to "inform us of this order in a new letter which refers to the last letter." This remarkable instruction was contained in a cable from Hammarskjold to Khiary on August 23, 1961.[15] The government obediently issued the decree, known as *Ordinance 70*, the next day, using almost exactly Hammarskjold's language.

Four days later, on August 28, using Ordinance 70 as legal support, the UNF at five o'clock in the morning launched *Operation Rumpunch*, which in twelve hours captured 338 mercenaries in Elisabethville and north Katanga. With the backing of Sture Linner, the Swedish U.N.

---

[13] CRISP, *Congo: 1961*, prepared by Benoit Verhaegen (Les Dossiers du CRISP, n. d.), p. 233.

[14] U.N., *SCOR*, Supplement for July, Aug., Sept., 1961, S/4923 (August 13, 1961), p. 76.

[15] The full cable is reproduced in Appendix G. The cable and the ordinance both took into account the April 17, 1961 agreement between Hammarskjold and President Kasavubu which explicitly exempted foreign advisers hired by the central government from falling under the February 21 Resolution.

Officer in Charge in Leopoldville, Conor Cruise O'Brien, the U.N. Representative in Katanga, suspended the operation before all arrests were made. He did this under pressure from the Belgian Consul who promised to repatriate promptly all prohibited personnel—the 338 under U.N. arrest and the 104 who were still at large according to a U.N. list.[16]

The promise of the Belgian Consul was largely empty, partly because he had full legal authority only over the small number of remain Belgian seconded officers, not over Belgian nationals recruited directly by Tshombe. The French and British consuls were in a similar predicament. By September 8, some 273 mercenaries were reported to have been sent home (some of whom later returned); another sixty-five awaited repatriation. A considerable number remained. The job was not finished.

In planning Operation Rumpunch, the UNF actively co-operated with Leopoldville, but it did not take orders from the Adoula government. On the contrary, the origin of Ordinance 70 suggests that Hammarskjold was giving very specific advice to Adoula, though the U.N. initiative in this matter could be described as technical assistance. Neither party was using the other since they had a common immediate objective—eliminating mercenaries—and a common ultimate goal— ending secession. The latter goal was usually referred to in official U.N. pronouncements by euphemisms such as "solving the Katanga problem."[17]

During Operation Rumpunch, U.N. troops occupied the Elisabethville post office and radio station, and threw a guard around the home of Interior Minister Godefroid Munongo. This was direct action against the Katanga regime, though no blood was spilled, and its net effect was to aid the fortunes of Adoula at the expense of Tshombe. But since the Council resolutions called for the end of Katanga secession, without specifying what authority the UNF had in achieving this result, Operation Rumpunch could be described as legitimate intervention on behalf of the Congo's territorial integrity.

THE SEPTEMBER 13, 1961 CRISIS

By early September, O'Brien, Khiary, and other U.N. officials came to regard the suspension of arrests during Operation Rumpunch as a

[16] U.N., *SCOR,* Supplement for July, Aug., Sept., 1961, S/4940, Add. 1 (September 14, 1961), p. 106.
[17] See Appendix G, para. 6.

blunder, and were determined to finish the job by direct action, though
U.N. negotiations on the mercenary problem with the Belgians and
others were continuing in the Congo, Brussels, and New York. Fearing
a resumption of direct U.N. action, preparations were being made on
the Katanga side.

Khiary and O'Brien appeared to exercise the greatest initiative
within U.N. circles, though Linner, Lieutenant General Sean McKeown,
the Force commander, and Brigadier K. A. S. Raja, the Katanga commander, were involved in the planning of the follow-up to Operation
Rumpunch. It was given the code name *Operation Morthor* (the Hindi
word for "smash"), and from the U.N. side was an attempt to dupli-
cate, build upon, and go beyond the bloodless and partially successful
Rumpunch.

The collaboration between the UNF and Leopoldville was even
closer in Morthor (or Round One), than in Rumpunch.[18] On September 8, the Congolese Parliament held a secret session of the Chamber
and apparently agreed on a plan to be executed largely by the UNF.
The plan included: (1) the arrest of the remaining mercenaries in
Katanga; (2) the arrest of Tshombe and his key ministers; (3) disarming of the Katanga gendarmerie; (4) and concurrently with these actions, the dispatch of a Central Government commissioner to take
control of Katanga.

With the aid and probably on the initiative of U.N. authorities, the
government prepared warrants for the arrest of Tshombe, Munongo,
and three other Katanga ministers. The warrants were given to O'Brien
in Elisabethville on September 11 by Vladimir Fabry, an American
who was the U.N. legal adviser in Leopoldville.

As the plans for Operation Morthor were nearing completion,
Linner made a quick but unsuccessful trip to Brussels to stave off what
appeared to be a collision course in Katanga, but this did not prevent
him from being fully informed of the new plan. In fact, he cabled
details of the plan to Hammarskjold and received his approval in

---

18 A brief summary of Round One is found in Appendix H. For fuller accounts
and interpretations, see the official U.N. documents; A. L. Burns and Nina Heathcote, *Peacekeeping by U.N. Forces: From Suez Through the Congo* (New York:
Praeger, 1963), pp. 100–31; King Gordon, *The United Nations in the Congo: A Quest
for Peace* (Carnegie Endowment for International Peace, 1962), pp. 122–32; Conor
Cruise O'Brien, *To Katanga and Back* (New York: Simon and Schuster, 1962), pp.
68–330; Hoskyns, *Congo Since Independence*, pp. 413–35; and Ernest W. Lefever,
Crisis in the Congo (Washington: Brookings Institution, 1965), pp. 79–88.

principle for putting it into effect if the situation remained as described. The Secretary-General left the timing to his subordinates in the Congo.

At four o'clock on the morning of September 13, Morthor was launched. On that fateful day, the U.N. operation was more severely tested than at any other point in the Congo mission. It was the beginning of an eight-day clash in which some fifty Katangan and eleven U.N. troops were killed. More important, the UNF was widely believed to have initiated the fire-fight, and was accused of committing atrocities. The peace organization was denounced in black headlines around the world for "waging war."

O'Brien expected his major objectives in Elisabethville to be achieved by mid-afternoon of the thirteenth. They included the arrest (or house detention) of five ministers, using the government warrants as legal authority; the securing of the post office, and the radio studios and transmitters; raiding the *Sureté* offices and the Information Ministry; and, most important, an agreement from Tshombe to end secession. Other U.N. officials—at least outwardly—shared his optimism. But the very timing of the operation to coincide with Hammarskjold's flight from New York to the Congo suggests that there may have been unacknowledged misgivings about the quick success of the operation or about Hammarskjold's views on some of the measures undertaken by the UNF. Hammarskjold was due to arrive in Leopoldville just about the time the job was to have been accomplished. O'Brien has frankly stated that the Secretary-General would doubtless have suffered embarrassment "if fighting were actually going on in Katanga while he was in Leopoldville," and he recalled Khiary's warning as the latter left Elisazethville on September 12: "Above all, no half measures."[19]

Rapidly unfolding events did not conform to O'Brien's expectations. Unlike Operation Rumpunch, Morthor did not take Tsombe by surprise and was not bloodless. Tshombe had been informed of the secret September 8 meeting, and was expecting the UNF to take action similar to Operation Rumpunch. The Katanga gendarmerie, now led by the mercenaries rather than regular Belgian officers, had taken precautionary measures. By September 12, Katanga paracommandos trained by the French mercenary, René Faulques, were guarding the Elisabethville post office.

---

[19] O'Brien, *To Katanga and Back*, pp. 246–251.

Within twenty minutes after Morthor got under way, there was an exchange of fire in the vicinity of the post office. It is still not certain whether the Indians or a Katanga sniper fired first. A fight followed:

. . . the Katangans fought fiercely but were inexorably driven out of their positions by Indian soldiers using hand-grenades and bayonets. Once the Indians were inside [the post office] they had to repulse a counterattack by Katangan troops and mercenaries who drove into the square in armoured cars. As a result of this incident, the Indians were in a highly nervous state and seem to have shot at any vehicles moving past, including a Katanga police jeep and an ambulance.[20]

The Indians captured the radio station in hand-to-hand fighting in which twenty gendarmes and policemen were killed. Eyewitness reports suggest the Indians, possibly because of panic, were brutal and shot a number of gendarmes and policemen in cold blood.[21]

By eight o'clock that evening, the post office and radio station were in the hands of the UNF. Swedish troops had occupied the *Sureté* offices. Only one minister, Vice-President Jean-Baptiste Kibwe, had been captured. Tshombe, with the aid of the British Consul, had escaped to Northern Rhodesia. The official Central Government party which had flown to Elisabethville in a U.N. plane was waiting impatiently at the airport under UNF protection.

In spite of these setbacks, and particularly the failure to arrest Munongo, O'Brien announced at 8:00 P.M. to startled reporters that the "secession of Katanga is ended," that the province was now under the authority of Leopoldville, and that a special commissioner would be coming from Leopoldville to take over.[22] He said the purpose of his action was to prevent civil war between Katanga and the ANC, and

[20] Hoskyns, *Congo Since Independence,* p. 419.

[21] *Ibid.,* Miss Hoskyns notes that "public opinion in Britain was considerably influenced by the fact that Richard Williams of the BBC" stated "he personally had seen Indian troops acting with 'brutal savagery' and firing on Red Cross vehicles, and that this story was backed up by Gavin Young of the *Observer,*" pp. 427–28. See also *Katanga Government White Paper* (Elisabethville, 1962), pp. 47–51. In an interview with the author in Elisabethville (February 10, 1965), a British resident of Elisabethville during Round One said that of the gendarmes and police killed in the taking of the radio station, eighteen were found face-down in the grass with their hands over their heads, having been shot in the back by the Indians. He referred to Brigadier Raja as an "inefficient swine." In an interview with the author in New Delhi (February 23, 1965), Brigadier Raja denied any brutality on the part of his troops on September 13, 1961. He said that the UNF did not violate the Red Cross symbol at any time, "though we shot at one 'Red Cross' truck on which a bazooka had been mounted. Our men were civilized," he said. "Our conscience is clear. My conscience is very clear."

[22] *New York Times,* September 14, 1961.

that he acted in accordance with the February 21 Resolution which authorized the use of force to prevent civil war.

The U.N. operation went somewhat better in North Katanga. The UNF captured gendarmerie posts in Albertville, Manono, and Nyunzu, and held on to the vital Kamina base.

On September 20, a provisional cease-fire was signed between Tshombe and Khiary in Ndola, Northern Rhodesia.[23] The agreement provided for prisoner exchange; the return of the radio facilities, post office, and other public buildings held by the UNF; and a joint commission of four members to supervise the agreement, including the inspection of all military centers in Katanga. Before the cease-fire was approved by the Secretariat on September 24, U.N. officials made it clear that it did not imply a recognition of the Elisabethville regime, and that its provisions applied only to Tshombe's forces and the UNF in Katanga.[24]

In legal, political, and military terms, Round One was a great embarrassment to Hammarskjold who arrived in Leopoldville on the afternoon of September 13, just when O'Brien had hoped the action would be over. Hammarskjold was distressed because the UNF had used force, because the effort failed, and because O'Brien had announced that its purpose was to end secession and that he cited the civil war paragraph of the February 21 Resolution as his authority to use force. Hammarskjold was also chagrined because O'Brien and Khiary apparently had tried to present him with a *fait accompli*.

Hammarskjold was further upset by the criticism of the world press which accused the United Nations of launching a war to settle an essentially internal problem in the Congo. He was also under great political pressure to explain what had happened and what he was going to do about it. The displeasure of the British government was expressed fully and directly to the Secretary-General by Lord Lansdowne who had just arrived in Leopoldville to assess the situation in the wake of Operation Rumpunch.

Hammarskjold had no easy way out. No simple explanation would serve the various interests he felt compelled to serve. If he had fired O'Brien for exceeding the authority of the UNF to use force, or for declaring that the end of secession was his purpose, or for plain ineptitude, this might have injured the entire U.N. operation and alienated

[23] Khiary was substituting for Hammarskjold (who was killed in the crash of a U.N. plane on September 17, 1961, on his way to Ndola).

[24] U.N., *SCOR*, Supplement for Oct., Nov., Dec., 1961, S/4940, Add. 11 (October 13, 1961), pp. 9–10.

the Afro-Asians and the Central Government.[25] If he condoned both O'Brien's action and O'Brien's legal interpretation, he would have lost the support of the British, the Belgians, and others who insisted on the restrained use of force and on a stricter definition of the noninterference rule. His own position up to this point made it impossible for him to support either the direct action or O'Brien's interpretation of it.

The Secretary-General moved quickly to repair the damage to his reputation as a scrupulous observer of legal constraints. After consulting with his advisers in Leopoldville and New York (but not with O'Brien), he issued a public statement on September 14, the relevant portion of which was summarized in the next *Annual Report of the Secretary-General:*

> At dawn of 13 September, the United Nations forces began once again to apprehend and evacuate foreign military and paramilitary personnel, for this purpose taking security precautions similar to those adopted on 28 August. At that juncture, the United Nations garage was set on fire, and troops proceeding to the garage to extinguish the blaze were fired on from the building in which the Belgian Consulate was located and from houses occupied by non-African residents in which a number of Belgian military personnel were known to be staying.[26]

Hammarskjold's explanation said nothing about ending secession, emphasized that Operation Morthor was simply the continuation of Operation Rumpunch, and portrayed the use of U.N. force as purely defensive. O'Brien said the reference to a fire in a U.N. garage was a fabrication. Linner said he knew of no such fire.

The Secretary-General's public explanation was less than candid, though it must be said it was issued before the details were fully known. Morthor was not simply a continuation of Rumpunch. The use of force was not simply in self-defense. The sending of well-armed troops to capture strategic points in a city and to apprehend cabinet ministers at four o'clock in the morning is hardly a use of force in self-defense. The U.N. statement made no reference to what appears to be well-authenticated cases of UNF brutality. Hammarskjold also knew that O'Brien acted to end secession, an objective the United Nations had no authority to pursue by force. In fact, the UNF was not specifically authorized to use force to arrest mercenaries until the subsequent Security Council Resolution of November 24, 1961.

---

[25] O'Brien resigned from U.N. service December 1, 1961, after he had been called to New York for consultations. He was never publicly reprimanded.

[26] U.N., *GAOR, Annual Report of the Secretary-General on the Work of the Organization, June 16, 1961–June 15, 1962,* A/5201, p. 4. (The full statement is found in U.N. Document S/4940 (September 14, 1961), p. 103.

Hammarskjold did not explain how the warrants for the arrest of the Katanga ministers were written, or why O'Brien used them as his legal authority. Nor did the Secretary-General attempt to justify the use of a U.N. plane to carry an official Central Government delegation to Elisabethville, even though he had explicitly told Gizenga on an earlier occasion that it would be illegal for a government party to be transported to Elisabethville on a U.N. plane.

Hammarskjold's relation to Leopoldville had clearly shifted in the direction of greater co-operation since the days of Lumumba, though probably not enough to condone the degree of collaboration which actually took place in the preparation for Morthor. This closer identification between the U.N. operation and Leopoldville had also been underlined by Linner on August 3, 1961, when he said that "if the government used military force to impose its control on the entire national territory, and if resistance by local authorities led to bloodshed, the 'United Nations would not regard this as a civil war' and would do nothing to prevent it."[27] Presumably these remarks referred to Katanga. Further, Hammarskjold had suggested the adoption of Ordinance 70, and then used it to justify Operation Rumpunch.

Even more than Rumpunch, Operation Morthor was an example of close collaboration in which it is not possible to say with certainty where the initiative lay. Given the weakness and inexperience of the Adoula government, it would seem safe to conclude that the concrete plans for dealing with Katanga came from U.N. sources. The execution of these plans were almost exclusively in U.N. hands. The use of government arrest warrants by the UNF, and the use of a U.N. plane by the government delegation obscured the independence of each party, but it did not mean that the UNF had become an agent of Leopoldville, since the UNF had a vague mandate to do something about Katanga from the Security Council. Here again, the U.N. operation took sides, but was it not required to do so under the directives of the Council? Questions may be raised about the propriety and legality of certain specific measures, particularly the nature and use of force in Elisabethville, but as far as the U.N.–host-state rules are concerned, there appears to have been no significant violation on either side.

ROUNDS TWO AND THREE

For the U.N. Mission, Round One was a military and political setback. Secession had not been ended. In spite of the truce, tension con-

[27] Report by Henry Tanner, *New York Times*, August 4, 1961, p. 6.

tinued between the U.N. presence and Tshombe. UNF units were harassed. On December 2, 1961, Katanga gendarmes fired on UNF troops at the Elisabethville airport. The Indian officers, who had the largest national contingent in Katanga, were becoming restive under the politically imposed constraints on the Force. The Indian government was also concerned about the failure to settle the Katanga problem.

On December 5, the UNF undertook action to defend its position in Elisabethville, and Secretary-General U Thant authorized "all counter-action—ground and aerial—deemed necessary" to restore complete freedom of movement in the area. The State Department supported him. After an Indian unit removed the roadblock between the airport and U.N. headquarters, the Katanga forces opened fired with heavy mortars, machine guns, and rifles against UNF positions. This was the beginning of the second clash—Round Two—which lasted fourteen days. At its peak, the December operation involved 6,000 UNF troops, compared with 1,400 in September. About fifteen jet and other U.N. planes were used. Offensive tactics were employed in the air and on the ground, and U.N. troops were *not* under orders to shoot only in self-defense. Some 206 Katanga troops, 50 civilians, and 25 U.N. soldiers were killed. The fifty civilians (which reportedly included a few atrocity cases), were killed by U.N. troops, due in part to the fact that the Force was taking a defended town from which civilians had not been evacuated.[28]

The new U.N. initiative drew severe criticism. After the air strikes of December 6, 1961, a number of Western European states accused the UNF of going beyond self-defense, carrying on warlike operations, and violating the Geneva Conventions. Thant publicly regretted civilian casualties, but denied other charges, citing "the campaigns of violence, abduction of hostages, assault and battery, murders, the setting up of roadblocks, etc." by Tshombe's gendarmerie. He insisted that the UNF had shown "great self-restraint," and would not have used military action at all had not the roadblocks prevented "freedom of movement." Thant noted that officials of *Union Minière* have proudly admitted the manufacture of gendarmerie armored cars and of bombs, and that the mining firm had made it possible for mercenaries to go underground by putting them nominally on its payroll. He denied that the

---

[28] This is the judgment of representatives from several Western governments in Elisabethville. See *The Katangese Government's White Paper on the Events of September and December, 1961* (Elisabethville, 1962), pp. 53–84.

U.N. aim was "to force a political solution to the Katanga problem."[29] Thant's assertion was hardly the whole truth because he was obviously eager to have Tshombe acknowledge the authority of the Central Government. He also believed that the exercise of "freedom of movement" by the UNF in Katanga would contribute to this political objective.

In Round Two, the U.N. Command carefully avoided certain pitfalls of Round One. Militarily the UNF was much better prepared. Legally, U.N. authorities sought to avoid the close identification with Leopoldville which had seemed to compromise its independence in September. Again, the UNF took the side of Leopoldville and again the operation failed to end secession.

This objective was not to be achieved until a full year later, and only after a protracted period of complex and frustrating negotiations in the Congo, Washington, Brussels, London, and New York. In August, 1962, Thant promulgated a Plan for National Reconciliation based on proposals prepared by the State Department in co-operation with the Belgian and British governments.[30] The Plan made little headway. The chasm between Leopoldville and Elisabethville seemed unbridgeable by peaceful means.

During the fruitless negotiations, there was a gradual military build-up by both sides in Katanga. By early December, U.N. troops there numbered 13,500. On December 11, Belgian Foreign Minister Paul-Henri Spaak characterized Tshombe as a "rebel," and said that he was prepared to support the UNF and the Central Government if they resorted to armed force to end Katanga's secession.[31] Spaak's statement was an important turning point. Though it was a declaration of one statesman of one small state—obviously a highly interested state—it reflected an increasingly widespread frustration with Katanga and a disposition to place a broader interpretation on the authority of the UNF to use force.

On December 21, an eight-man U.S. military mission, headed by Lieutenant General Louis Truman, arrived in Leopoldville for a five-day survey of the needs of the UNF. This State Department trip caused some apprehension in diplomatic circles in Leopoldville and Elisabeth-

---

[29] U.N., *SCOR*, Supplement for Oct., Nov., Dec., 1961, S/5025 (December 15, 1961), pp. 195–199 and *The Annual Report of the Secretary-General on the Work of the Organization, June 16, 1961–June 15, 1962*, U.N. Document, A/5201, p. 16.

[30] *New York Times*, August 21, 1962. For text of the Plan, see U.N. *SCOR*, Supplement for July, Aug., Sept., 1962, S/5053, Add. 11 (August 20, 1962), pp. 16–17.

[31] Cited in "Chronologie des Événements," *Études Congolaises* (Brussels), Vol. 4, No. 2 (February, 1963), p. 48.

ville. But it was warmly welcomed by the U.N. Command in Katanga. After assessing the situation, General Truman prepared a list of needed supplies, including a temporary bridge, trucks, armored personnel carriers, mine-clearing gear, and transport and tanker planes for immediate delivey to Elisabethville by air. This equipment arrived in early January, too late to make a military difference. Major General Prem Chand, the new Indian commander in Elisabethville, was convinced that the mission meant not only increased U.S. logistical assistance, but also signaled Washington's determination to support U.N. military action since persuasion, negotiation, and economic measures apparently had failed. Prem Chand's interpretation of the mission was correct. After a thorough reappraisal of U.S.–Congo policy in November, President Kennedy concluded that direct U.N. action was required.

The Truman mission, and Spaak's endorsement of military action, plus growing neutralist pressures for stronger measures; the disposition of the Indian officers to finish what, in their view, was the unfinished task of Rounds One and Two; the expected withdrawal of the large Indian brigade in early 1963 because of Red China's attack on India's northern border; and the financial plight of the United Nations were all factors which pointed toward the final solution of the Katanga problem by force.

For some months, the U.N. Command had been developing a plan for ending Katanga's secession by force, though in legal terms it was called a plan for extending "freedom of movement" throughout the province. A date was set, but as matters developed, Round Three started several weeks prematurely in response to the one-sided harassment of U.N. troops by Katanga gendarmes. After four days of intermittent firing which Tshombe seemed powerless to control, the UNF on December 28 started to move against strong points in Elisabethville. In the first instance the UNF was literally moving in self-defense.

What fortuitously started as a defense of existing UNF positions soon became *Operation Grandslam,* the code word given by the Indian officers to the existing three-phase plan. The operation was completed on January 21, 1963, when the U.N. troops entered Kolwezi without resistance and were received by Tshombe personally. This marked the end of the military phase of bringing Katanga under the control of the United Nations and the Central Government.

Round Three, in contrast to the two previous clashes, was conducted with discipline and restraint. Major General Prem Chand was a competent and respected commander. Throughout the operation, the UNF encountered little resistance. The mercenaries, now largely French and South African, were considerably less organized than in the earlier rounds. During or shortly after Round Three, most of the remaining mercenaries left Katanga by the way of Angola. Tshombe's appeals for a scorched-earth policy went largely ignored. For these reasons, casualties on both sides were light. Noting this fact, Thant said: "For a peace force, even a little fighting is too much, and only a few casualties are too many."[32]

This successful use of U.N. military force to end secession was applauded on almost all sides; Moscow and Washington were pleased. In Leopoldville there was joy, and in Brussels and London a sigh of relief.

In all three rounds, UNF military action was exercised without any parallel or supporting action by Congolese troops. On the planning level, however, there was a degree of co-operation with the Adoula regime, though progressively less with each operation. It is doubtful that the Adoula government or even General Mobutu knew about the U.N. plans for Operation Grandslam. There was always the hope that the ANC could be involved in ending secession and thus share in the honor, but this was denied Adoula. Nevertheless, he certainly benefitted politically by the success of Round Three.

While force was used with commendable restraint—this is attested to by all observers, notwithstanding the Jadotville[33] and Lufira River[34] incidents—it was used by the UNF for purposes beyond self-defense narrowly defined, and arresting mercenaries. In the official U.N. White Book, the Secretariat declared that force was used in Round Three in self-defense and "to establish complete freedom of movement."[35] Any reasonable definition of "freedom of movement," sufficient to accomplish its objective of maintaining order throughout the Congo, gave the UNF the legal authority to establish a military presence in all the key points in Katanga. Having failed to achieve this objective by two-and-one-half years of negotiation, the UNF finally used limited force to exercise this admittedly vaguely defined right.

[32] U.N., *SCOR*, Supplement for Jan., Feb., March, 1963, S/5240 (February 4, 1963), p. 95.
[33] After the UNF peacefully took Jadotville, two Belgian women in a civilian car were shot and killed by Indian soldiers at a U.N. checkpoint on the edge of the city when the male driver suddenly accelerated the car rather than slowing down or stopping. This unauthorized shooting greatly embarrassed U.N. officials.
[34] See Chap. 10.
[35] *The United Nations and the Congo: Some Salient Facts* (United Nations: February, 1963), p 9. One-hundred-thousand copies of this nineteen-page booklet were printed in English, and 25,000 in French.

THE UNF–ANC PROBLEM

The disunity and irresponsibility of the Congolese National Army (ANC) were symptoms as well as causes of the political fragmentation of the Congo. The 1960 mutiny of the ANC was the proximate cause of the crisis which invited U.N. intervention. Since then ANC lawlessness, indiscipline, and factionalism have been major disruptive factors. The ANC has never been a united national army. As late as 1966, only a portion of Congolese troops were under effective Central Government control.

Incidents of ANC indiscipline include extortion, wanton murder, and rape, attacks on UNF units, mutiny, and the arrest and attempted assassination of the army's Commander in Chief, Mobutu. In a four-month period, from May through August, 1963, one unpublished U.S. tabulation (admittedly incomplete) of events "traceable to the instability of Congolese security forces" lists sixty unlawful incidents, excluding "ordinary" crimes. Thant summarized the situation as of June, 1964, with diplomatic understatement:

> . . . the ANC is still insufficiently trained and officered to cope with any major crisis. Most of the Congolese troops still show, in emergency situations, inadequate discipline and devotion to duty or country. Good officers, who are competent and earnest, would seem to be the exception rather than the rule. The result is that there is little authority at the top and little soldierly spirit in the ranks. The lack of adequate leadership and of an organic chain of command is perhaps the main cause for the present ineffectiveness of the ANC.[36]

This situation confronted the Secretary-General and the UNF with three difficult and interrelated problems. The most immediate one was caused by incidents in which Congolese soldiers took hostile action against UNF personnel.[37] The second question had to do with U.N. responsibility for training and reorganizing the ANC. The third, underlying the first two problems, concerned the basic relation between an invited foreign military presence and the domestic military establishment of a legally sovereign state. This root problem was greatly complicated during the first three months of the U.N. operation when there were three separate and independent military forces in the Congo: the mutinous ANC with 25,000 men in the process of firing its Belgian officers; Belgian forces numbering about 10,000 men; and the

---

[36] U.N., *SCOR*, "Report by the Secretary-General on the Withdrawal of the United Nations in the Congo and on Other Aspects of the United Nations Operation There," Document S/5784, p. 30 (Mimeographed June 29, 1964.)

[37] A number of such incidents are briefly described in Appendix H.

quickly improvised UNF of 16,000 men. In a sense, the UNF was intended to replace both Belgian and Congolese troops, but it lacked authority to expel the Belgians or to disarm the Congolese. Under diplomatic pressure Belgian forces were speedily withdrawn, except for the small number of seconded officers and men who remained in Katanga for a year. But the tense and undefined relationship between the UNF and the ANC continued to be one of the most perplexing problems confronting the Secretary-General.

The Ndjili Airport (Leopoldville) incident,[38] and Major General H. T. Alexander's subsequent disarmament of ANC troops, illustrate most legal and political facets of the UNF–ANC problem. On August 18, 1960 Congolese soldiers surrounded the U.N. plane, interrogated the crew, and mistreated the four Canadians, whom the Congolese accused of being Belgian paratroopers. After some delay, the U.N.-Ghanian unit guarding the airport succeeded in releasing the Canadians.[39] Hammarskjold protested to the Leopoldville government and criticized the Ghanian unit for passive behavior in the face of the assault.

General Alexander, the British commander of the Ghanian contingent, acknowledged the facts of the unfortunate airport incident, but strongly repudiated "any criticisms of Ghanian officers and men." Noting this was but one of many cases of ANC atrocities and indiscipline, Alexander said the "immediate and also long-term possibility of getting the country back to normal hinges on the retraining and disciplining" of the Congolese army. The first task, he said, was to disarm the ANC, implying that force should be used if persuasion failed. He pointed out, however, that he and two Ghanian officers had completely and peacefully disarmed the ANC units in Leopoldville, suggesting that a general policy of disarming Congolese would probably meet with little or no resistance. Alexander also criticized Major General von Horn, the UNF commander, for failing to issue specific orders on how to deal with such situations, and for his unwillingness to "exercise any military authority at all, thus putting Ghanian and other U.N. troops in an impossible position." He added: "The situa-

[38] ANC soldiers entered a U.N. aircraft, marched the Indian crew away at gun point, manhandled three Moroccan civilians, and beat four out of fourteen Canadian members of the UNF.

[39] CRISP, *Congo: 1960*, II, prepared by J. Gérard-Libois and Benoit Verhaegen (Les Dossiers du CRISP, 1961), 620.

tion is not irretrievable, but it will certainly be hopeless unless something drastic is done."[40]

Undersecretary Bunche, who was the Acting Officer in Charge in Leopoldville, took strong exception to Alexander's interpretation of U.N. authority. He admitted there was "much room for valid criticism" of the UNF, but insisted that the General's criticisms were unjustified because he did not understand that the UNF was a "peace force, not a fighting force," that it could use arms only in self-defense, and that U.N. troops should avoid getting into the "extreme position of having to shoot Congolese."[41] This was before the permissible use of force was broadened by the February 21, 1961 and November 24, 1961 Resolutions.

On the difficult problem of training the unruly ANC, Bunche insisted that nothing could be done without the active co-operation of the Central Government. He acknowledged that "a reorganized and disciplined Congolese National Army is a most, perhaps *the* most, vital problem," but the "way of force offers no possibility for an international body operating in a soverign country at the invitation of that country." Bunche added:

> The United Nations in the Congo has neither sought to replace the Congo Government nor to make it a captive. The UNF is in the Congo as a friend and partner, not as an army of occupation. It has studiously avoided any suggestion of replacing in any way the former colonial administration.[42]

Bunche's legally correct and authoritative view was supported by Hammarskjold. There was no systematic effort by the UNF to disarm ANC units, but Bunche's words did not dispel the suspicions of certain Congolese leaders who tended to regard the UNF as an occupying army bent on disarming the ANC on the slightest pretext. The passive disarmament which had occurred during July and early August, 1960, was short-lived, and the process was actually reversed in mid-August when the U.N. Command gave in to Lumumba's demand that certain disarmed units be permitted to recover their weapons.

The persistent fear of ANC disarmament among Congolese leaders was dramatically illustrated by President Kasavubu's reaction to some

[40] U.N., *SCOR*, Supplement for July, Aug., Sept., 1960, S/4445 (August 19, 1960), pp. 101–102.

[41] U.N., *SCOR*, Supplement for July, Aug., Sept., 1960, S/4451 (August 21, 1960), pp. 113–15. Alexander maintains that Bunche backed him "completely in my attempt to persuade the Congolese soldiers to hand in their weapons." See Major General H. T. Alexander, *African Tightrope: My Two Years as Nkrumah's Chief of Staff* (New York: Frederick A. Praeger, 1966), p. 38.

[42] *Ibid.*

incidents involving U.N. personnel in February, 1961. In response to several assaults by Congolese soldiers against U.N. personnel, including the rape of a civilian woman and the beating with rifle butts of two Canadian officers and two Canadian enlisted men, a U.N. spokesman said an investigation was under way to determine whether "the sudden outburst of outrages" had any connection with "certain threats" made by leaders of the Ileo regime. The statement referred to "bestial behavior" and "brutal assaults" by ANC soldiers.[43]

In reply, Kasavubu angrily warned that the ANC "will open fire if need be against anyone who opposes its mission" and announced that his government had decided to organize a battalion of reservists "in face of a U.N. threat to place the Congo under its tutelage." He added: "We must act. The U.N. is betraying us."[44]

Nearly all competent observers, including Bunche and Alexander, agreed on the desirability of disarming the ANC, but they differed on the feasibility of doing so, given the necessity for government consent. In retrospect, however, it appears that disarmament without coercion might have been possible in the first hectic weeks if the Secretary-General had given high priority to this objective, if it had been vigorously pursued at the diplomatic level in New York and the political level in Leopoldville, and if all U.N. commanders had been instructed to engage in active persuasion toward this end. Evidence suggests that the physical presence of a competent military unit commanded by white officers might well have been sufficient in the great majority of cases to achieve pacific disarmament.

Laying speculation aside, the cold fact is that neither Lumumba nor any of his successors consented even to the temporary disarmament of the ANC and the UNF had to live with this basic fact.

From the beginning it was assumed that one of the major tasks of the U.N. mission was to assist the government in reorganizing and retraining the ANC. A request for such assistance was explicit in the first informal communication from Lumumba to Hammarskjold, transmitted by Bunche on July 11, 1960. The indiscipline of the ANC, however, was not mentioned in the two formal requests on the following day which focused on Belgian "aggression." No Security Council resolution ever specifically authorized the Secretary-General to reorganize or retrain the ANC, but the Congo Advisory Committee, the Secretariat,

43 *New York Times*, February 28, 1961, and *Washington Post and Times Herald*, February 28, 1961.
44 *Ibid.*

the United States, and other supporting states assumed the U.N. mission should assist the government to do precisely this.

The fundamental problem was to secure a competent officer corps to replace the departed Belgian officers. This problem was usually refered to by the euphemism "training and reorganizing" the ANC. The polite language did not lead to cordiality or mutual confidence between U.N. and Congolese officials, and General Mobutu's sensitivity on this matter persisted until the end.

The crucial issue was host-state consent. A U.N. training program for Congolese troops was begun in late August, 1960, under General Hammou Kettani of Morocco, the deputy UNF Commander. It was brought to an abrupt halt by the Mobutu coup the following month. In October, 1961, at the request of Leopoldville, Major General Iyassu Mengesha of Ethiopia made preparations for a U.N. officer training school with a multinational staff. General Mobutu never sent any cadets because he preferred direct assistance from governments of his own choice. From the outset he retained a small group of Belgian advisers on his staff and in the Defense Ministry, and he was anxious to get additional officers from Brussels. On the wall of his office in 1962 hung the pictures of all but one of the past commanders of the Belgian *Force publique;* the exception was the last one, the blunt General Janssens. When Mobutu was asked why the pictures were there, he replied that even though there was political discontinuity in the Congo, there should be military continuity.[45]

Incidental training was provided for some six to eight hundred Congolese when the Thirteenth ANC Battalion was attached to the UNF at Kamina Base, from September, 1962, until it withdrew in February, 1964, but some observers believed they were "integrated" mainly to keep them out of trouble.

The United Nations failed either to disarm or to retrain the ANC. This failure to make any significant provision for the maintenance of internal security after the departure of the UNF was a serious one. There is disagreement as to where the fault lies. Most U.N. officials place the blame on the government. Many observers, including U.S. officials and some U.N. officials, believe that the United Nations was also at fault. Actually, the failure was largely inherent in the situation.

THE GREENE PLAN

Recognizing that the United Nations was making no progress in reorganizing the ANC or providing a reliable officer corps for it, the

45 Author interview in Leopoldville, September, 1962.

United States and other interested governments were eager to find an alternative plan which would yield some positive results before the inevitable withdrawal of the UNF. In July, 1962, Washington sent a military advisory team to the Congo to appraise the situation. The Greene Plan—named after Colonel Michael J. L. Greene, USA, who led the team—was the result.

The purpose of the Greene Plan was to assist the Congo to modernize and train officers for the ANC and the provincial gendarmerie through a series of bilateral assistance programs. The Plan included measures to eliminate unnecessary and unreliable elements from the ANC. These bilateral programs were to be channeled through and coordinated by the United Nations in accordance with Security Council resolutions. The U.N. command was to serve as an umbrella for this multinational technical assistance effort in the security field.

After considerable debate within the U.S. government, discussion in Leopoldville, and confidential consultation with U.N. officials, the United States approached five governments interested in assisting the Congo: Belgium, Canada, Israel, Italy, and Norway. Privately, Thant encouraged the Greene Plan and on February 4, 1963, he said it had become "advisable and desirable" to increase "bilateral aid" to the Congo.[46]

On February 26, 1963, Adoula's office informed Robert A. K. Gardiner, the U.N. Officer in Charge in Leopoldville, that his government had decided to request the following states "for assistance in modernizing the ANC: (1) Canada, for technical schools (communications); (2) Italy for the Air Force; (3) Norway, for the Navy; (4) Israel, for the training of paratroopers; (5) Belgium, for technicians for ANC Headquarters and the various units. Belgium will also assist us in the matter of our bases, the Gendarmerie, and our various military schools." The letter added that the United States "will do no more than provide the equipment necessary to ensure the success of these technical assistance measures."[47]

This was a controversial communication because it introduced the prospect of direct military assistance to the Congo which ran counter to Hammarskjold's original rule against external aid not provided through the U.N. channels. The prohibition was reaffirmed by the November 24, 1961 Council Resolution. While it was directed primarily against states

---

[46] U.N., *SCOR*, Supplement for Jan., Feb., March, 1963, S/5240 (February 4, 1963), p. 101.

[47] S/5240, Add. 2 (May 21, 1963), p. 2. The official U.N. version of this question is summarized in the *Annual Report of the Secretary-General on the Work of the Organization: June 16, 1962–June 15, 1963*, A/5501, pp. 14–15.

assisting Katanga, the implications were broader. Further, U.S. participation, though only through the provision of equipment, raised the
question of direct Big Power involvement, but perhaps no more so
than the U.S. logistical support of the U.N. operation from the
beginning.

The public announcement of the Greene Plan for military assistance
from Belgium, Canada, Italy, Norway, Israel, and the United States
under a U.N. umbrella drew criticism from several quarters. The
Soviet Union called the Plan a NATO scheme to impose colonial
shackles upon the Congo. The United Arab Republic attacked the
plan because of Israel's involvement. Some African leaders were distressed at Belgium's participation. All of this caused Thant to have
second thoughts about the matter. On March 20, 1963, he discussed the
Greene Plan with the Congo Advisory Committee which concluded
that the urgently needed training of the ANC "could be most appro-
priately given" by the states which had contributed troops to the UNF.
This advice ruled out the United States, Belgium, and Israel, and was
probably meant to rule out Canada and Norway as well, both of
which had sent only specialized personnel to the Congo. As it turned
out, none of the neutralist states with troop contingents in the UNF
offered such assistance. On April 29, 1963, Thant informed Adoula
that he could not support the Plan. Adoula replied that the Congo as
a sovereign state had the right to negotiate bilateral agreements and
would do so. The Greene Plan, as such, was dead. Subsequent efforts
to resuscitate it proved fruitless.

Adoula went ahead with bilateral military aid programs to train,
modernize, and streamline the 35,000-man ANC. They were very slow
in getting underway. By June 30, 1964, Israel had trained 220 paratroopers, including General Mobutu himself. Italy had just begun pilot
training with twelve Congolese cadets. Norway and Canada did not
participate.

The most significant program is the officer training effort conducted
by Belgium. As of June 30, 1964, some seventy-five Belgian officers and
advisers were in the Congo. Since Independence Day, about 300 Congolese have gone to Belgium for military training. The United States
provided vehicles, communications gear, and other supporting equipment.

CONCLUSIONS

Returning to the three rules that governed United Nations–host-
state relations, to what extent did each party observe them? There was

always a degree of tension and sometimes hostility between the two actors. That this tension never resulted in a complete break is a tribute to the skill of Hammarskjold and Thant, the quiet supporting diplomacy of the United States and several other countries, and a recognition on the part of Congolese leaders that, in spite of the constant embarrassment, there was no immediate alternative to the U.N. presence. After the UNF arrived, Leopoldville had little choice but to accept it and make the most of it. Hammarskjold summed up the relationship accurately on March 8, 1961, when he said it was:

. . . not merely a contractual relationship in which the Republic can impose its conditions as a host State and thereby determine the circumstances under which the United Nations operates. It is rather a relationship governed by mandatory decisions of the Security Council.[48]

Hammarskjold's interpretation was never seriously challenged. The Congo requested a UNF and never formally asked it to leave. Though Lumumba demanded that the UNF, or at least the white U.N. troops, leave the Congo, and other Congolese leaders occasionally criticized the behavior of U.N. personnel, these criticisms had little or no effect on the operations of the Force or the duration of its mission.

As far as explicit consent from Leopoldville for specific actions or operations of the UNF was concerned, the record indicates that such consent was neither sought nor given for the great bulk of its activities. Nor was it required, since consent refers primarily to the question of initial entry. Thereafter there was bilateral negotiation on significant issues. There was occasional co-operation, but the instances were few. There was no direct co-operation between the troops of the ANC and the UNF, except for the incorporation of the Thirteenth ANC Battalion into the UNF for eighteen months, and the transfer of responsibility from U.N. units to ANC units during the phaseout of the UNF after Round Three.

There was one sensitive area where the absence of government consent made a significant difference—the disarmament and training of the ANC. The Secretary-General knew he had substantial support from Leopoldville when the UNF moved against the mercenaries and the Katanga gendarmerie. He was prepared to take some initiative in calming down local unrest. But when the U.N. mission tried to do something about disarming, training, or reorganizing the ANC, the government balked. Leopoldville's reluctance was natural and understandable. Historically, states needing military assistance have turned to a

---

[48] Message of March 8, 1961, U.N., *SCOR*, Supplement for Jan., Feb., March, 1961, S/4775 (March 30, 1961), pp. 261–65.

close ally or friendly state, and not to an internationally authorized multinational staff. Collaboration in the vital matters of national security implies a degree of mutual trust and some common political objectives. Such mutuality is virtually impossible between a sovereign government and a multinational U.N. mission. Even at best, relations between two close allies tend to be strained on sensitive national security problems. The Congo experience suggests that an international instrumentality is probably not psychologically and politically competent to assist effectively in a task as sensitive as the building of the military establishment of a sovereign state.

According to the second rule, the UNF should cooperate with the Central Government without becoming its instrument. Hammarskjold successfully resisted Lumumba's attempt to use the UNF for his purposes. When the UNF, at the request of Adoula, assisted the government in consolidating its position in Stanleyville and in arresting Gizenga, the UNF in a literal sense was acting as an instrument of the host government. But, given the mandate to help maintain territorial integrity and order, the modest U.N. police assistance in this case could hardly have compromised the essential integrity of the U.N. mission.

If U.N. integrity and independence was ever compromised by collaboration with Leopoldville, it was during Round One when O'Brien used the government's warrants as his legal basis for attempting to arrest Katanga ministers and when a U.N. plane was used to transport a government party to Elisabethville to take control of the province. Tacitly acknowledging this was at least a formal violation of U.N. independence, U. N. authorities in Rounds Two and Three—undertaken for the shared objective of ending Katanga's secession—carefully avoided the appearance of collaboration with Leopoldville. It is doubtful that the government was privy to the U.N. plans which underlay either of these two operations.

The third and most difficult rule governing the U.N. operation was the prohibition against taking of sides in the internal political struggle. It was impossible for the U.N. mission to observe this rule in the Congo where internal and external factors were inextricably intertwined. The net impact of the U.N. peacekeeping mission over the four years was clearly to support the fortunes of the Central Government over the rival centers in Stanleyville, Katanga, and South Kasai which challenged its authority. The U.N. effort tipped the scales in favor of the moderates over the extremists and in favor of those seeking a unified state over those supporting a loose confederation. This was hardly surprising because the coalition of states supporting the U.N. effort also sought the same objectives. And to a considerable extent these very objectives found expression, implicitly or explicitly, in the Council resolutions.

To say that the UNF had a significant impact on the internal affairs of the Congo is not to say that U.N. authorities quickly and easily chose sides. The controversial closing of the Leopoldville radio station and airports by Cordier could be justified on the law-and-order mandate; his action was no fundamental violation of the noninterference rule. The resolutions themselves were not impartial as far as the domestic struggle was concerned; they were strongly anti-Tshombe. Hammarskjold was unusually circumspect in the manner and interpretation of his initial entry into Katanga. His impartiality was attested to by the fact that he was strongly criticized by both sides. The UNF also had a clean bill of health as far as the peaceable roundup of prohibited foreigners was concerned; there were repeated resolutions authorizing this, though not until November 24, 1961, was the use of force for this purpose authorized.

In the three clashes with Katanga forces, the UNF was undoubtedly assisting the cause of the Central Government, but by the time of Round One, the end of secession was an objective repeatedly called for by the Security Council, though it never gave the UNF authority to use force for this purpose. U.N. authorities wanted to end secession. They also wanted to observe the Council constraints on the use of force, constraints strongly reinforced by Britain, Belgium, and other states that opposed the imposition of a political solution by military means. There was a legal way out—the right to use force in self-defense, to prevent civil war, and to exercise freedom of movement. Laying aside the question of the political wisdom of the three rounds in Katanga or the merits of the dispute between Elisabethville and Leopoldville, there were ample legal grounds for the three U.N. operations, with certain exceptions. The use of the arrest warrants and the U.N. plane for government officials in Round One was questionable. The overuse of force by the UNF in Rounds One and Two was obviously indefensible.

As a whole, the U.N. peacekeeping mission maintained its integrity in its relations with the host government. It was not captured, subverted, used, or even misled by Leopoldville or by any faction in the Congo.

4.

The United States: Coalition Leader

On December 15, 1961, President Kennedy designated his Ambassador to the Congo, Edmund A. Gullion, as a special representative to help arrange an agreement between Prime Minister Adoula and secessionist Katanga's Tshombe. Four days later, Ambassador Gullion escorted Tshombe in the presidental plane *Columbine* dispatched especially for that purpose—from Ndola to Kitona, a U.N. military base at the mouth of the Congo, to meet with Adoula. Whatever may be said of the wisdom of this dramatic gesture, usually reserved for heads of state, it does illustrate the deep interest of the United States in the Congo crisis. The American commitment was greater than that of any other state, with the sole exception of Belgium.

During its first four years of independence, the Congo was on the front burner at the White House and the State Department, sharing with Berlin, Cuba, and Vietnam the distinction of having a special task force devoted to its problems. The role of the UNF was a matter of considerable controversy within the State Department. Congress joined in the debate. Senator Thomas J. Dodd's advocacy of Tshombe's cause earned him the sobriquet, "Ambassador to Katanga," to the discomfort of the U.S. Ambassador in Leopoldville. Portions of the press and public were passionately partisan, though no American blood was being spilled. In 1960 Walter Lippmann called the U.N. peace-keeping effort "the most advanced and sophisticated experiment in international co-operation ever attempted,"[1] and four years later, Arthur Krock referred to UNF action as "the bloody war to suppress the establishment of Katanga as a separate state."[2]

This inquiry is not concerned with the Congo debate within the government or the impact of the Congo question on the American public, but rather with U.S. policy toward the U.N. operation in the light

[1] *Washington Post and Times Herald,* July 21, 1960.
[2] *New York Times,* December 4, 1964.

of the depth and sustained character of Washington's commitment to a crisis in a part of the world previously regarded as the periphery of American interest.[3]

INTERESTS AND OBJECTIVES

The Congo erupted six months before the end of the Eisenhower administration, but there was no significant difference between Eisenhower and Kennedy in the assessment of the crisis, or the nature of American interests in central Africa. From the first day of the crisis, Washington sought a united Congo with a stable and moderate government in Leopoldville, representing all major factions and capable of sustaining mutually beneficial relations with Western states. Both administrations wanted the new state to succeed politically and economically, and sought to ensure continued Western access to the vast economic resources of the country. The United States wanted to frustrate Soviet subversion, to avoid civil war, and to integrate Katanga peacefully. These specific objectives were compatible with the larger goal of stability and peaceful change in Africa.

In Washington, more energy was devoted to the Congo than to the rest of Africa combined because the immediate dangers and opportunities there characterized the continent as a whole. Wayne Fredericks of the State Department's African Bureau said: "If we don't have a Congo policy, we don't have an African policy."[4] The European Bureau kept insisting that U.S. African policy had to be orchestrated with America's far-flung commitments elsewhere, particularly in Europe. The government had to take seriously the interests of Belgium, Britain, France, and the other NATO countries that were unenthusiastic about U.N. intervention, as well as the views of the Afro-Asian leaders calling for more militant U.N. action in Katanga.

Washington was deeply concerned with the lawlessness and disorder that followed the ANC mutiny of July, 1960, Lumumba's dismissal of the Belgian officer corps, and the exodus of Belgian administrative and technical personnel. The State Department feared the Soviet Union would exploit the chaos for purposes inimical to stability and the best interests of the Congolese, and regarded Moscow, not Brussels, as the chief threat to independence. Though the only government to

---

[3] The internal Congo debate in Washington is summarized briefly in Arthur M. Schlesinger, Jr., *A Thousand Days* (Boston: Houghton Mifflin, 1965), pp. 574–79, and Theodore C. Sorensen, *Kennedy* (New York: Harper and Row, 1965), pp. 635–39.

[4] Cited in Schlesinger, *A Thousand Days*, p. 575.

receive a formal invitation from Leopoldville for military assistance to restore law and order, Washington from the outset and for a variety of reasons chose to channel its assistance through the United Nations.

Direct U.S. military aid was quickly ruled out for fear it might be used as a pretext for more substantial Soviet intervention in behalf of Lumumba, which could lead to an unsought confrontation of the two great powers. U.S. leaders did not fear a political contest with the Communist bloc in the Congo, but they wanted the contest to be conducted by acceptable rules and with a minimum risk. The fear of Soviet bloc involvement persisted throughout the U.N. period, and not without reason. The real Communist danger was the subversive exploitation of civil strife and chaos, and not a direct military confrontation as implied in some American statements.

The U.N. option was supported also by the disposition of Washington to share the responsibility for security in Africa with other states, particularly with the former metropolitan powers. American leaders recognized that the new states would continue to rely heavily on their European ties, and saw themselves as allies of the British, French, and Belgians (and other states for that matter) in a common effort to strengthen and protect the fledgling regimes.

With its commitment to decolonization and its increasing interest in the Third World, Washington was anxious not to alienate the leaders of the emerging states by political, military, or economic policies which carried overtones of control or excessive influence. Regardless of what the United States did, there would be Communist charges of neo-colonialism, but it was believed that the United Nations, "like a lightning rod"—to use the image of a former U.S. ambassador to Leopoldville—would help to absorb these charges.

The United States had long advocated U.N. peacekeeping in principle, and had been the most consistent supporter of UNEF and other U.N. missions involving military personnel. This largely favorable experience with multilateral peacekeeping reinforced a general disposition to turn to the United Nations in certain types of crises where bilateral or alliance action was held to involve unacceptable political costs.

A final and significant factor which weighed on the side of the U.N. option was the sheer confusion of the situation. The reports from the Congo in those early hectic days were distorted and exaggerated by rumor, panic, and sensational headlines. No one knew how much or what kind of external assistance was needed.

Given these considerations, U. S. Ambassador-designate Clare H. Timberlake advised President Kasavubu and Prime Minister Lumumba to appeal for U.N. aid. That was on July 10, 1960. On July 12, a group of Congolese cabinet members formally requested in writing the assistance of 3,000 American troops to restore order and insure the departure of Belgian forces. The matter was already before the Secretary-General, and President Eisenhower declined to provide direct U.S. assistance. Two-and-one-half years later, Assistant Secretary of State Harlan Cleveland summed up the initial U.S. response: "Should the Congo's chaos be attacked by a hastily assembled international peace force; or should we send in a division of United States Marines; or should we just sit on our hands and wait for our adversaries to exploit the situation?" We wisely decided, he continued, "not to risk a confrontation of nuclear powers in the center of Africa." We believed, he added, that a U.N. force would serve "the national interest" of the United States.[5]

DANGER OF COMMUNIST PENETRATION

The U.S. emphasis on the restoration of internal order was based on the premise that chaos would be exploited by Communist states and their allies. In the Security Council debate that preceded the first three U.N. resolutions, Washington succeeded in stopping the Communist effort to brand Belgium as an aggressor. U.S. Delegate Henry Cabot Lodge quickly denied charges of Belgian aggression, and insisted that the withdrawal of Belgian troops be contingent upon the capacity of the U.N. forces to restore order.[6]

America's repeated warnings that the introduction into the Congo of military assistance not under the U.N. Command or any other unilateral aid would be "in defiance of the United Nations" and would "seriously jeopardize any effort to bring stability and order to the Congo," reflected the overriding concern with Soviet penetration.[7] When Lumumba asked for technical and financial help during his visit to Washington on July 27, 1960, he was told that all U.S. assistance would be given through U.N. channels.[8]

Lumumba's strident attacks against Belgium and the United Nations, his unwillingness to co-operate with the U.N. Mission, his willingness

---

[5] U.S. Department of State, Press Release No. 34, January 17, 1963, p. 34.
[6] U.N., *SCOR*, S/PV 873 (July 13, 1960), pp. 15 and 42–43.
[7] U.N., *SCOR*, S/PV 877 (July 20, 1960), p. 38.
[8] *New York Times*, July 28, 1960.

to accept Soviet aid, and his increasingly evident emotional instability made Washington apprehensive about his capacity to govern responsibly. When Kasavubu dismissed Lumumba on September 5, Washington made no announcements but its private reaction was—according to the *New York Times*—"It's about time."[9]

The Council of Commissioners installed by the September 14 coup of Colonel Joseph Mobutu received U.S. support. Francis Monheim, a Belgian journalist and close friend of Mobutu, suggests that Mobutu acted on his own initiative.[10] Other reliable sources claim, however, that Mobutu was encouraged and even "discovered" by the CIA, and implied that the ANC chief had the Agency's full support.[11] The exact role of Washington is less important than the fact that the Council of Commissioners had U.S. support from the beginning. U.N. officials, on the other hand, were reluctant to work with the *de facto* regime. The U.S. Ambassador urged the Secretary-General to back the Council government.[12] Certain U.N. officials apparently continued to regard Lumumba as the legal Prime Minister, even though they no longer dealt with him as such. On this point, American views conflicted sharply with those of Hammarskjold and his Special Representative in the Congo, Rajeshwar Dayal.

On November 2, 1960, Dayal strongly attacked the Belgian advisers in Leopoldville and Elisabethville, and denounced the ANC for its lack of discipline and inability to maintain order. He all but ignored the Council of Commissioners and asserted that the only institutions "whose foundations still stand" were the Chief of State and the Parliament, the latter having already been suspended by Kasavubu. Only through them could a peaceful settlement of the constitutional crisis be found.[13] The State Department rejected Dayal's criticism of Belgium, and pointed out that the Congolese Parliament was unable to act normally "because of existing conditions" (implying that Lumumba's reinstatement was unacceptable).[14] This view reflected the widely held suspicion that the U.N. operation might be used to reestablish Lumumba.

[9] *Ibid.*, September 6, 1960.
[10] Francis Monheim, *Mobutu, l'homme seul* (Brussels: Editions Actuelles, 1962), p. 132ff.
[11] Hoskyns, *Congo Since Independence*, p. 201. See also Andrew Tully, *CIA—The Inside Story* (New York: W. Morrow, 1962), pp. 220–22.
[12] Hoskyns, *Congo Since Independence*, p. 242.
[13] U.N. *SCOR*, Supplement for Oct., Nov., Dec., 1960, S/4557 (November 2, 1960), pp. 7–34 *passim*.
[14] *New York Times*, November 5, 1960.

Washington's misgivings about the impartiality of Dayal strained its relations with the U.N. Secretariat. In Leopoldville, there was frequent friction between Dayal on the one hand and Ambassador Timberlake and other Western diplomats on the other. Eventually it became evident that Dayal's continued presence in the Congo prevented an effective co-operation between the UNF and the Leopoldville authorities. The latter repeatedly insisted that Dayal be replaced. On March 10, 1961, Hammarskjold recalled Dayal to New York for consultations. Two months later Dayal's resignation was announced. His withdrawal was accomplished by a "deal" that also called for the transfer of the U.S. and British ambassadors.[15] Timberlake left the Congo in June.

THE "AMERICAN PLAN"

One of President Kennedy's first decisions in African affairs was to order a reassessment of the government's Congo policy. Under Dayal, the situation had deteriorated. Congolese troops continued their lawlessness. The intense dissatisfaction among the militant African states over the ouster of Lumumba led to the Casablanca Conference in early January, 1961, which demanded the disarmament of Mobutu's troops, the release of political opponents arrested by Leopoldville, the reconvening of Parliament, and the expulsion of all foreign advisers from the Congo. Pressured on all sides, Hammarskjold requested on February 1 that the Security Council strengthen the mandate of the UNF so it could more effectively protect the Congo from outside interference and remove ANC factions from political life.[16]

Against this background, the State Department developed a series of tentative proposals which the European allies called the "American Plan." The Plan included four major elements:[17]

1. That all Congolese troops be neutralized by the UNF. This disarmament—or limitation of arms—should be accomplished by negotiation if possible, but by force if necessary.

2. That all foreign interference in the Congo outside the U.N. framework cease.

---

[15] See Hoskyns, *Congo Since Independence,* p. 365. O'Brien also discusses U.S. efforts to oust Dayal in his book: see Conor Cruise O'Brien, *To Katanga and Back,* pp. 63–64. This conclusion was confirmed by U.S. officials in author interviews.

[16] U.N., *SCOR,* S/PV 928 (February 1, 1961), pp. 11–18 *passim.*

[17] See *London Times,* February 4, 1961; *New York Times,* February 4, 1961; *Washington Post and Times Herald,* February 3 and 8, 1961; *CRISP, Congo: 1961* (Brussels: Les Dossiers du CRISP, n.d.), p. 320. See also Adlai E. Stevenson's statement, U.N., *SCOR,* S/PV 934 (February 15, 1961), pp. 12–13.

3. That if the neutralization of the ANC proved to be effective, all political prisoners, including Lumumba, be released and allowed to participate in domestic politics.

4. Subsequently, that a broadly based government under the authority of Kasavubu, and representing all major factions, be established.

The "American Plan" was designed to further the U.S. objectives of internal security and political moderation by making the formation of an all-Congo government contingent upon the neutralization of the ANC and the restoration of domestic order. This new approach reflected Washington's effort to strengthen the moral stature of the Secretary-General and to increase his authority in the Congo. Hammarskjold was under severe and constant Soviet attack at that time. The new Kennedy administration also sought to demonstrate its desire to improve relations with the Afro-Asian bloc.

The announcement of Lumumba's death on February 13 produced an atmosphere in which Washington felt it had to lean closer to the more militant Afro-Asian leaders who insisted on "energetic measures" to expel the Belgians and on reconvening the Congo Parliament. It was generally believed that Parliament would probably support the Stanleyville forces against Leopoldville. On February 17, the Afro-Asians introduced a draft resolution in the Security Council which neither referred to President Kasavubu, nor associated Hammarskjold with its implementation. It put the emphasis on the withdrawal of foreign advisers rather than on the disarmament of the contending ANC groups as the best way to restore order. The neutralization of Army units and internal order were no longer made a condition for national reconciliation. Ambassador Adlai E. Stevenson argued for the consolidation of the Ileo-Kasavubu government, and objected to the draft which seemed to exclude a prohibition against the foreign arms which Stanleyville continued to receive. Although the language differed from the original U.S. proposal, under pressure of the Afro-Asian states the U.S. delegate finally endorsed the resolution.[18] Washington also accepted the paragraph authorizing the use of force to prevent civil war.

THE KATANGA PROBLEM

In the beginning, Washington insisted that the UNF should not become involved in the Congo's domestic affairs. In a Council debate, Ambassador Lodge warned that the U.N. mission should not be drawn

18 U.N., *SCOR*, S/PV 941 (February 20, 1961), pp. 16–17.

into the political struggle between Lumumba and Tshombe which, he held, was essentially an internal dispute.[19]

After Lumumba's ouster, Washington began to fear that U.N. policy in the Congo tended to favor the Lumumba cause, but on the question of Katanga's secession, Eisenhower was generally satisfied with Hammarskjold's cautious approach. The Kennedy administration supported more vigorous U.N. measures to create an environment in which the Congolese factions, particularly Leopoldville and Katanga, could reach an accord.

There were six factors that figured strongly in the American opposition to an independent Katanga: (1) Under Belgian rule, Katanga had always been an integral part of the Congo. The Brussels Round Table Conference in 1960 had accepted this. (2) If Katanga were allowed to secede, other regions might follow suit. The result would inevitably be fragmentation and chaos which would invite Communist penetration. (3) If the problem of Katanga secession were solved, it would, as George W. Ball maintained, "contribute decisively to the ability of the Leopoldville government to cope with the diversionary activities of Antoine Gizenga."[20] (4) Secession would disrupt the Congo's economic fabric and destroy its potential for economic viability. (5) Though Tshombe was anti-Communist, a number of moderate leaders in Leopoldville, especially Adoula, met this description equally well. (6) To enhance America's stature in the eyes of the emerging nations, Washington had to oppose Tshombe's secession effort which most Afro-Asian states believed to be a simple expression of Western "neocolonialism."[21]

For all these reasons, Washington sought to encourage the development of a moderate regime in Leopoldville. The installation of Cyrille Adoula as Prime Minister on August 2, 1961, seemed to vindicate U.S. policy. "Adoula had been the Americans' choice for this job from the start," Assistant Secretary G. Mennen Williams reportedly admitted.[22]

---

[19] U.N., *SCOR*, S/PV 885 (August 8, 1960), p. 8.

[20] George W. Ball, Undersecretary of State, *The Elements in our Congo Policy*, Department of State Publication No. 7326 (Washington: U.S. Government Printing Office, December, 1961), p. 19. This statement by Mr. Ball was the most complete and authoritative pronouncement of U.S. Congo policy during the first thirty months of the crisis.

[21] These factors are recalled by G. Mennen Williams, Assistant Secretary of State for African Affairs, in Department of State Press Release No. 84, April 25, 1965, pp. 1 and 6.

[22] *Welensky's 4000 Days*, p. 220.

Secretary of State Dean Rusk publicly praised Adoula's "intelligence, moderation, and nationwide stature."[23]

Washington's objectives for the Congo now called for the ending of the secessionist movements in Elisabethville as well as in Stanleyville. When Williams met Sir Roy Welensky, Prime Minister of the Federation of Rhodesia and Nyasaland, in August, 1961, he apparently told Welensky that the United States sought to end Katanga secession by peaceful means if possible, but by force if necessary:

He [Williams] told me that if the Katanga [Government] did not come to an accommodation with the Central Government soon, it was to be expected that that Government would seek to impose its will by force of arms and that the U.N. forces would be justified in intervening on the side of the Central Government on the grounds that it was the only legal government.[24]

After Round One was launched on September 13, 1961, Washington refrained from making any public comment, but according to the *New York Times,* State Department spokesmen regarded the U.N. action as falling within its mandate.[25] While not implying approval for everything U.N. troops may have done in the September action, Washington clearly supported a firmer approach by the UNF. As a manifestation of its commitment to a strong U.N. presence in Katanga, the United States provided four transport planes to the UNF for use inside the Congo.[26]

Washington's desire to back a U.N. effort to end the secessionist threats of both Tshombe and Gizenga was evident in the debates on the November 24, 1961 Resolution which authorized the use of force for the apprehension of prohibited foreigners. Although Stevenson tried unsuccessfully to amend the draft to authorize action against *all* secessionist movements, and not only Katanga, he voted for the more limited resolution. Another U.S. draft amendment which requested Thant to use negotiations and conciliation to settle the Congo problems was withdrawn under the threat of a Soviet veto. This amendment was designed in part to allay fears among the Western allies. Since the November 24 Resolution affirmed all previous ones, including those providing for U.N. conciliation efforts, Stevenson said: "This

---

23 *New York Times,* December 9, 1961.
24 *Welensky's 4000 Days,* p. 222.
25 *New York Times,* September 14, 1961.
26 A *Globemaster* C–124 and a *Hercules* C–130 arrived on September 21, a few hours after the cease-fire went into effect. Two more C–130s followed shortly. Heretofore, the United States had provided airlift facilities for the UNF only to and from the Congo. (*New York Times,* September 22, 1961.)

new resolution can in no way be a diminution of, but only an addition to, authority previously granted."[27]

The United States apparently supported Round Two from the outset. It began on December 5, 1961. The next day, in compliance with a U.N. request, Washington disclosed that it would provide some twenty additional transport planes to fly troops and equipment to Katanga. "It was this internal airlift that permitted the rapid U.N. buildup in Katanga," according to the State Department.[28]

Brussels, London, and Paris reacted strongly against the December UNF action. At the Western Foreign Ministers Conference then meeting in Paris, and at the subsequent NATO Council session, several European allies tried to persuade the United States to join them in a call for an immediate cease-fire. Washington said it opposed a cease-fire until the UNF had attained its "minimum objectives"—the need and right of the UNF "to protect itself, to maintain its freedom of movement and communications."[29] This unequivocal demonstration of American approval of the U.N. action helped Thant to resist the European demands for a halt to the fighting. The UNF continued its military operation in Katanga until December 19, and achieved most of its immediate "minimum objectives."

Faced with the threat of a military defeat, and with the strong advice of the American, Belgian, and British consuls, Tshombe agreed to meet with Adoula. On December 14, Tshombe requested the intervention of President Kennedy, who designated Ambassador Gullion in Leopoldville as his personal representative to arrange a meeting between Adoula and Tshombe. After preliminary discussions in Leopoldville, Gullion met Tshombe in Ndola, Northern Rhodesia. He then escorted the Katanga leader in the President's plane to Kitona to meet Adoula. Only then did Thant order the UNF to cease firing. At Kitona, Gullion and U.N. Undersecretary Ralph Bunche tried to convince the two parties of the need for reconciliation. An eight-point agreement was reached.

Back in the United States, there was considerable debate within the government on the proper role of the UNF in Katanga. During the December fighting, an American Committee for Aid to Katanga Freedom Fighters had been organized, listing some eighty well-known

---

[27] *U.S. Participation in the U.N.: 1961,* Department of State Publication No. 7413 (Washington: U.S. Government Printing Office, August, 1962), p. 83.

[28] *Ibid.,* p. 87.

[29] *New York Times,* December 14, 1961.

persons as members.[30] Known as the "Katanga Lobby," and designed to put pressure on the administration, the Committee declared that U.N. "action against Katanga," as well as U.S. "logistical support," was "illegal." Among the Senators opposing Kennedy's support of Round Two were Thomas J. Dodd, Everett McKinley Dirksen, Thurston B. Morton, Richard B. Russell, Strom Thurmond, and James O. Eastland.[31] In a syndicated column, Richard M. Nixon declared that the administration's policy in the Congo was "the worst foreign policy blunder since its handling of the Cuban invasion."[32]

On December 27, 1961, Assistant Secretary Williams and Carl T. Rowan, Deputy Assistant Secretary of State for Public Affairs, denounced Katanga's propaganda campaign. Williams accused the "propaganda machine" of fabricating "horrendous tales of indiscriminate mayhem" committed by the UNF. Rowan said: "There has been a clever big-money campaign to convince Americans that they ought to support Katanga's secession" and accused Michel Struelens, former director of the Tourist Office of the Belgian Congo, of running the campaign from "plush quarters in New York." Four days later, Undersecretary of State George C. McGhee said that the Williams and Rowan speeches "were not cleared at the highest levels of the Department." The controversial Mr. Struelens provoked a drawn out dispute between the State Department and several members of the internal security subcommittee of the Senate Committee on the Judiciary. Finally, in December, 1962, he was ordered to leave the country or face deportation. "After a series of legal battles, he left voluntarily in August, 1963."[33] He returned to the United States in 1964, after Tshombe became Prime Minister of the Congo as a special representative of Leopoldville.

The Kitona Accord led to long and fruitless negotiations between Leopoldville and Elisabethville. By mid-1962, the United States decided stronger measures were required. After discussions with Brussels and London, Washington drafted a plan for integrating Katanga. Unlike its allies, the United States was prepared to recommend the imposition of economic sanctions against Katanga if Tshombe refused to accept peaceful integration and recognize Leopoldville's authority. In early

[30] In January, 1962, full-page advertisements of the American Committee for Aid to Katanga Freedom Fighters appeared in leading United States newspapers. Max Yergen, 79 Madison Avenue, New York City, was listed as chairman.

[31] *New York Times,* December 15, 1961.

[32] *Washington Post and Times Herald,* December 19, 1961.

[33] The activities of Mr. Struelens are summarized in a news analysis, "Tshombe's Spokesman," *New York Times,* August 3, 1964.

August, Washington submitted its proposals to the Secretary-General. On August 20, Thant officially presented his U.N. Plan for National Reconciliation which was, in fact, a slightly modified version of the U.S. draft. Five days later, the United States pledged its full support of the Plan.

Although both Adoula and Tshombe endorsed the Thant Plan—as it was called—they still could not come to terms. Failing to solve the Katanga problem, Adoula's position had become highly precarious and the fall of his government, which would open the door for a left wing regime, was a distinct possibility.[34] These developments moved Washington to further action. In October, George C. McGhee, Undersecretary of State for Political Affairs, went on a three-week mission to the Congo to encourage a *rapprochement* between Leopoldville and Elisabethville, and to convince Tshombe that the United States did not seek his downfall as the leader of the richest province in the Congo. By the end of November, Washington secured Belgian acquiescence to institute more coercive measures under the Thant Plan. At the conclusion of the talks between President Kennedy and Foreign Minister Paul-Henri Spaak in Washington on November 27, the Belgian leader agreed that unless "substantial progress within a very short period" were made, it would be necessary "to execute further phases under the United Nations Plan, which include severe economic measures."[35] After some persuasion, Washington also managed to get London to promise it would not prevent the imposition of sanctions against Katanga if they were considered necessary.

The situation continued to deteriorate. Tshombe was building up his forces. Observers were predicting Adoula's early collapse. Ambassador Gullion was afraid that Adoula would yield to alleged offers of Communist bloc aid. Some State Department officials, who Theodore C. Sorensen identified as "doves," came up with the hawk-like proposal to send to the Congo "a squadron of U.S. fighter aircraft" manned by U.S. Air Force pilots to "end Katanga's resistance in a hurry."[36] The President was skeptical of the proposal, and on December 9, 1962, ordered a thorough-going reappraisal of alternatives for dealing with the situation, ranging from direct U.S. military intervention to the withdrawal of U.S. support for the U.N. effort to end secession. The appraisal opposed the use of a U.S. air squadron, either by

[34] See address by G. Mennen Williams, November 2, 1962, Department of State Press Release No. 670, p. 5.

[35] *New York Times*, November 28, 1962.

[36] Sorensen, *Kennedy*, p. 638. See also Schlesinger, *A Thousand Days*, p. 578.

Washington or under U.N. auspices, but the proponents of this drastic measure continued to press for it in one form or another. Both Adoula and Thant had reservations about the proposal, and on December 17, Kennedy postponed action pending the finding of a U.S. military mission he dispatched to the Congo three days later. Headed by Lieutenant General Louis W. Truman, the eight-man team was to "determine what additional forms of assistance the United States could provide to ensure the ability of the United Nations to maintain peace in the Congo."[37]

The Indian commanders of the UNF in the Congo rightly interpreted the Truman Mission, which arrived in the Congo on December 21, as a clear sign of Washington's determination to support U.N. military action to end secession. After recurrent provocations, the UNF launched Round Three on December 28, several weeks ahead of schedule. As a direct outgrowth of the Truman Mission thirty trucks, six armed personnel carriers, mine-clearing equipment, transport aircraft, and other U.S. military materiel began arriving early in January, but not in time to affect the outcome of Round Three. With the entry of U.N. troops in Kolwezi on January 21, 1963, the secession of Katanga was finally ended.

The initial U.S. position that the Leopoldville-Elisabethville conflict constituted a domestic dispute which the UNF should not attempt to solve by force had undergone a substantial change. The problem was seen increasingly as a threat to stability in Central Africa. When negotiation and other diplomatic means proved ineffective, Washington supported the use of force by the UNF under its right of "self-defense" and "freedom of movement" to oust the secessionist regime in Elisabethville. On January 17, 1963, Assistant Secretary of State Harlan Cleveland said the U.N. military action in Katanga was justified, even though it was opposed "in varying degrees by several of the larger nations." Because of the Congo operation, he said: "There are no uninvited foreign troops, no Communist enclaves, no army of liberation, no reason for a single American soldier to die there, no excuse for a Soviet soldier to live there."[38]

After heading a U.S. fact-finding mission to the Congo, Cleveland declared in Leopoldville on February 12 that the two major problems confronting the Congo were "catastrophic inflation" and the retraining and streamlining of the Congolese army.

[37] *New York Times,* November 28, 1962.
[38] Address, January 17, 1963, U.S. Department of State Press Release No. 34, p. 2.

BILATERAL MILITARY ASSISTANCE

In 1960, the United States expected the U.N. mission to make a serious effort to discipline and retrain the ANC. The fundamental problem then and since has been to provide a competent officer corps which, under the circumstances, meant the recruiting of European officers. In its so-called "American Plan," Washington explored the possibility of having all Congolese troops disarmed. In November, 1961, Adlai Stevenson argued in vain for explicit U.N. authority to train and reorganize the ANC. He also recommended that the Security Council assist the Congo by providing a small air force.[39]

In face of the failure of the U.N. mission to make any headway in streamlining, training, or officering the ANC, Washington developed the Greene Plan which called for a series of bilateral aid programs to be channeled through, and co-ordinated by, the United Nations.[40] After intensive discussion within the U.S. government, negotiations with Leopoldville, and consultation with U.N. officials, Washington approached Belgium, Canada, Italy, Norway, and Israel, each of whom agreed to participate. The Plan was rejected by Thant in April, 1963, because of objections from the more militant Afro-Asian states, and because it may have stretched the U.N. mandate too far. As a result, Belgium, Italy, and Israel eventually entered into conventional bilateral military aid agreements with Leopoldville, which was a literal violation of the Security Council prohibition against direct assistance.

Even before the failure of the Greene Plan, the United States had informally and quietly started its own bilateral aid effort in October, 1962, and concluded in July, 1963, a bilateral military aid agreement with the Adoula government. The following month, a U.S. military aid mission was established in the Congo. The program was confined mainly to the provision of vehicles and communications equipment.

The U.S. aid effort received a boost at the end of March, 1964, when Undersecretary of State W. Averell Harriman recommended, after a six-day mission in the Congo, that more ground vehicles, transport aircraft, and communications equipment be sent.[41] By June, 1964, the United States had contributed $6.1 million in bilateral assistance compared to $170 million in military assistance it provided to the UNF.[42]

---

[39] U.N. SCOR, S/PV #975 (November 16, 1961), p. 10.
[40] The origin, character, and ultimate failure of the Greene Plan are discussed in Chap. 3.
[41] *New York Times*, April 1, 1964.
[42] *Ibid.*, June 22, 1964.

By that date, Washington had sent almost 100 military technicians to the Congo to train ANC personnel in the use and maintenance of the equipment furnished.[43] American bilateral efforts, initiated long before the UNF withdrew, were motivated by the same objective of internal stability that underlay its support of the U.N. Mission, and reflected Washington's belief that the UNF had failed in one of its most important assignments—making the Congolese army a responsible instrument of internal security.

FINANCIAL AND LOGISTICAL SUPPORT

America's political endorsement of the UNF was consistently under-written by financial and logistical support. The total cost of the military operation from July, 1960, through June, 1964, was some $411 million, of which the United States provided, or will provide, 41.5 per cent (or about $170 million). U.S. support included both assessments and voluntary contributions. Washington also became the largest purchaser of U.N. bonds, issued to meet the peacekeeping debts. It bought $100 million in bonds on a matching basis with other states on the condition that annual payments of the interest and principle for the next fifteen years would be included in the regular U.N. budget.[44]

The United States continued its logistical support of the UNF to the end. As of June 30, 1964, the Defense Department had transported 118,091 troops and 18,569 tons of cargo into or out of the Congo, and airlifted 1,991 troops and 3,642 tons of cargo within the Congo. The breakdown of external logistical support follows:[45]

U.S. Airlift: 1960–1964

Troops into the Congo	43,303
Troops out of the Congo	31,093
Cargo into the Congo (tons)	8,542
Cargo out of the Congo (tons)	1,904

U.S. Sealift: 1960–1964

Troops into the Congo	20,352
Troops out of the Congo	23,343
Cargo into the Congo (tons)	5,322
Cargo out of the Congo (tons)	2,801

[43] *Washington Post and Times Herald,* June 17, 1964.

[44] Further details of U.S. financial support are found in Chap. 11, and in Appendix I.

[45] These figures were provided by Captain William Alexander, USN, J–3, Joint Chiefs of Staff, Department of Defense (September 16, 1964).

IMPACT ON THE PEACEKEEPING MISSION

By virtue of its power and active involvement, the U.S. government had a greater impact on the character, effectiveness, and duration of the U.N. Congo operation than any other government. Though it sent no troops and was not a member of the Secretary-General's Congo Advisory Committee, without Washington's assurance of U.S. political, financial, and logistical support, the operation would not have been authorized. It certainly could not have been mounted on anything approaching the scale it was without substantial U.S. aid. Had American support been withdrawn at any point, the effort would have collapsed or have been greatly reduced in size. The widespread assumption of consistent U.S. support made possible the political, financial, and manpower support from many other states. Vitally important were the troop contributions of India and Ethiopia, each of which made available more than 100,000 man-months, and the Canadian communications unit.

Washington became the informal leader of a relatively stable coalition of states that supported, for somewhat different reasons, the U.N. resolutions and their interpretation and implementation by Hammarskjold and Thant. As the only great power and the only permanent member of the Security Council that consistently backed the operation, the United States was thrust into the position of greatest influence and responsibility. This leadership role was further strengthened because there was almost a complete concurrence between the U.S. goals of stability in Central Africa and the prevention of Communist penetration, and the Security Council resolutions calling for the restoration of law and order and prohibiting states from unilateral intervention.

Washington served both as generator and balance wheel. It generated ideas and plans and constantly sought to achieve a working consensus among the associated states. The Secretary-General, the senior members of his staff in the Congo Club,[46] and U.N. officials in Leopoldville and Elisabethville frequently sought American counsel. U.S. officials also offered technical, military, and political advice, as did the officials of other interested states. The United States acted as a balance wheel between the sometimes irreconcilable positions of the militant Afro-Asian leaders and the more conservative European spokesmen. It was precisely this mediating role that drew criticism from both sides, and at the same time assured Washington's leadership of the

---

[46] The Congo Club (which included three Americans) is discussed in Chap. 3.

coalition. The State Department and White House both led and reflected the changing interpretation of what the UNF should do.

This does not mean that the U.N. Secretariat was an appendage to the State Department, or that the Secretary-General failed to exercise initiative in his own right. It means rather, that in spite of occasional differences in tactics and timing, the Secretary-General and the President saw the situation in substantially the same terms. Nor does this concurrence of objectives mean that U.N. officials were unresponsive to the advice from other governments. The fact is that both the Secretary-General and the President took into account the same range of internal and external forces bearing in on the Congo drama, and came to similar conclusions.

There is no evidence that the U.S. government ever exerted improper influence on U.N officials or advocated measures contrary to the resolutions. The presence of three Americans among the Secretary-General's close staff advisers was cited by the Russians and others as proof that Hammarskjold—and to a lesser extent Thant—was taking orders from Washington. In connection with the Kitona Conference in December, 1961, for example, the Soviet delegate to the United Nations Valerian A. Zorin accused Washington of "direct interference" in the Congo to "save" Tshombe and asserted that Ambassador Gullion "gave instructions" to Ralph Bunche, a U.S. citizen.[47] Bunche replied: "Gullion and I worked together amiably. I in no way affected him, and he in no way affected me. I neither took nor gave instructions to Gullion . . . I am proud that in sixteen years of U.N. service my government has never attempted to give me advice or instructions on my U.N. duties."[48]

THE U.N. AS AN INSTRUMENT OF U.S. INTERESTS

On balance, the U.N. peacekeeping mission served American interests and objectives in the Congo, but this does not necessarily mean that U.S. policy might not have been served equally well or better by other options.[49] In retrospect, there were only two plausible alternatives to U.N. intervention.[50] One was an assertion of Belgian authority

[47] *Washington Post and Times Herald,* December 23, 1961.
[48] Hearst Headline Service dispatch by Pierre J. Huss (December 22, 1961).
[49] See Ernest W. Lefever, "The U.N. As A Foreign Policy Instrument: the Congo Crisis," in Roger Hilsman and Robert C. Good (eds.), *Foreign Policy in the Sixties: The Issues and Instruments* (Baltimore: The Johns Hopkins Press, 1965), pp. 141–157.
[50] These alternatives are also discussed in Chap. 12.

to nip the army mutiny in the bud, and the other was the dispatch of a small U.S. military force in response to the July 12 invitation from the Congolese ministers. Forthright Belgian action at an early stage, with or without the invitation of Lumumba, could have arrested the mutiny. Even later, after the situation had deteriorated, Brussels could have restored order if it had had the support of Britain, France, and the United States, as President Charles de Gaulle had suggested.[51] The judicious exercise of Belgian authority—unilaterally and without an invitation from the Lumumba government—with such an invitation, or backed up by one or more NATO allies, would doubtless have been effective in restoring order. But it would have evoked outraged cries of neo-imperialism from predictable quarters, even if it had not cost a single Congolese life. No one can say, of course, what the long-range consequences of Belgian action would have been.

U.S. military assistance, though in response to a formal invitation from Leopoldville, would likewise have evoked charges of neo-colonialism. But in either case, order could have been restored and probably at less financial, political, and human cost than the four-year U.N. operation. Very early action may well have forestalled Katanga's secession. This speculative and retrospective judgment takes into account the largely successful and relatively low cost of three exercises of Western military authority in tropical Africa in 1964—the invited dispatch of British troops to the three new East African states to put down army mutinies in January, the not-so-clearly-invited use of French military power in Gabon the following month, and the invited Belgian-American paratroop mission to rescue hostages in the Stanleyville area in November. The British and French military actions accomplished their immediate goal of restoring order at a low political and human cost. The five-day Stanleyville operation successfully achieved its objective of rescuing some 2,000 persons of eighteen different nationalities with little loss of life.[52] Despite the barrage of criticism against the essentially humanitarian Stanleyville rescue mission from Communist and militant neutralist leaders, including organized attacks against U.S. embassies and legations in a half dozen capitals, the gains far outweighed the temporary political cost.

---

[51] President de Gaulle's proposal is discussed in Chap. 6.

[52] The foreign hostages rescued included Africans and Asians as well as Europeans and Americans. See address by Ambassador Adlai E. Stevenson before Security Council, U.S. Mission to the United Nations, Press Release No. 4479, Dec. 14, 1964, p. 2.

Turning from the hypothetical options for dealing with the Congo crisis to the actual alternative pressed by Washington, it can be said that the U.N. peacekeeping mission, despite its inefficiency and duration, contributed to American goals at an acceptable financial, political, and human cost. Along with other elements including U.S. diplomacy, the UNF contributed to the central U.S. objective of a united and stable Congo with a moderate government capable of having mutually beneficial diplomatic and economic relations with the West. This was also a Western objective generally, and was not incompatible with legitimate African interests or the larger interests of international peace.

The more extravagant expectations and hopes for the UNF entertained by some U.S. officials were not fulfilled. The U.N. effort, along with parallel forces, did not achieve peace in the Congo. After four years of peacekeeping, the Congo was rent by tribal conflict and rebellion. Without a competent officer corps, the ANC remained a source of disorder and lawlessness. The UNF helped to impose ground rules that made it difficult for the Soviet Union to capture the Lumumba-Gizenga movement and thus establish a base for subversion in Africa, but by 1963 the Chinese Communists had succeeded in penetrating the Congo and were giving material support and direction to rebel groups committed to overthrowing the Central Government. In the latter half of 1964, the lives of Americans in the Congo were in greater danger than at any time since independence. U.N. officials, unable to make any headway in building a competent ANC officer corps, actually held up progress in this vital area by opposing the use of Belgian training officers and advisers.

Those State Department officers who believed that U.S. aid through the U.N. channel, as opposed to direct military assistance, would protect the American diplomatic "image" among the new African political elites, were destined to be disappointed. Before long U.N. troops were being called "American mercenaries"—and worse. Ironically, some of these image-conscious persons were among the strongest advocates of direct U.S. military action to destroy Tshombe's regime in Katanga in 1962, going so far as to urge the President to dispatch a squadron of fighter aircraft. This apparent contradiction on the question of direct U.S. military action in the Congo can be attributed in part to the belief that in 1960, U.S. military assistance to restore law and order would have been resented by the African nationalists while direct and forceful U.S. military action against Tshombe in 1962 would have been welcomed by them. This is implied by Assistant Secretary

Williams: "Our generally good image in Africa reached a remarkable apogee when we fully supported the U.N. in ending the secessionist movement in Katanga. That effort at secession was regarded by other Africans as counter-revolutionary and a return to colonialism."[53]

These shifting positions on the use of force in Africa among American officials can be explained largely by the proponent's views of the relative justice or injustice of a particular cause for which coercion is being considered. In some policymakers there is also a persistent, though not fully substantiated assumption that a "just" but "unpopular" course of action, especially if it involves military force, can be made more palatable by a sugar-coating of U.N. legitimacy. It was this assumption that permitted some Americans outside of government to give moral support to the exercise of U.S. military power in Korea. The formal endorsement of President Truman's initiative in Korea by the Security Council enabled them to sanction a use of force which they would have condemned had it been carried out under a normal bilateral arrangement between Seoul and Washington.

The U.N. endorsement of a military operation, whatever moral and political assets such an endorsement may have, is hardly an effective device for warding off hostile propaganda attacks from those governments that oppose the operation. It is doubtful that a U.N. authorized and executed Stanleyville rescue mission in 1964, with the inevitable side effect of strengthening the central Congolese government, would have been any more popular in Moscow, Peking, or Cairo than the actual one authorized by Leopoldville and carried out by the Belgians and the Americans. This is not to say that the channel for implementing a policy is unimportant, because the instrument is a part of the policy, even if only a small part. But the intent of the actor and the effect of the policy on the interests of other parties are more important morally and politically than the formal legal or quasilegal arguments or instruments employed to justify or implement the policy.

[53] Address by G. Mennen Williams, April 25, 1965, Department of State Press Release No. 84, p. 1.

5.

The Soviet Union: Ambiguous Adversary

The Soviet diplomatic mission was twice expelled from the Congo—first by Colonel Joseph Mobutu in September, 1962, and then by Prime Minister Cyrille Adoula in November, 1963. In the summer of 1961 the U.S.S.R. temporarily recognized the rebel regime in Stanley-ville. This turbulent diplomatic relationship between Moscow and Leopoldville reflected the deeper contradictions in Russian policy during the four years of the U.N. effort. These contradictions in turn were rooted in the failure of the Soviet Union to "radicalize" the Congo (i.e., transform it into a radical socialist state such as Cuba), or to gain the support of the Afro-Asian states for its policies designed to move in this direction.

The policy of Moscow toward the U.N. peacekeeping effort was also ambiguous, ranging from initial support, to passive acquiescence, to active opposition, depending on the circumstances. The record would have been one of more consistent obstruction had it not been for Moscow's desire to keep on good terms with the Afro-Asian states which by and large supported the UNF.

INTERESTS AND OBJECTIVES

Moscow's chief objective was to "radicalize" the Congo and use the Lumumba regime as an instrument for pursuing its wider goals in Africa. "This process of political radicalization," said a Soviet commentator, "is one of the salient features of present-day Africa."[1] To further this inevitable "political radicalization," the Soviet Union worked toward three specific objectives in the Congo—the expulsion of Belgian economic influence, the neutralization of American political influence, and the support and "socialization" of the Lumumba

[1] Yuriy Zvyagin, *New Times* (Moscow), April, 1965.

regime. As the self-styled chief advocate of "national liberation," the U.S.S.R. was eager to demonstrate its zeal in promoting efforts to expel the "Belgian colonialists," especially from Katanga, and to frustrate the efforts of the American "neo-colonialists."

For tactical and pragmatic reasons, Moscow decided that its goals could be accomplished at less risk by going along with a U.N. peace-keeping presence, which it apparently felt would preclude neither normal Soviet diplomatic and economic activities in the Congo nor covert operations designed to "radicalize" the Lumumba government. It appears that Moscow's immediate reason for supporting the July 14, 1960 Resolution was to prevent direct U.S. assistance, which was considered a serious barrier to the achievement of Soviet objectives in Central Africa.[2]

Khrushchev wanted to establish a base in the Congo from which the anti-colonial forces could undermine "reactionary" Western political and economic influence, establish "progressive" regimes in the newly independent African states, and subvert the "imperialist" governments of Angola, the Rhodesian Federation, and South Africa.

Like the United States, the Soviet Union invested a great deal of energy and prestige in the Congo. And like Washington, Moscow in the late 1950's for the first time directed serious attention to the unfolding drama in tropical Africa. The presumed unity of purpose among the emerging African states soon broke down under conflicting internal and external pressures. Pan-African solidarity became a slogan with little substance. It became clear that the U.S.S.R. could not pursue identical policies in the different African states. Soviet diplomacy supported increasingly the more militant African regimes, and at the same time tried not to alienate other nonaligned states. The Congo crisis forced Khrushchev to choose between Lumumba and Kasavubu, and between the Casablanca powers and moderate African countries.

The Congo represented for Moscow the classical example of a colony exploited by Western imperialists and ripe for a "nationalist revolution" or "liberation," the first step toward genuine "socialism." Patrice Lumumba, who seemed a perfect instrument of Soviet objectives in the underdeveloped world, had been carefully cultivated and vigorously promoted by the Communists before he became the Congo's first Prime Minister.

---

[2] A brief summary of Soviet interests in Africa is found in "The U.S.S.R. and Africa in 1965," *The Mizan Newsletter* (London: May, 1965), pp. 1–9. (Reprinted in *Africa Report* [November, 1965], pp. 30–32.)

The Soviet Union welcomed the Security Council debate on the Congo crisis, not because it wanted the Council to act, but because open discussion would expose to the world the "colonialist plot" of the Western powers against the new state. As Khrushchev said on July 12, 1960, the Council could "hardly be expected to give sympathetic consideration to the justified demand of the people of the Congo" because it "has been turned by the U.S.A. into an instrument for suppressing the freedom-loving peoples and keeping the peoples in colonial bondage."[3] During the debate, the Soviet delegate charged the NATO powers with "treacherous aggression" and warned his audience against the "machinations" and new-style "colonialism" of the United States and its allies.[4]

The July 14 Resolution was strongly endorsed by the Afro-Asian bloc, and the Soviet Union felt it had to vote for it, even though it had profound misgivings about U.N. military aid. With its frequently expressed commitment to "decolonization," Moscow could not fail to support a resolution backed by the Afro-Asians.

Direct military aid from Moscow was ruled out for some of the same reasons that underlay a similar decision by Washington. Khrushchev did not want to provide a pretext for direct U.S. intervention. The Kremlin, like the State Department, was anxious to court the favor of African nationalists. Moscow, however, faced a practical problem Washington did not face. The Soviet Union lacked the logistical structure to dispatch and sustain a significant military force in the heart of Africa. There was no assurance that the necessary overflight and refueling rights would have been granted by the countries en route. The lines of communication would have been long and vulnerable.

Despite the physical and political realities, President Kasavubu and Lumumba invited Soviet military aid on July 14 if Western "aggression" continued. With this request on file, Moscow was in a better position to respond bilaterally and on a small scale, even though it had nominally backed the U.N. mission.

The withdrawal of Belgian troops through a U.N. effort would be a desirable achievement at no political cost to Moscow. Since the Soviet delegate made clear that Belgian forces were to be withdrawn "immediately" and "unconditionally," his government could later claim major credit for this accomplishment.[5]

---

[3] Cited by Richard Lowenthal, "China," in Zbigniew Brzezinski (ed.), *Africa and the Communist World* (Stanford: Stanford University Press, 1963), p. 179.
[4] U.N., *SCOR*, S/PV 873 (July 13, 1960), pp. 16–21 *passim*.
[5] U.N., *SCOR*, S/PV 873 (July 13, 1960), p. 44.

In the Council debate, the U.S.S.R. also castigated Katanga's secession, declaring that it was a colonialist plot "to dismember the young Republic."[6]

Moscow's early position on the UNF embraced three intertwined strands which characterized its subsequent policy: support for the Lumumba forces through the United Nations when possible, but unilaterally when necessary; vigorous opposition to Katanga secession; and a mounting mistrust of the U.N. system which reached its height in the vituperative attack on the Secretary-General in 1961. Complicating the Soviet policy was the desire to avoid an open split with the moderate Afro-Asian states.

SUPPORT FOR THE LUMUMBA FORCES

Having endorsed the July 14 Resolution, the Soviet Union made a show of co-operation with the U.N. effort. On July 23, Moscow informed Hammarskjold that it had authorized the use of five IL–18 planes, assigned to the Ghana government, for the transport of Ghanian troops and equipment to the Congo in support of the mission. Since the planes remained under complete Soviet control, they could be used unilaterally for purposes other than those of the UNF.

Moscow continued to promote the thesis that Belgian "aggression" in the Congo was part of a larger Western plot: "The bayonet was Belgian, but the bosses were the United States, Belgian, British, and West German big monopolies," Khrushchev said on July 15, 1960.[7]

As events unfolded, Moscow saw the danger of being outmaneuvered by the Western allies and the U.N. Mission, and quickly decided to support Lumumba directly. On July 22, Moscow announced that it would ship 100 trucks complete with spare parts, a repair shop, and supporting technicians to the Congo. The shipment followed, plus additional equipment and personnel, including agents, medical teams and supplies, and reportedly also arms.[8] By the end of August, ten twin-engined IL–14 planes with Soviet crews had arrived in the Congo. Earlier, one such plane had been presented to Lumumba for

[6] *Ibid.*, p. 20.

[7] *New York Times,* July 16, 1960.

[8] Pierre Houart, *La pénétration communiste au Congo* (Brussels: Centre de documentation internationale, 1960), p. 64. See also Michel Borri, *Nous . . . ces affreux* (Paris: Editions Galic, 1962), p. 48. [Borri is the pseudonym of a French Intelligence agent, whose book is generally regarded as accurate.]

his personal use. Ostensibly these actions were under the aegis of the United Nations. In fact, they constituted bilaterial assistance. When Hammarskjold reminded the Soviet Union that its actions violated U.N. resolutions, he was accused of exceeding his mandate by attempting to control the relations between the "sovereign" government of the Congo and other states. Moscow asserted that the resolutions do not restrict "in any way the right of the Congolese government to request assistance directly from the governments of other countries and to receive such assistance, just as they do not and cannot restrict the rights of states to render assistance to the Republic of the Congo."[9]

On August 15, Lumumba specifically asked the Russians for transport planes and crews, trucks, various weapons "of high quality," and other equipment.[10] Lumumba used the planes and trucks to bring troops to Kasai in preparation for his attack against Bakwanga and later against Katanga.[11] The closing of the airports in the Congo to all except U.N. traffic by Andrew W. Cordier on September 5 stopped further direct Soviet military aid to Lumumba.[12]

The Soviet Union reacted sharply to Cordier's measures. It charged Hammarskjold and the U.N. Command with violating the Council resolutions by this "flagrant interference" in the Congo's internal affairs and with undermining the position of the "lawful" Lumumba government.[13] The Soviet attack boomeranged. Disturbed by Moscow's campaign against the Secretary-General, and interested in eliminating all Big Power intervention in the Congo, Ceylon and Tunisia drafted a Council resolution reaffirming the previous ones and outlawing military aid outside U.N. channels.[14] The Russians vetoed the resolution.

Confronted by a Security Council deadlock, the General Assembly met in a special emergency session at the request of Washington. In spite of their disquiet over Lumumba's ousting by Kasavubu, the Afro-Asian leaders were more interested in effective U.N. action to insure decolonization than in direct support for Lumumba. The resulting September 20, 1960 Resolution prohibited all military assis-

[9] U.N., *SCOR*, Supplement for July, Aug., Sept., 1960, S/4503 (September 10, 1960), p. 156.

[10] A reproduction of Lumumba's letter requesting Soviet aid can be found in Houart, *La pénétration communiste,* App. VI.

[11] The Soviets withdrew most of their planes from the Congo when Mobutu on September 14 expelled all Russians and broke diplomatic relations with the Soviet Union.

[12] This incident is discussed in Chap. 3.

[13] U.N., *SCOR,* S/PV 901 (September 14, 1960), pp. 2–16 *passim.*

[14] U.N., *SCOR,* Supplement for July, Aug., Sept., 1960, S/4523 (September 16, 1960), pp. 172–73.

tance to the Congo except through the United Nations. It was adopted by a vote of 70–0. The Soviet bloc, France, and the Union of South Africa abstained. This was a clear defeat for Moscow which had maneuvered itself into an open split with the Afro-Asian members. Even Yugoslavia, which otherwise followed the Soviet lead on the Congo question, deserted Moscow and cast its lot with the majority.

The Soviet abstention in the Assembly indicated that Moscow was not prepared to break completely with the U.N. effort. The Russians now sought to mend their fences with the Afro-Asians. In his September 23 Assembly speech, Khrushchev demanded that only African and Asian troops be permitted in the Congo and that they be used only "at the discretion of" the Lumumba government. He did not elaborate what role, if any, the U.N. Command was to play. Khrushchev also threw his weight behind the Lumumba regime as the only "lawful" government that "enjoys the confidence of the Congolese people." But he clearly avoided any specific commitment that would imply direct Soviet involvement in the Congo conflict, because "the Congolese people themselves will be able to deal with the difficulties . . . in restoring order."[15]

Khrushchev's speech indicated that Soviet support for Lumumba would remain largely diplomatic, though some military aid was continued. Soviet bloc advisers remained active in Stanleyville; some bloc weapons, including shipments from the United Arab Republic, were delivered to the Stanleyville forces;[16] and some financial aid was given to the rebel Stanleyville regime.[17] But Moscow concentrated mainly on a propaganda campaign designed to support Lumumba and to turn the Afro-Asian states against the West over the Congo issue.

When Lumumba was arrested on December 1, 1960, by Mobutu's soldiers, the Russians blamed the NATO powers and the U.N. Command and called for Lumumba's release, the disarmament of Mobutu's troops, and the creation of a special Afro-Asian committee to investigate "the sources of financing and supplying arms to the Mobutu

[15] U.N., *GAOR*, A/PV 869 (September 23, 1960), pp. 71–72.

[16] *New York Times*, February 2, 1961. *New York Herald Tribune*, February 17, 1961.

[17] According to an American spokesman, a Soviet officer in Cairo transmitted $3 million in European currency to a Congolese representative of the Stanleyville regime. American agents, however, were able to snatch the case containing the funds from the Congolese when he was in Khartoum on his way to Stanleyville to deliver the money to Gizenga. The Soviet officer responsible for the transfer of the funds was reportedly shot by his government.

gang."[18] Soviet diplomatic efforts at U.N. headquarters, gained some Afro-Asian support, but failed to secure Lumumba's release.

The dramatic announcement of Lumumba's death on February 13, 1961, provided Moscow with the ammunition to bring its anti-West and anti-U.N. campaign to a climax. In a violent statement, the U.S.S.R. demanded that the UNF immediately arrest Tshombe and Mobutu, "the henchmen of the colonialists," disarm all their troops, and expel all Belgians from the Congo. Moscow also insisted that the U.N. operation be ended within one month.[19] The Russians did not explain why or how they expected the UNF, portrayed as the tool of the "colonialists," to take action against the "colonialists." Nor did they submit plans for withdrawing the UNF or for maintaining law and order in its absence. The February 21, 1961 Resolution, which strengthened the U.N. mandate, presented Moscow with a dilemma. The Afro-Asians—except for the Brazzaville bloc—supported it, and Moscow ended up by abstaining on (rather than vetoing) the resolution. Prime Minister Jawaharlal Nehru's negative response to Khrushchev's letter of February 22, seeking Indian support for Moscow's anti-Western stand, also dramatized Moscow's miscalculations.

Soviet diplomatic support of the Stanleyville rebel regime was ambiguous. On February 14, the Russians pledged to "give all possible help" to the "lawful" government of the Congo, headed by Antoine Gizenga.[20] This statement was widely interpreted as diplomatic recognition, and some Western powers feared that Gizenga might receive substantial material assistance from the Soviet bloc. This fear did not materialize. Not until July, 1961, did the Soviet Union establish a diplomatic mission in Stanleyville.[21]

When the Adoula government was established in Leopoldville on August 5, 1961 (it subsequently included Gizenga as Deputy Prime Minister), Moscow promptly recognized the new regime. The Afro-Asian states, including the Casablanca group, did likewise. The Soviet Union took this step, even though its diplomatic relations with Leopoldville—broken by Mobutu in September, 1960—had not been restored. The new Soviet Chargé d'Affaires arrived on September 19,

---

[18] *New York Times,* December 7, 1960.

[19] U.N., *SCOR,* Supplement for Jan., Feb., March, 1961, S/4704 (February 14, 1961), p. 115.

[20] *Ibid.*

[21] The Soviets, however, did not accord Gizenga formal recognition. The dispatch of the mission in July was not even formally announced in Moscow. See Alexander Dallin, "The Soviet Union: Political Activity," in Brzezinski, *Africa and the Communist World,* p. 240, n46.

1961, in Leopoldville; the formal presentation of credentials did not occur until December 2, 1961.

By that time, Gizenga had again left the Leopoldville government and shifted his political base to Stanleyville. In January, 1962, with the help of the UNF, Leopoldville ended Stanleyville's rival regime.[22] Given its former support of Lumumba and Gizenga, the Russian reaction was mild, confined to a complaint about Thant's "hasty" decision to send U.N. forces to help restore order in Stanleyville.[23] The Soviet press, on the other hand, forecast another "Lumumba-style" murder with the arrest of Gizenga, but Moscow's official comments on Adoula were restrained and the prior invitation for him to visit the Soviet Union was not withdrawn. This Soviet swing toward the more moderate Adoula reflected the change in the balance of forces in the Congo as well as within the Afro-Asian group.

The only period of spectacular Russian intervention in the Congo was during the last few weeks of the Lumumba regime. After Lumumba's fall and subsequent death, Soviet support of Stanleyville was limited largely to inflamatory declarations against the moderates. For Soviet propaganda purposes, a dead Lumumba was probably more useful than a live Lumumba.

THE CAMPAIGN AGAINST KATANGA

Soviet policy in the Congo from the outset was characterized by an unremitting opposition to Katanga's secession. On August 8, 1960, the Russians backed Lumumba's request to use the UNF against Katanga. Contrary to their professed concern for the Congo's sovereignty, the U.S.S.R. insisted that the Secretary-General could use "any means" and the UNF had an "unconditional" right to clear Katanga of Belgian troops, arrest Tshombe and his followers, and suppress all Katangan resistance.[24] The August 9 Resolution did not go nearly this far, but the Russians endorsed it again, largely because it had the support of the Afro-Asian states.

Soviet fulminations against Tshombe and his followers held pace with Soviet attacks against the West. Moscow's charges that Katangan leaders were the pliant instruments of the "colonialist" powers met a ready response among most Afro-Asian leaders.

22 This incident is discussed in Chap. 3.
23 *Washington Post and Times Herald,* January 16, 1962.
24 U.N., *SCOR,* S/PV 885 (August 8, 1960), pp. 19–22.

When Moscow recognized the new Adoula government in August, 1961, it sought to justify its switch in support from Stanleyville to Leopoldville by attempting to identify the new Central Government with Lumumba's heritage. Soviet leaders quickly urged Adoula to act vigorously against Katanga, and backed his requests for U.N. assistance for this purpose.[25] Predictably, the Soviet Union deplored the failure of Rounds One and Two to eliminate all mercenaries and end Katangan secession. The cease-fire agreement of October, 1961, and the Kitona Accord of December, 1961, were denounced as a "colonialist" endorsement of the "mercenary and separatist bands" and an attempt to "rescue Tshombe, the protégé of the foreign monopolies in Katanga."[26] The Russians asserted that the Thant Plan for National Reconciliation of August, 1962, was designed to strengthen Tshombe's position and weaken the Leopoldville government, and submitted a substitute which called upon the UNF to arrest and expel all mercenaries immediately. The Soviet plan also demanded that Katanga be reintegrated into the Congo within one month, after which the U.N. troops should be withdrawn.[27] Little interest was shown in the Soviet proposal, even by the Afro-Asian states; the U.S.S.R. finally went along with the more gradual approach of the Thant Plan.

On the whole, the Soviet Union was frustrated in its repeated efforts to pressure the UNF into crushing Katanga secession with military power. For two-and-one-half years Moscow was forced to accept Hammarskjold's and Thant's more moderate interpretation of the U.N. mandate as endorsed by the supporting coalition. The U.S.S.R. was, of course, delighted with the initiative of the UNF in Round Three which ended Katanga's secession. At this point in the drama, there was little difference between the U.S. and the Soviet view.

ATTACK ON THE SECRETARY-GENERAL

The Soviet Union's resentment over its failure to save the Lumumba regime and to use the UNF for its own purposes, exploded into a shoe-thumping attack against Secretary-General Hammarskjold and several of his chief aides. Despite its initial support, the Kremlin never believed that the UNF and U.N. personnel could be politically im-

[25] Lowenthal, "China," in Brzezinski, *Africa and the Communist World*, p. 181.
[26] U.N., *SCOR*, Supplement for Oct., Nov., Dec., 1961, S/4962 (October 16, 1961), p. 62. U.N., *SCOR*, Supplement for Jan., Feb., March, 1962, S/5064 (January 25, 1962), p. 53.
[27] *New York Times*, September 7, 1962.

partial. This view was rooted in the Communist doctrine that there are no neutral men. Given this assumption, Moscow feared the Secretary-General would pursue policies in the Congo contrary to Soviet interests. As Khrushchev explained to an American journalist: "You would not accept a Communist administration and I cannot accept a non-Communist administrator."[28]

As early as July 13, 1960, Moscow denounced U.N. Undersecretary Ralph J. Bunche, an American, as a tool of Western intervention operating under the cloak of the U.N. flag.[29] The first serious conflict between Moscow and Hammarskjold occurred when the Secretary-General criticized Soviet unilateral assistance to Lumumba. When Cordier closed the Congo airports on September 5, 1960, Moscow bitterly attacked Hammarskjold for playing the colonialist game and insisted that the entire U.N. Command be removed.[30] Soviet efforts to censure Hammarskjold and to dismiss the U.N. Command were defeated by the September 20, 1960, Assembly Resolution which reaffirmed the U.N. Mission.

Failing to gain political support in the United Nations, the Soviet Union thereafter blamed Hammarskjold personally for the "disgraceful state of affairs" in the Congo. On September 23, 1960, Khrushchev submitted his famous Troika Plan to the General Assembly. He proposed that the Secretary-General's post be abolished and replaced by a "collective executive organ" consisting of three persons who would represent the Western, the socialist, and the neutralist blocs.[31]

The tripartite formula would have extended the Security Council veto to the Secretariat. The executive implementation of all Council and Assembly resolutions would henceforth be subject to a veto. Specifically, no action in the Congo or in any future peacekeeping missions could be taken against Soviet objections. This would prevent or paralyze all operations which the Russians did not support. The Troika Plan applied to the sixteenth century, Adlai Stevenson once observed, would be like administering international affairs by "a triumvirate consisting of the Pope, the Sultan, and Martin Luther."[32]

The troika scheme was partly motivated by Moscow's insistence on protecting its national sovereignty. The tripartite concept was also a

28 *New York Herald Tribune,* April 17, 1961.
29 U.N., *SCOR,* S/PV 873 (July 13, 1960), p. 19.
30 U.N., *SCOR,* S/PV 901 (September 14, 1960), pp. 14–15.
31 U.N., *GAOR,* A/PV 869 (September 23, 1960), pp. 82–83.
32 Adlai Stevenson Address, May 17, 1961, U.S. Mission to the United Nations Press Release No. 3724.

logical extension of the conviction that the organization and its structure should mirror the world alignment of forces. In Soviet ideology, there were the Western and socialist camps with a neutralist bloc gravitating towards the Communist world. No single person could be independent of or impartial toward these three camps. Khrushchev once said: "It is said that God alone was able to combine three persons in one. But then, no one has ever seen him, and so let him remain in the imagination of the people who invented him. But we can see the Secretary-General."[33]

Khrushchev's hostility toward Hammarskjold was also a response to Soviet setbacks in the larger world. In May, 1960, the U–2 incident had adversely affected Moscow's prestige in the world, and in Communist China in particular. The Geneva disarmament negotiations were broken off in June, which indicated Moscow's failure to impose its disarmament proposals on the West. By September, 1960, the split between the Soviet Union and Communist China had visibly deepened. The fall of Lumumba and the persistence of Katangan secession compounded Soviet reverses and seemed to vindicate China's rigidly consistent opposition to the U.N. operation.

The bitter Soviet vendetta against the Secretary-General continued and culminated in the demand for Hammarskjold's dismissal immediately after the news of Lumumba's death. Moscow said Hammarskjold was responsible for Lumumba's "murder," and declared that it would have no further relations with him or recognize him as a U.N. official.[34] Again Khrushchev miscalculated the mood of the African states whose "overwhelming opinion" was that Hammarskjold should remain in office.[35] The Soviet dilemma was also illustrated in the April 15, 1961 Assembly Resolution, which expressed continued confidence in Hammarskjold's handling of the Congo mission. Moscow found itself voting with the more conservative Brazzaville bloc against the resolution endorsed by the majority of the Afro-Asian states, including the more militant Casablanca group. By this time, the Soviet Union had come to realize that its attack against Hammarskjold was alienating the Afro-Asians. In contrast to earlier speeches, the Soviet delegate was now more moderate. Although he continued to refuse to recognize Hammarskjold, he no longer urged the Secretary-General's dismissal.

[33] *New York Times,* October 4, 1960.
[34] U.N., *SCOR,* Supplement for Jan., Feb., March, 1961 (February 14, 1961), pp. 113–115.
[35] This view was expressed by the delegate from Liberia. U.N., *SCOR,* S/PV 938 (February 17, 1961), p. 5.

The Soviet attack on Hammarskjold and the U.N. system can be understood only in light of the Russian belief that the Secretary-General was a tool of the "colonialists" who were trying to obstruct the inevitable march toward socialism in Africa. Hammarskjold's effort to restore stability in the Congo, which would permit constructive evolutionary change, led to policies that favored the moderate forces represented by Kasavubu. The U.N. system was seen as a barrier to the decolonialization and "radicalization" of the Congo, and its eventual incorporation into the Communist bloc. The culprits, said Khrushchev to Nehru, were "those who would like to hold back the march of history."[36]

Moscow's opposition to the U.N. mission found logical expression in its refusal to pay its assessed share of the expenses. The U.S.S.R. contended that the "colonial powers and their accomplices" should bear the full burden.[37] The unwillingness of the U.S.S.R. and France to pay their quotas precipitated the U.N. financial crisis.

THE MINIMAL ROLE OF COMMUNIST CHINA

As a nonmember of the United Nations, Communist China had a small impact on the peacekeeping operation. Peking adopted a diplomatic posture toward the Congo crisis similar to that of the U.S.S.R. But China's support of the Lumumba faction was less tangible than Russia's. In September, 1960, during the power struggle between Kasavubu and Lumumba, and after Cordier had deprived Lumumba of the use of the radio station and the airfields, Gizenga appealed to Peking for volunteers and equipment "to defend the territorial integrity of the Republic of the Congo."[38] In response, China made no attempt to send men or material to aid Lumumba. On February 20, 1961, after Lumumba's death, Peking recognized the Stanleyville government, but the Chinese Chargé d'Affaires did not arrive until July 31, which was even later than the arrival of the Soviet mission.[39] When Gizenga accepted an invitation to join the Leopoldville government, the Chinese withdrew their mission from Stanleyville with the explanation that the legal government of Gizenga had "terminated its existence" and the

[36] Cited by Alexander Dallin, *The Soviet Union at the United Nations* (New York: Praeger, 1962), p. 150.

[37] *New York Times*, April 9, 1963.

[38] Cited by Richard Lowenthal, "China," in Brzezinski, *Africa and the Communist World*, p. 180.

[39] The Soviet Mission arrived in Stanleyville "about July 6," according to the Elisabethville radio. (*Ibid.*, p. 260, *n*66.)

Leopoldville government was maintaining diplomatic relations with "the Chiang Kai-shek clique."[40] Moscow, on the other hand, accepted the new Adoula-Gizenga regime, and transferred its diplomatic mission from Stanleyville to Leopoldville.

Several Congolese leaders continued to maintain contact with Communist China. Among them was Pierre Mulele who had served as Gizenga's representative in Cairo in 1961. After Gizenga's fall, Mulele went to Peking, where he studied Mao's guerrilla warfare tactics. In the summer of 1963 Mulele returned to the Congo, and subsequently headed the insurgent movement in Kwilu province which led to the January, 1964, uprising. By that time Chinese agents had become subversively and significantly involved in the Congo, operating from Peking's embassies in the Kingdom of Burundi and in the Congo (Brazzaville). These agents provided Congolese rebel groups political and technical advice, money, equipment, and weapons, though the Chinese never succeeded in fully controlling the disparate rebel elements. In June, 1964, Peking's *Jenmin Jih Pao* publicly welcomed the "excellent revolutionary situation" in the Congo.[41] These developments, however, had no significant effect on the U.N. peacekeeping mission which withdrew on June 30, 1964. After the Belgian-American rescue mission in November, 1966, Chinese influence declined.[42]

SOVIET IMPACT ON THE UNF EFFORT

Although the Soviet Union was one of the two super powers, the effect of its opposition on the U.N. peacekeeping mission was, on the whole, remarkably small. Like any other state, the U.S.S.R. had to take into account the broader ramifications of its Congo policy. These larger considerations, including Soviet relations with the more moderate Afro-Asian states and the deepening rift with Peking, deterred the Russians from carrying their opposition to the UNF to its logical conclusion. Confronted by reverses, Moscow was prepared to end its unilateral aid to the Congo, to continue in the United Nations, and to refrain from vetoing key Security Council resolutions which did not meet its approval.

Moscow undergirded its political nonsupport of the Congo effort with a consistent refusal to pay any of its assessed share of the costs, in-

---

[40] *New China News Agency,* September 18, 1961.
[41] Cited in the *New York Times,* June 25, 1964.
[42] For a brief appraisal of Peking's influence in Africa, see George T. Yu, "China's Failure in Africa," *Asian Survey,* VI, No. 8 (August, 1966), 461–468.

cluding the interest on the U.N. bonds issued to underwrite the peace-keeping deficit. It is interesting to note, however, that the Soviet Union did provide some initial airlift and supplies for U.N. troops which, according to its own testimony, amounted to $1.5 million. Moscow never made a claim for this expenditure against the United Nations. While it is impossible to determine how much of this airlift actually assisted the U.N. effort and how much was used to support Lumumba, the Russians insist it was undertaken in behalf of the UNF. Consequently, the Soviets claim to have supported the effort to the extent of $1.5 million. This may be taken as a symbol of their ambiguity on the operation, especially in the early days.

In the Security Council, the Soviet position forced the adoption of compromise resolutions, and the threat of a Soviet veto on one occasion resulted in the transfer of the Congo issue to the General Assembly. The Russians, however, never succeeded in gaining majority Council or Assembly support for their Congo policies.

Soviet hostility inevitably influenced the Secretary-General in his interpretation and execution of the mandate. But the Soviet Union failed to force its own interpretation of the mandate on Hammarskjold or Thant, and it had to accept reluctantly their more gradual and moderate policies.

Moscow's strident calls for Hammarskjold's resignation and for the adoption of a troika arrangement were bound to erode the authority of the Secretary-General. They tended to weaken the position of Hammarskjold's successor, who also had to take into account Soviet views if he wished to avoid a demand for his dismissal. Thant was more inclined to play a passive role than Hammarskjold, and due primarily to changing circumstances he did not undertake major initiatives in the Congo which met with strong opposition in Moscow. On the contrary, two of his most important decisions met with Russian approval—Round Three, and his rejection of the Greene Plan.

The Soviet assault on the Secretary-General forced the Afro-Asians to rally to Hammarskjold's banner. This development offset to some degree the damage of the Soviet attack. In spite of Russian pressures, the Secretary-General was never censured by the Security Council or the General Assembly for his Congo policies.

In the Congo itself, direct Soviet material support to the Lumumba regime and its successor jeopardized the U.N. objectives of reestablishing order and maintaining territorial integrity and clearly violated the U.N. resolutions. Soviet diplomatic support of the Stanleyville leaders was contrary to the intent of the resolutions because it encouraged rebellion against the Central Government.

Moscow's policies did not substantially alter the course of the U.N. operation, though its hostility to the UNF made the Secretary-General's task more difficult, and its refusal to pay its assessments contributed to the termination date. The Soviet experience in the Congo doubtless strengthened Moscow's determination to limit the U.N. role in future conflict situations.

Throughout the Congo crisis, Soviet policy was characterized by ambiguity and miscalculation. Both Moscow and Washington had been taken by surprise. Neither was prepared. Both improvised. But in contrast to the United States, the Soviet policies in the Congo led largely to frustration and failure. The UNF stood in the way of Russian attempts to prolong and capture the Lumumba regime. Instead of being "radicalized," the Congo became more moderate. Moscow certainly gained some propaganda mileage out of the Congo affair, particularly from Lumumba's death and Tshombe's close connection with European financial interests, but this short-term advantage was offset to a significant extent by Moscow's failure to become the acknowledged voice of the Afro-Asian states on other, less dramatic issues. Khrushchev was confounded by the fact that the views of the Afro-Asians were closer to those of Washington than to those of Moscow.

The failure of Moscow's Congo policy and the expulsion of Soviet security guards and diplomats from Ghana in February, 1966, must surely rank as Russia's two greatest political disasters in tropical Africa. If the United States was the chief beneficiary of the U.N. Mission, the Soviet Union was the chief loser.

6.

France and Britain: Reluctant Allies

Though Britain and France were allies of the United States on European matters, and though all three had parallel objectives in Central Africa, there were wide differences among them on the desirability and performance of the U.N. peacekeeping operation in the Congo. Both London and Paris wanted a stable Congo with a politically moderate government. Both wanted to frustrate Communist designs, and to contain the chaos at minimum risk.

London had serious reservations about the initial authorization of the mission, and was concerned about Secretary-General Hammarskjold's interpretation of the resolutions. His advocacy of speedy decolonization in Africa had occasioned misgivings in the Foreign Office. London also feared that the U.N. effort might interfere in the Congo's internal affairs, thus establishing an unfortunate precedent for U.N. intervention in the Rhodesian Federation and elsewhere in Africa. Britain abstained on the first Security Council resolution, but supported most of the subsequent ones. It also paid its full assessment. British policy as a whole can be described as reluctant and critical support.

Embracing all the critical elements of the British view, France carried its position considerably further because, unlike London, it was opposed to U.N. intervention in principle. President Charles de Gaulle proposed that the Congo crisis be settled instead by a troika composed of Britain, France, and the United States. Paris abstained on all the Congo resolutions except one, and like the Soviet Union, it has refused to pay its assessment. President de Gaulle's basic position was closer to that of the Soviet Union than the United States. Unlike Moscow, he did not constantly denounce the UNF and threaten to veto Congo resolutions, but his sustained posture of non-co-operation and occasional acts of obstruction had very much the same effect.

FRANCE'S DEEP INTEREST IN THE CONGO

France's aloofness and disdain toward the U.N. operation did not imply disinterest in the Congo. On the contrary, Paris was deeply interested in maintaining stability as well as increasing French influence in the former Belgian colony. During the Brussels Round Table Conference in February, 1960, Foreign Minister Couve de Murville informed the Belgian Ambassador in Paris that his government still considered the Ferry–Leopold II *Accord of 1884* to be in force.[1] The *Accord* gave France the right of first option if Belgium were to withdraw from the Congo. It is doubtful that France seriously contemplated replacing Belgian authority with her own in the blatant and atavistic manner suggested by the nineteenth century agreement. But Couve de Murville's reminder did indicate that France would watch Congo developments with more than passing interest.

When France terminated the imperial ties with her African territories, she sought as a minimum to prevent her former colonies from slipping into an anti-Western bloc. As a more ambitious goal France hoped to retain a significant measure of economic, political, and cultural influence in Africa. French interests were more likely to be achieved in an atmosphere of stability. The failure of the Congo to develop into a viable state would present a threat to its neighbors, particularly to Congo (Brazzaville), a former French colony. A basic tenet of French policy in 1960 was the protection of the strategic axis which ran from Paris through Algiers to Brazzaville. For these reasons, France sought a regime in Leopoldville that would get along with the moderate Youlou government in Brazzaville.

PARIS OPPOSES U.N. INTERVENTION

When the Congo crisis erupted, Paris was immediately and profoundly concerned. Sharing the broad objectives of her Western allies —the reestablishment of order, the preservation of the unity and territorial integrity, and the prevention of Communist intervention, France opposed the instrumentality of the United Nations to deal with the problem. She abstained on the July 14, 1960 Security Council Resolution, but voted for the July 22 Resolution at the explicit request of Brussels, and because it did not "imply the slightest criticism" of the Belgian government.[2] France consistently abstained on all subsequent Council and Assembly resolutions.

[1] CRISP, *Congo: 1960*, I, 235.
[2] U.N., *SCOR*, S/PV 879 (July 21, 1960), pp. 14–15.

The French opposition to U.N. intervention was firmly rooted in de Gaulle's understanding of the rights and responsibilities of the state, which he regards as the preeminent reality in world politics. He also differentiates between long established states that are "endowed with cohesion and unity" and understand "the traditions, obligations, and responsibilities" of international relations, and newly "improvised" states that lack maturity and experience.[3] In important matters of peace and war, de Gaulle tends to think in terms of a concert of the Big Powers. Given political realities, the Security Council can act effectively only when there is unanimity among the permanent members. The General Assembly can debate, but not act, on basic security questions. The substitution of the Assembly to deal with enforcement measures is regarded by Paris as contrary to the U.N. Charter.

France also sees the United Nations increasingly dominated by small and irresponsible African and Asian states which can line up against the larger more mature powers. This, she believes, can ultimately serve only the Communist states and their allies. As a result, there is an *a priori* disinclination to employ U.N. machinery to handle conflict situations.

France's doctrine of nonintervention also affected her Congo policy. U.N. intervention in 1960 was seen as a threat to the sovereignty of the Congo. Armed intervention in an internal struggle served to encourage conflict and to prevent the state from settling its own problems in its own way and in its own time. French spokesmen contended that the U.N. Mission might lead to interference in the Congo's domestic affairs. The French wanted to avert a civil war in the Congo in which the United States would support one camp and the Soviet Union the other, and insisted that U.N. intervention would increase rather than decrease, the probability of such a confrontation. In short, U.N. intervention would insure the introduction of the Cold War into the Congo.

Associated with its nonintervention doctrine, Paris advocated that the Western powers respect the views of the most directly concerned ally, Belgium. Her sympathy for the dilemma of Brussels was undoubtedly influenced by her own experience in the U.N. debates which, since 1952, deepened France's estrangement from the United Nations. In 1960, the French-Algerian war was in its sixth year, and each year France had been bitterly denounced. France had consistently argued that the Algerian question was a matter of French domestic

---

[3] André Passeron, *De Gaulle parle* (Paris: Plon, 1952), pp. 406–407.

jurisdiction and thus, outside the purview of the United Nations. There was some concern in Paris that U.N. intervention in the Congo would create a precedent for interference in Algeria or other parts of French Africa.

In the first months of the Congo crisis, one of the salient features of French policy was the complete endorsement of Belgian actions. In July, 1960, de Gaulle personally assured the Belgian ambassador in Paris of his total support for the defense of Belgian interests,[4] and said the use of paratroopers to restore order was fully justified. He also asserted that the presence of Belgian troops remained indispensable as long as U.N. forces were unable to control the situation.[5] On July 25, Prime minister Michel Debré publicly reaffirmed Belgium's right to protect her citizens.[6] In the Congo, Paris demonstrated her sympathy with Belgium's problems by representing Belgian interests when Leopoldville broke its diplomatic ties with Brussels.

In the Security Council debate on the August 9 Resolution, France espoused the Belgian cause. Bérard asked bluntly: "Which of our governments would have acted differently if it had been placed in the same position?"[7]

DE GAULLE'S TROIKA PROPOSAL

In July, 1960, de Gaulle proposed that the United States, Britain, and France act in concert to prevent further deterioration in the Congo and to block Communist intervention.[8] He recommended that the three Western powers exert pressure on Brussels and Leopoldville to come to terms under their Treaty of Friendship. This meant that a significant cadre of Belgian administrators, technicians, and probably military officers would remain in the Congo to carry on the functions of the state until a sufficient number of Congolese had been trained to take over. In his view, only Belgium was in a position to provide experts familiar with the local problems. If the Belgians were quickly replaced by others—Congolese or foreigners—anarchy would ensue. The three Western allies would guarantee that Belgium would respect

---

[4] *The Times* (London), July 21, 1960.

[5] *Le Monde,* July 21, 1960.

[6] *Ibid.,* July 27, 1960.

[7] U.N., *SCOR,* S/PV 886 (August 8, 1960), p. 37.

[8] A few days after de Gaulle made his proposal, Prime Minister Debré repeated it in the National Assembly on July 25, 1960. (*Le Monde,* July 27, 1960.)

the independence and freedom of the Congo. De Gaulle stated his position openly at his September 5, 1960, press conference:

If the United States, Great Britain, and France had concerted their positions in this matter from the beginning of the crisis; if these three powers had first encouraged the Belgians and the Congolese to establish their mutual relations on a practical and reasonable basis; and if these three powers had also taken steps to help the young state of the Congo get started and finally to make it understood that once the emancipation of the Congo had been assured and guaranteed by the West, no intervention from elsewhere would be permitted—I feel that the result would have been preferable to the bloody anarchy that now exists in this new state. I believe, furthermore, that the prestige and cohesion of the West would have been better assured in this way than by playing second fiddle to the so-called "United" Nations, whose action is inadequate and very costly.[9]

Within NATO circles, France urged increased consultation among the Western allies for a joint strategy toward the Congo. French pressures mounted when the situation in the Congo deteriorated and a civil war threatened to break out among the Leopoldville, Stanleyville, and Elisabethville factions. At a NATO meeting in January, 1961, France argued along with Belgium for the adoption of a common Western line of action and for a firmer pro-Western policy against the Afro-Asian states favoring the Lumumba cause.

Washington's reaction to de Gaulle's troika arrangement for the Congo was cool, reflecting a similar response to the General's original proposal for a tripartite NATO directorate in 1958. In a letter to President Eisenhower on September 17, 1958, the French leader proposed a troika of the United States, Britain, and France to deal with security problems in Africa and elsewhere outside the immediate NATO theatre. Eisenhower's reply of October 20 acknowledged the continued need for consultation among the three Western powers, but rejected the idea of a formal directorate. "We cannot afford to adopt," said Eisenhower, "any system which would give our other allies, or other free world countries, the impression that basic decisions affecting their own vital interests are being made without their participation."[10]

President Kennedy, like Eisenhower, rejected the troika, but affirmed the need for consultation. France contended, however, that Washington did not consult sufficiently with its major Western allies on Congo

---

[9] Passeron, *De Gaulle parle,* p. 475.
[10] The Eisenhower letter was released by the State Department in August, 1966. *New York Times,* August 15, 1966.

matters. Other NATO allies joined in this criticism as far as the so-called "American Plan" was concerned.[11]

FRANCE URGES A LIMITED U.N. ROLE

Though on principle Paris opposed U.N. intervention, once the operation was authorized, she did not wash her hands of the matter. French spokesmen repeatedly invoked the doctrine of noninterference and insisted on a U.N. mandate restricted primarily to the restoration of order. France objected strongly to the September 20 Assembly Resolution because it provided for an Afro-Asian conciliation group to help the Congolese resolve their internal problems.[12]

Paris opposed the "American Plan" recommendation to neutralize all Congolese troops, including those loyal to the moderate Kasavubu government, on two counts. First, no sovereign state could be deprived of its army and remain sovereign. Second, indiscriminate disarmament would place the Central Government, which Hammarskjold and the Western powers were trying to uphold, on an equal footing with internal adversaries bent on its destruction. From the time of the Kasavubu-Lumumba rupture, Paris consistently upheld Kasavubu as the Congo's lawful Chief of State whose constitutional authority should be accepted, not only by Stanleyville, but also by Elisabethville. Although the French were by no means hostile to the Tshombe regime, they did favor an *entente* between Kasavubu and Tshombe, with Kasavubu remaining President.

In one instance French advocacy of noninterference by the UNF in internal disputes was overruled by France's desire to prevent the militant Stanleyville regime from consolidating its position. In early 1961, the French delegate said that U.N. contingents "were duty bound to resort to coercion" to stop the brutality of the Stanleyville troops against Congolese in parts of Kivu and Orientale in the presence of U.N. soldiers.[13] This was the one time Paris openly recommended the interjection of armed force in the internal Congo rivalries, justifying her departure from strict nonintervention in the name of the U.N. obligation to maintain order.

In dealing with the Katanga problem, France consistently opposed U.N. military action and contended that the secessionist province should be reintegrated by persuasion. Paris condemned U.N. coercion

---

[11] The "American Plan" is discussed in Chap. 4.
[12] U.N., *GAOR*, A/PV 861 (September 19, 1960), p. 62.
[13] U.N., *SCOR*, S/PV 932 (February 7, 1961), p. 17.

in Rounds One and Two. In December, 1961, during Round Two, France and Britain tried to get U.S. support for an immediate cease-fire in Katanga. Failing in this effort and with the fighting continuing, Paris on December 15 prohibited planes carrying U.N. supplies to the Congo from flying over her territory. This directly affected U.S. planes based in France which were providing logistical support for U.N. troops in Katanga. All planes from Europe had to circumvent Algeria and secure overflight rights from neighboring countries. This French move did not measurably affect U.N. military capability in Katanga, but it was a mild harassment and, combined with the political pressures of other Western states, contributed to the ceasefire two days later. U.N. action in Round Two was terminated without ending Katanga's secession.

During 1962 Paris became increasingly convinced that the United States exercised a decisive and unwarranted influence over U.N. policies in the Congo. The Thant Plan for National Reconciliation was regarded as an instrument of U.S. foreign policy. France opposed the Plan because it interfered in domestic affairs and the boycott of Katanga exports was impracticable. In December, when Thant appealed for economic sanctions, Paris directed its criticism primarily against Washington. The French also disapproved the increased U.S. military support to the UNF resulting from the mission of Lieutenant General Louis W. Truman. Since Tshombe now appeared to be more inclined to compromise, the French argued, it would be singularly ill-timed to push him. Paris also regarded with a great deal of skepticism American warnings of intensified pro-Russian activities in the Congo.[14] The Paris daily, *Le Figaro,* reflected these views:

> The United Nations was literally pushed bodily into the use of force in Katanga by the United States. For the last year, the Americans have taken charge of the Congo, which had entered into their sphere of influence. Not that they are particularly interested in it, but because they want to prevent the Communist bloc from getting hold of it . . . This is the way things started in Laos and we remember how that worked out.[15]

PARIS OFFICIALS SUPPORT TSHOMBE

Sympathy for Tshombe's secessionist cause in high French circles was doubtless an element in the government's hostility to a military solution of the Katanga problem. Within the French administration

14 *The Times* (London), December 21, 1962.
15 Cited in the *Washington Post and Times Herald,* January 6, 1963.

there were factions that encouraged Tshombe's independence aspirations, but this did not mean that the Gaullist regime supported Katanga secession.

Several officials in the Ministry of the Armed Forces co-operated with Tshombe by facilitating the acquisition of military equipment for the Katangan gendarmerie and by permitting the recruitment of mercenaries in France. The purchase of arms for Katanga through French channels occurred primarily in the early stages of the Congo crisis and was probably completely halted by the summer of 1961.

In February, 1961, three *Fouga-Magisters* (French jet trainers) were delivered to the Katanga government. When this fact leaked to the press, the French Foreign Ministry denied having authorized the shipment. The Ministry admitted knowledge of an order for *Fougas* placed by Belgium before June, 1960, for its forces in the Congo, and promised it would ask Brussels to explain why these planes had been shipped to Elisabethville after the Congo became independent.[16] According to one scholar, in the fall of 1960 the Katanga Defense Secretary arranged to purchase the *Fougas* as part of the original Belgian order for the *Force publique*.[17] The sellers of the *Fougas* probably received export licenses from French Ministry officials. The planes were transported to Katanga by Stratocruiser (Boeing C–97) under contract with the Seven Seas Airlines, a private American firm which flew from Luxembourg via Brazzaville to Elisabethville.

In addition to the *Fougas,* some weapons from France and elsewhere reached Katanga and South Kasai via Pointe Noire in Congo (Brazzaville). In the summer of 1961, the French government appears to have decided to block further shipments through Brazzaville. A French intelligence agent explained that in the spring of 1961, the Brazzaville government ordered arms in Rome on behalf of the secessionist regime of South Kasai. Part of the shipment was stopped by the Italian government before it left Genoa; the part which reached Brazzaville was eventually confiscated by French officials and stored in French arsenals at Pointe Noire.[18]

The story of Colonel Roger Trinquier highlights the ambiguity surrounding the recruitment of French mercenaries for Katanga which started in the fall of 1960. A French paratroop officer well-known for his theory of guerrilla warfare and counterinsurgency, Trinquier had

[16] *Le Monde,* February 18, 1961.
[17] J. Gérard-Libois, *Sécession au Katanga* (Brussels: CRISP, 1963), p. 188.
[18] Michel Borri, *Nous . . . ces Affreux* (Paris: Editions Galic, 1962) pp. 326–27 and 349–55.

fought in Indochina and Algeria. His opposition to de Gaulle's Algerian policies led to his transfer from Algeria to metropolitan France. On January 5, 1961, still on active service in Nice, Trinquier received an invitation from the Katanga regime to take command of its armed forces. He went to Paris to discuss Tshombe's proposal with Pierre Mesmer, the Armed Forces minister, who had also served in French Africa. According to Trinquier, he never would have gone to Katanga if he had encountered any resistance from the French government.[19] In any event, the Colonel received permission from Messmer to go on a fact-finding mission to Katanga, although apparently someone in the Ministry raised objections. On orders from de Gaulle's office, Trinquier was told that if he decided to enter Tshombe's service, he would have to resign his French Army commission.

Trinquier left Paris for Katanga on January 25, 1961, to investigate the situation. In Elisabethville he met with intense hostility from Belgian officers who resented the appointment of a Frenchman to the senior post. After Tshombe assured Trinquier of his complete support, the French officer agreed to become Commander in Chief of the Armed Forces of Katanga. After a few days in Elisabethville, he returned to Paris and gave Messmer a personal account of his visit. Trinquier argued that Katanga was the last bastion of the West against Communist infiltration in Central Africa. This passionate identification of Katanga's cause with the defense of the West was later made by the majority of French mercenaries. Trinquier submitted his resignation which was immediately accepted and made retroactive to January 24, the day before he left for Elisabethville. At about the same time, he opened an office in Paris to recruit mercenaries for Katanga.

Partly as a result of the publicity these developments received in France and abroad, Paris took measures against Trinquier's activities. Early in February, the government decreed that French soldiers who served a foreign power could lose their citizenship.[20] About a week later, the Prime Minister's office issued a press release which said that in the light of Article 85 of the Penal Code which forbids the recruitment of soldiers in France for a foreign regime, the recently opened enlistment office for volunteers for Katanga had to be closed.[21] The office in question was closed, but recruiting reportedly continued at

19 Colonel Roger Trinquier *et al., Notre Guerre au Katanga* (Paris: Editions de la pensée moderne, 1963), pp. 53–54.
20 *Le Monde,* February 7, 1961.
21 *Ibid.,* February 14, 1961.

another address by Katanga officials with the assistance of a retired French officer.[22]

Despite the government decree, Trinquier left for Katanga at the end of February with Commandant René Faulques and two other officers. Each of his three companions had made his reputation in the Algerian war, and each resigned from the French Army to join the Katanga gendarmerie. As a result of Belgian pressures, however, President Tshombe broke his agreement with Trinquier. He was forced to leave Katanga on March 9, but he did not abandon his new cause there. He went to Greece and prepared recommendations for the organization of Katanga's military establishment. Realizing he could accomplish little without the support of his own government or the co-operation of the Katanga regime, Trinquier returned to France in April, 1961.

Commandant Faulques and the other two French officers remained in Katanga. Faulques took charge of the training center in Shinkolobwe. Gradually other mercenaries from France joined Tshombe's volunteer forces. After the putsch of April, 1961, in Algeria, some disillusioned officers left Algeria for Katanga. The number of French who served in the Katanga gendarmerie was not large. Pierre Davister, the Belgian reporter, maintains that at least twelve French officers were attached to Tshombe's staff.[23] Conor Cruise O'Brien gives one of the highest estimates, suggesting there were about thirty French mercenaries in Katanga.[24]

The effectiveness of the French officers compensated for their small numbers. Their experience in Algeria had trained them well in the techniques of guerrilla warfare. They were much better equipped to fight in Katanga's political and geographical environment than the other mercenaries. The failure of the U.N. military operation in Round One, September, 1961, was largely the result of the opposition organized by the French officers. Colonel Muké, the illiterate former sergeant major was the official commander of the Katanga gendarmerie; Faulques was "in theory his Chief of Staff, but in fact, the real commander," according to the French journalist Jacques le Bailly.[25]

[22] See Justin Bomboko's statement to the Security Council on November 17, 1961. (U.N., *SCOR*, S/PV 976 [November 17, 1961], pp. 40–41.)

[23] Pierre Davister and Philippe Toussaint, *Croisettes et casques blues* (Brussels: Editions actuelles, 1962), p. 153.

[24] O'Brien, *To Katanga and Back*, p. 201.

[25] Trinquier, *Notre Guerre au Katanga*, p. 112.

Faulques and his team continued to play a key role in Katanga's resistance until the end of 1961. After Round Two, several French mercenaries, including Faulques, left Katanga. The French component of the mercenary force had never been large; the even smaller remaining group consisted of the most extreme OAS types, the *Ultras,* as they were called.

In the course of 1962, the mercenaries became increasingly disorganized. When Round Three began on December 28, 1962, mercenary resistance was no longer effective against the U.N. troops. After the fighting, most remaining mercenaries fled to Angola and Rhodesia.

In January, 1962, Article 85 of the French Penal Code was applied for the first time. A French paratroop captain, Paul Ropagnol, who had fought with Faulques in Katanga and who had been sent to France to recruit additional volunteers, was arrested in Toulouse and later sentenced to six months in prison. In the following months, an order for the arrest of Commandant Faulques was issued. By June, however, the proceedings against Faulques had been dropped because of "insufficient grounds" for prosecution.[26]

French support for Tshombe came also from officials in de Gaulle's Presidental office. Foccart, a member of de Gaulle's office from the beginning, was originally charged with the coordination of internal security and intelligence activities. In 1960 he became the Secretary-General for African and Malagasy Affairs in the Office of the President. Foccart belonged to the informal nerve-center of the Gaullist regime. He was one of de Gaulle's principal advisers on African matters, though his influence varied. He gathered information on all African questions, and controlled a network of intelligence agents in Africa. It is not certain that Foccart himself supported Tshombe, but several of his agents did, particularly those attached to the Youlou regime in Brazzaville.[27] Foccart was a staunch supporter of President Youlou who, in turn, was one of Tshombe's closest allies.

The significance of the clandestine support for Katangan secession that came from Foccart's office is difficult to determine. It consisted of political advice, generally via Brazzaville; of aid to the recruitment of mercenaries in France; and probably of co-operation with some of the weapons shipments to Katanga.

26 *Le Monde,* June 9, 1962.
27 Michel Borri, reportedly one of Foccart's agents, testified in his *Nous . . . ces Affreux* of the strong pro-Tshombe sentiment among the French agents in Brazzaville.

Certain French foreign service officers in the Congo also collaborated with Tshombe. The French Consul in Elisabethville, Joseph Lambroschini, was one. O'Brien accuses him of being a "dangerous adversary" of the United Nations, and of supporting the Katanga regime.[28] The whole demeanor of the French Consul suggests that O'Brien's charge was essentially correct. Like his British and Belgian counterparts, the French Consul gave friendly political advice to Tshombe. He also sought to obstruct the apprehension of mercenaries by the UNF. Lambroschini probably knew all the mercenaries, but refused to reveal their identity or whereabouts to U.N. officials in Katanga. On August 28, 1961, Lambroschini and the other European consuls persuaded O'Brien to halt the arrest of the mercenaries and pledged to take the responsibility for their repatriation themselves. This promise amounted to a play for time which enabled many of the mercenaries to take off their uniforms and reappear as civilians. Of the twenty-one French officers who were on the list to be expelled, only ten were awaiting repatriation or had left Katanga by September 8, and some of them returned shortly thereafter.

This does not necessarily mean there was collusion between the French Consul and his superiors in Leopoldville and Paris. The Foreign Ministry adhered to France's official position. French diplomats in the Congo found themselves in a rapidly changing and chaotic situation, and communications between Leopoldville and Elisabethville were not always good. France's official representatives, particularly in Katanga, lived in an atmosphere where the overwhelming majority of the European population was vehemently against the U.N. presence and passionately in favor of Tshombe. These factors at least partly explain the difference between Paris and Elisabethville.

IMPACT OF FRANCE ON THE MISSION

France's official position of critical aloofness toward the Congo effort changed little during the four years. In the early months, French policy was marked by strong support for Belgium. Later, as the UNF became increasingly active in Katanga, Paris became more critical of Washington. France's basic distrust of the U.N. system and her preference for working through Western Big Power channels persisted. Except where the Stanleyville regime was concerned, Paris adhered to the principle of nonintervention. She also insisted upon respect for

---

[28] O'Brien, *To Katanga and Back,* pp. 108 and 128.

the Central Government as represented by President Kasavubu and opposed the use of force to effect a political settlement in the Congo.

As a tangible manifestation of her opposition to the UNF, France refused to pay her assessed share of the expenditures. Her reasons were political, but her justification was couched in legal terms. U.N. peace-keeping operations, Paris argued, are the exclusive responsibility of the Security Council. Since the financial assessments were made by the General Assembly, there is no legal obligation to honor them. Further, the July 20, 1962, opinion of the International Court of Justice on the financial question was advisory and hence not obligatory.[29] These arguments are almost identical to those advanced by the Soviet Union to support its nonpayment position.

Taken as a whole, French policies placed a restraint on the U.N. Mission, but they did not seriously alter its course. Lacking the endorsement of Paris, the U.N. effort suffered some loss in the prestige that broader diplomatic support would have brought. France's refusal to pay her share of the cost contributed to the financial crisis, but the political consequences of this refusal were far more significant than its material effect.

The Secretary-General was never free from France's restraining influence in the interpretation or execution of his mandate. In the absence of unanimous consent from the permanent members of the Security Council, Hammarskjold and Thant had to move with greater caution in the exercise of their authority.

In a strict legal sense, the *official* policies of the French government may not have been contrary to the U.N. mandate, but an assessment of the total impact of public statements and specific acts of non-co-operation could lead to the opposite conclusion. General de Gaulle's calling the United Nations a *"petit machin,"* France's unwillingness to pay her assessment, its insistence on limited U.N. authority in Katanga, its prohibition of U.N. overflights, the tacitly permitted pro-Tshombe activities of certain French officials—taken together these elements suggest a pattern of opposition to the U.N. operation, particularly in Katanga.

The covert, and apparently unofficial, political and military support to the Katanga regime from certain French government quarters was a distinct breach of the U.N. mandate. The French mercenaries clearly strengthened Tshombe's military capability, especially in Rounds One

---

[29] The French position is summarized in *France and the United Nations,* French Affairs, No. 178 (New York: The French Press and Information Service, June, 1965).

and Two, and thus delayed the integration of Katanga. Their presence and activities were in direct violation of the U.N. resolutions. The French government, by looking the other way when mercenary recruitment and other activities in support of Tshombe occurred, acted against the spirit and intention of the Council mandate.

Ironically, France's own interests were served by the U.N. Mission to the extent that it succeeded in frustrating Soviet ambitions and in reestablishing order and stability in the Congo.

BRITISH INTERESTS IN THE CONGO

Britain like France participated in the Western concern that the Communists would exploit the Congo's chaos to the detriment of her interests in Africa. London was particularly concerned with the impact of the crisis on the Federation of Rhodesia and Nyasaland which was created under British sponsorship. Northern Rhodesia, now Zambia, shared an eleven-hundred-mile frontier with Katanga. The exploitation of the rich mineral deposits on both sides of the border had led to close economic ties between the Federation and Katanga.

Federation Prime Minister, Sir Roy Welensky, wanted a stable and Western-oriented regime in Elisabethville, and believed that this could best be guaranteed by supporting Tshombe's secessionist ambitions. He sought to enlist support for Tshombe in London. From a strictly British viewpoint, however, two factors argued against a commitment to Katanga's independence. First, in so far as London was still trying to hold the Federation together, it could not very well endorse a secessionist movement in a neighboring state. More important, British support for Tshombe would jeopardize London's carefully forged relationships with the nationalist leaders in British Africa.

Compounding the British predicament was a strong pro-Tshombe sentiment in official and private circles in London. Britain had industrial and financial interests in the Congo; about 45 per cent were in Katanga. The spokesmen for British investments in Katanga were vociferous. On the whole, their outlook leaned towards the more conservative European-governed regimes in Africa. Their views were expressed by the right wing of the Conservative party. As a result, the Conservative government found itself torn by internal pressures. It was also assailed from the outside by spokesmen from the Rhodesian Federation. Much of the ambivalence in Britain's Congo policies stems from this situation.

LONDON'S POLICY OF CRITICAL SUPPORT

Britain's first reaction to the proposal to dispatch a U.N. Force was ambivalent. Unlike Paris, London had a positive view toward U.N. peacekeeping and felt that the mission could be constructive. But like France, Britain was worried about Hammarskjold's probable interpretation of his mandate and the precedents set by U.N. interference, particularly military action, in Congolese internal affairs. London abstained on the July 14 Resolution, but Prime Minister Harold Macmillan nevertheless promised his full support.[30] As events developed, London gained more confidence in Hammarskjold's handling of the Congo situation and endorsed the second and third Council resolutions as well as the more far-reaching February 21, 1961 Resolution.

Throughout the operation, British leaders frequently registered their critical views on U.N. policies. In general, Britain expressed the same reservations about the breadth of U.N. authority as France did. Britain also opposed the indiscriminate disarmament proposals of the "American Plan."[31] She observed the nonintervention principle, which she enjoined on the UNF, by refusing to recognize Katanga as a state, in spite of Welensky's pleas to give at least *de facto* recognition.[32] When officers of British origin began volunteering for service in the Katanga gendarmerie, London announced on April 12, 1961, that "any United Kingdom national who takes up a military engagement in the Congo, other than under U.N. command" would have his passport invalidated.[33] The majority of the English-speaking mercenaries in Katanga were South Africans. Some came from Rhodesia. Probably less than a dozen came from Britain. The recruitment of English-speaking volunteers took place primarily in South Africa. The Rhodesian Federation permitted the passage of mercenaries across its territory. There was no recruitment in Britain.

Britain's insistence on noninterference of the UNF in the Congo's internal conflict reflected a concern that such interference would create a dangerous precedent which would place the Organization "at the beck and call of any state with the problem of a dissident minority within its own borders."[34]

---

[30] *The Times* (London), July 15, 1960.

[31] U.N., *GAOR*, A/PV 952 (December 17, 1960), p. 1349; and U.N., *GAOR*, A/PV 980 (April 7, 1961), p. 258.

[32] *Welensky's 4000 Days,* p. 210.

[33] U.N., *SCOR,* S/PV 976 (November 17, 1961), p. 30.

[34] *Ibid.,* p. 34.

London applied the noninterference formula most rigorously on the Katanga question. The pragmatic argument against forcing Elisabethville to bow to the authority of Leopoldville centered on the fact that there was already a semblance of order and a functioning government in Katanga. The liquidation of Tshombe's regime would open Katanga to the chaos that had submerged the rest of the Congo. The United Nations would do well to leave Katanga alone and concentrate its resources on restoring stability where they were needed most.[35]

Apart from strong pro-Tshombe pressures from Welensky and Conservative party quarters, the British government itself did not want to weaken the Katangan regime, particularly in view of the rivalry between Leopoldville and Stanleyville. The position of the Kasavubu government was highly precarious. Its overthrow by the Stanleyville forces was a distinct possibility. A militant regime in Leopoldville would jeopardize Britain's economic interests in the Katanga–Rhodesia Copperbelt and its political interests throughout Central and Southern Africa. If Tshombe could come to terms with Leopoldville, the moderate Central Government would be strengthened and Stanleyville could be kept effectively in check. On several occasions, London requested Welensky to use his influence with Tshombe to persuade him to reach an accord with Kasavubu.[36] The British also pressed for the recall of Dayal, the U.N. Representative in Leopoldville, whose attitude they believed reflected irreconcilable hostility toward Elisabethville, contempt for Leopoldville, and sympathy for Stanleyville.[37]

THE KATANGA PROBLEM

British criticism of the UNF centered almost exclusively on its role in Katanga. London sought diligently to prevent the exercise of U.N. force there. After Round One began on September 13, 1961, the British government, partly to silence the protests of its right wing faction and to allay the fears of Welensky who had promptly ordered Rhodesian troops to the Katanga border, used "all their influence to urge a ceasefire."[38] London's ambassador in Leopoldville reportedly warned Hammarskjold that Britain would withdraw its suport from the U.N. operation unless he could offer an acceptable explanation of the events

---

[35] See Alport, *The Sudden Assignment*, p. 105.
[36] Alport, *Sudden Assignment*, p. 107; *Welensky's 4000 Days*, pp. 220 and 229.
[37] Hoskyns, *Congo Since Independence*, p. 349.
[38] Hansard, H. C., *Debates*, Vol. 534 (October 17, 1961), col. 22.

in Katanga and promise to halt the fighting.[39] In a conference with Hammarskjold in Leopoldville British Undersecretary of State, Lord Lansdowne, was "highly critical" of U.N. action on September 13.[40]

Lord Lansdowne also discussed with Hammarskjold the U.N. request to Britain to permit Ethiopian jets on their way to join the UNF in Katanga to overfly Uganda. The rights were not granted, but London never officially admitted that it refused to grant them. In a House of Commons debate three months later, the government spokesman said that if these planes had reached Katanga, there would have been the danger of an escalation of the fighting at the very time that Hammarskjold was seeking to arrange a cease-fire.[41] British diplomacy deserves considerable credit for arranging the cease-fire negotiations between Tshombe and Mahmoud Khiary, Chief of U.N. Civilian Operations, who took over after Hammarskjold's death.[42] The British government also played an important role in the forced resignation of Conor Cruise O'Brien, whom the Foreign Office regarded as irresponsibly "anticolonial."

Britain and France abstained from the November 24, 1961, Council Resolution because it went "dangerously far in encouraging" the U.N. command in Katanga "to use an added measure of force." Britain warned that its continued support would depend on the "skill and wisdom and the conciliatory manner with which the United Nations carries out its mandate."[43] Within a fortnight Round Two started.

On October 21, shortly after Round One the Secretary-General had asked London for a supply of 1,000-pound bombs, presumably 24, for the Indian Canberra bombers in the UNF. On December 7, the request was repeated. This unusual request posed a dilemma for the Macmillan government. India, which had the largest contingent in the UNF and whose officers were in command in Katanga, would have regarded a negative response as one more irritant to Anglo-Indian relations. If Britain refused, she would have drawn further criticism from other Commonwealth and U.N. members that were accusing her of encouraging Katangan secession. On December 8, the Foreign Office

---

[39] Arthur L. Gavshon, *The Mysterious Death of Dag Hammarskjold* (New York: Walker and Co., 1962), pp. 129–31.

[40] Hansard, *Debates*, Vol. 534 (October 18, 1961), cols. 445–54 *passim*.

[41] Hansard, *Debates*, Vol. 542 (December 14, 1961), col. 657.

[42] Lord Alport, the British High Commissioner to the Federation, gives a detailed account of the efforts of the British representatives in Elisabethville and himself to arrange a meeting between Tshombe and Hammarskjold and subsequently between Tshombe and Khiary. Alport, *Sudden Assignment*, pp. 108–33.

[43] U.N., *SCOR*, S/PV 979 (November 21, 1961), pp. 5 and 6.

announced that Britain would provide the bombs. In Rhodesia, Welensky issued an impassioned denunciation of London's decision and declared that the bombs would not be permitted to cross "one inch of Federal soil."[44] In the House of Commons, Viscount Hinching-brooke, a Conservative, filed a motion of censure against the government. Many Tories beyond those identified with the "Katanga Lobby" became deeply disturbed for fear that Britain might find itself in a position of supporting open war against Katanga. The Conservative government was compelled to take a right wing revolt seriously. On December 11, in the middle of Round Two London announced that the bombs would not be delivered until U.N. policy had been further clarified and urged an immediate cease-fire in Katanga. These moves closed the Conservative ranks in time to forestall a censure vote.

The initial decision to provide the bombs was made with obvious reluctance. Its reversal and the cease-fire call were the direct consequence of pressures from the right wing at home and from the Rhodesian Federation. These acts of non-co-operation with the U.N. effort also reflected more than current political pressures. They were rooted in part in the conviction that the U.N. Force should not be used to settle internal conflicts. This conviction inspired Lord Home's assertion that there was a "crisis of confidence in the United Nations."[45] On various occasions in 1962, the British government repeated this theme.

The long stalemate in the Congo and the failure of Elisabethville and Leopoldville to reach a settlement finally persuaded London that it was powerless to prevent coercive measures if the coalition supporting the UNF was prepared to resort to them. In August, 1962, Britain publicly endorsed the Thant Plan, although it still shied away from the associated economic boycott. By the end of November, London informed Tshombe that if he rejected a peaceful settlement with Leopoldville, Britain would not oppose economic sanctions against Katanga.[46]

Britain's reaction to Round Three was much more restrained than it had been to the previous two. A Foreign Office statement simply mentioned the futility of trying to impose a political pattern on the Congo by force, and appealed for an immediate halt in the fighting. In Katanga, British actions were confined to attempts to force Tshombe to return to the conference table and to dissuade him from carrying out his threatened scorched-earth policy. It was primarily due to the

[44] *Welensky's 4000 Days*, p. 248.
[45] *The Times* (London), December 29, 1961.
[46] *Welensky's 4000 Days*, p. 264.

efforts of the British and Belgian consuls at Elisabethville that most of Katanga's industrial complex was spared, although the Americans actively pursued the same objective.

BRITISH IMPACT ON THE MISSION

In spite of its misgivings about the use of force by the UNF in Katanga, Britain did not withhold its financial support of the operation. In addition to paying its full assessment, Britain voluntarily contributed $585,000 in cash and waived the cost of her initial airlift amounting to $520,000.[47] Britain also became the second largest buyer, after the United States, of U.N. bonds.

Britain's general policy of critical support had a significant restraining effect upon the action of the UNF. Her sustained diplomatic and financial support conferred a degree of authority and prestige upon the mission. For this reason the Secretary-General took more seriously the views of London than those of Paris which chose to criticize the effort from the outside without assuming any responsibility. British criticism, for example, had greater weight in terminating the inconclusive U.N. military operations of Rounds One and Two than similar criticism from France.

British diplomats in the Congo, as well as Sir Roy Welensky, had a moderating influence on Tshombe. They frequently persuaded him to continue negotiations with Leopoldville or to resume them when the dialogue was broken. These diplomatic activities created a climate more conducive to the achievement of U.N. objectives.

London's hostility to the use of force and the efforts to preserve Tshombe's position also nurtured Katanga's illusion that the British endorsed its secession. Here Britain's policy was similar to that of France, and had the effect of delaying the reintegration of Katanga into the Congo.

To the extent that the U.N. Mission forestalled a direct clash between the Big Powers in Central Africa and protected the Congo against Communist penetration, the peacekeeping effort served British interests in stability and peaceful change. Although the U.N. undertaking temporarily complicated British-Rhodesian relations, it also helped to prevent Rhodesian intervention in the Congo. Such intervention would have adversely affected the British position in Africa as well as the U.N. operation.

[47] See Appendix I. The financing of the UNF is discussed in Chap. 11.

7.

Belgium: Responsibility Without Authority

The Belgians were more intensely involved in the Congo crisis than any other people, except for the politically aware Congolese. As the former colonial power, Brussels had a profound political, economic, and psychological stake in the restoration of order and in the success of the new state. It had an immediate vital interest in protecting the lives of some 87,000 Belgian citizens who were living in the Congo on Independence Day. Of these, some 10,000 were administrators and technicians in the Congolese government, and some 17,000 were employed in the private economic sector.[1]

The Belgian government had a deep political interest in and moral commitment to the achievement of viable statehood in the Congo. Brussels wanted to prove to itself and to the world that it was not irresponsible in abruptly granting independence, though it felt this fateful decision was forced upon it. During the colonial era the Belgians developed a thesis which called for a step by step preparation of the Congolese for full participation in modern civilization. In accordance with this thesis, Belgium emphasized mass elementary education rather than the creation of a highly educated elite. Secondary and university training was to be stressed at a later stage. The Belgian administration provided the Congo with a living standard that compared favorably with most other tropical African countries, but political development did not keep pace with economic development. Brussels' plans for an effective but gradual transition of its colony to a functioning state were prematurely cut off by the fast-moving events of 1959 and 1960.

Belgian government and private investments in the Congo were substantial. The official colonial policy encouraged the development of the country's rich mineral and agricultural resources by granting exclusive

[1] CRISP, *Congo: 1960,* II, 518.

concessions to private, mainly Belgian, corporations. The Belgian holdings, known as the "Congo Portfolio," amounted to some $750 million in 1960. The largest Belgian financial grouping was the *Société Générale de Belgique,* which controlled directly or indirectly, about 70 per cent of the Congolese economy.[2] The Société's mining activities were concentrated in Katanga and Kasai. Through an intricate system of interlocking shareholdings and directorates, the Société had a controlling interest in the *Union Minière du Haut-Katanga,* which had a virtual monopoly on extracting in Katanga. The control of the Société over the Union Minière was not complete; another large shareholder was Tanganyika Concessions, the British-African giant company which held 20 per cent of the voting rights in Union Minière. German and French investment was also represented in the Katanga mining concern. American financial interests in the Congo were negligible.

In contrast to Great Britain and France, Belgium lacked a tradition of empire. The general public and the political parties were content to leave the management of Congolese affairs to the responsible ministries and the ministries were responsive to the interests of the investors. Colonial policy was rarely a matter of public debate in Belgium. The Congo seemed quiet and far away. This was a major reason the relatively small nationalist riots of January, 1959, in Leopoldville produced shocked concern throughout Belgium. There was a common desire to avoid a conflict that might degenerate into a Congolese Algeria. The Socialist opposition responded with an intensive campaign against the dispatch of metropolitan troops to the Congo, though some officials considered this necessary to control further disorder. These circumstances, plus the fear that international opinion would turn against Belgium, led the Liberal-Christian Democrat Coalition government to call the Brussels Round Table Conference in January, 1960, which resulted in the decision to grant full sovereignty to the Congo on June 30, with only five months' notice.

By accepting the principle and date of Congolese independence, and by providing the new state with a transitional Fundamental Law (embracing the goals of national unity and parliamentary democracy), Belgium hoped that the Congo would make a peaceful transition without a serious rupture in the traditional economic and cultural ties. According to this ideal expectation, the Congo would have all the attributes of sovereignty, but because of the lack of trained Congolese,

[2] CRISP, *Structures économiques de la Belgique: Morphologie des groupes financiers* (Brussels: CRISP, 1962), p. 150.

its civil administration and its army—the instruments of its unity—would depend for a long time on experienced Belgians serving as technical advisers and administrators.

The mutiny of the *Force publique* and its aftermath cruelly shattered this peaceful image. Belgian prestige fell in the international arena. It was accused by some critics of aggression, and by others of abandoning its colonial responsibility and inadequately preparing the Congo for statehood.

INITIAL POSITION TOWARD KATANGA

The fundamental minimum objective of Brussels from the beginning was to maintain a sufficient presence in the Congo to protect Belgian interests. A larger and compatible goal was to make decolonization succeed. If it failed, Belgian interests would suffer. Consequently, Brussels sought to give its nationals in the Congo a sense of security so they would remain at their posts and ensure the functioning of the new state.

The Belgian government justified its military intervention in mid-July, 1960, because of the total inability of the Congolese authorities to maintain order and guarantee the safety of Belgian citizens and other Europeans.[3] Brussels did not regard this temporary emergency measure as illegal interference in the internal affairs of the Congo, and certainly not an act of aggression.[4] No Belgian official seriously suggested the reimposition of Belgian authority in the Congo. This emergency action was much like the Stanleyville rescue mission in 1964, except that in the latter case the Belgians and Americans had an invitation from the Leopoldville government.

At the outset, Brussels regarded a U.N. military presence as an inevitable and potentially desirable form of collaboration with Belgian metropolitan troops to restore order. Since U.N. intervention did not constitute a sanction against Belgium, Brussels was prepared to en-

---

[3] By July 18, 1960, Belgian troops had intervened in twenty-three different places in the Congo. Belgian military strength in the Congo at its height consisted of 9,400 men; there were 3,800 Belgian metropolitan forces, including members of the auxiliary and supporting services, in the Congo before the mutiny started, and 5,600 men were flown in from Belgium to reinforce the metropolitan troops after the mutiny began. By August 7, 1960, 2,800 men had been withdrawn again. At that date there were 1,700 Belgian troops left in Katanga and 4,900 men at the bases in Kitona and Kamina and in Ruanda-Urundi. [Ganshof van der Meersch, *Fin de la Souveraineté Belge au Congo*, p.484.]

[4] U.N., *SCOR*, S/PV 873 (July 13, 1960), pp. 34–37.

dorse the July 10, 1960, request from Leopoldville for U.N. military aid and a similar request on July 12 from the Congolese Minister of Foreign Affairs. Brussels did not endorse the July 12 and 13 appeals of Kasavubu and Lumumba which placed the onus for the breakdown of order on Belgian intervention.

Hammarskjold's July 13 Security Council statement did not condemn Brussels, but did emphasize the need to restore order, so Belgium expressed its willingness to cooperate fully with the United Nations and to withdraw its troops as soon as the UNF was able to take over.[5] Brussels reserved the right to decide in each specific situation whether the UNF could in fact maintain law and order and to act directly in the event of imminent danger to its citizens. If it felt compelled to intervene, it promised to notify the U.N. command immediately.[6] The first Belgian units left Leopoldville for Brussels on July 17, but the major withdrawal did not start until July 20; it was completed in three days. Hammarskjold did not request Brussels to expedite this troop recall and did not formally criticize Belgium's unilateral interventions after July 14; he thus appeared to accept the policy of a gradual troop repatriation.

Brussels also indicated its desire to co-operate with the U.N. Mission by suggesting to Ralph Bunche, on July 16, that Belgian troops be employed by the UNF, particularly for the restoration of order in Stanleyville. This proposal was rejected. UNF officials agreed, however, that Belgian aircraft, painted with U.N. markings, would transport the Ethiopian troops from Stanleyville to other places in Equateur province. Further, during these early weeks Belgian troop units were offered to the U.N. Command for joint patrol operations, and some joint patrolling took place.

In secessionist Katanga, Belgian troops quickly restored law and order, and Brussels saw no need for U.N. intervention there. Belgian officials also opposed Lumumba's demands for U.N. military action against Tshombe. They felt that even the peaceful dispatch of U.N. troops to Elisabethville would constitute illegal interference in behalf of Lumumba.

The Belgians in Katanga constantly urged Brussels to grant recognition to the Tshombe regime and to keep the UNF out. If U.N. troops entered, they warned, the economy and administration would collapse. Many Europeans threatened to leave if the UNF came in.[7] Tshombe's

---

[5] *Ibid.*, pp. 36–37.
[6] U.N., *SCOR*, Supplement for July, Aug., Sept., 1960. S/4398 (July 18, 1960), p. 24.
[7] *Congo 1960*, II, 946–47.

supporters were more interested in tangible Belgian assistance which was feasible than in formal diplomatic recognition which was ruled out by international political realities. The Belgian Technical Mission, established in Elisabethville on July 20, served as the principal channel of Belgian influence and support in the early months.

Brussels agreed to provide Katanga with Belgian troops long enough to neutralize anti-Tshombe troops and tribal groups, particularly in North Katanga. Recognizing the impossibility of preventing the eventual entry of the UNF into Katanga, the Belgian government sought to delay the arrival of U.N. units until Katanga could assume the responsibility for its own administration, and was strong enough to resist a Lumumba invasion. The hostility of the Katanga regime to the UNF presence helped to promote Belgium's objective. Brussels, however, was not prepared to threaten force to delay the entry of the UNF, and Belgian troops were under strict orders not to resist U.N. troops and not to collaborate in any operation against the UNF.[8]

Fully aware of the Belgian position, Hammarskjold escorted a token U.N. presence of 240 Swedish soldiers into Elisabethville on August 12, where Belgian officials sought to obtain U.N. guarantees of noninterference in Katangan affairs. In consultation with the UNF commander, the evacuation of Belgian metropolitan forces in Katanga started on August 14.

During July and August, 1960, Belgium's policy was marked by a determination to intervene where its nationals were threatened, to delay U.N. entrance into Katanga, and to ensure its own continued military presence there. This course of action deepened Lumumba's hostility to any efforts to disarm ANC troops.[9] At the same time, it reinforced Katanga's position and encouraged Tshombe's obstruction to U.N. intervention. As a result, the relations between the UNF and the Lumumba regime deteriorated.

RELATIONS WITH LEOPOLDVILLE

Contrary to a widespread impression Belgian policy in the Congo was not to support secessionist Katanga against the Leopoldville gov-

---

[8] U.N., *SCOR,* Supplement for July, Aug., Sept., 1960, S/4417 (August 6, 1960), p. 53.

[9] On July 15, Major General Alexander, Belgian General Gheysen, and ANC Acting Chief of Staff Mpolo agreed to disarm ANC troops. On July 18, Mpolo appealed to Congolese troops to lay down their arms upon arrival of U.N. forces. Lumumba strenuously objected to any disarmament.

ernment, but simultaneously to support both. In the first turbulent months of independence, Brussels wanted to cover all bets. A high priority and immediate necessity was to isolate Katanga from the political influence of Lumumba and the chaos in the rest of the Congo. If the other five provinces were engulfed by conflict and confusion, at least Katanga should be saved. At the same time, Belgian diplomacy in Leopoldville was actively seeking to make the Congo as a whole a going concern. This seeming contradiction was little understood at the time, and Brussels drew charges of duplicity from some critics.

After Lumumba broke diplomatic ties with Brussels in July, Belgian policy, like Western policy generally, sought to encourage a moderate government in Leopoldville. Without a formal diplomatic mission in the Congo, Brussels worked through President Fulbert Youlou's French advisers in Brazzaville and other unofficial channels. After the ouster of Lumumba, the Belgians tried unsuccessfully to establish normal diplomatic relations with the moderate Council-Mobutu and Ileo governments.

Unofficial Belgian advisers of the Council-Mobutu regime were highly critical of what they regarded as U.N. support for Lumumba under Hammarskjold's "nonrecognition" doctrine.[10] Tension between the UNF on one side, and Brussels and Leopoldville on the other, was further inflamed by the Bukavu incident in late December, 1960.[11] On December 29 President Kasavubu requested Belgian authorities to permit ANC troops to pass through the Belgian Trust Territory of Ruanda-Urundi (now Rwanda and Burundi) on their way to Bukavu, the capital of Kivu province, where Lumumba supporters had taken over. Leopoldville also requested Belgian assistance in this move. Brussels gave the permission and provided the assistance. On January 1, 1961, Hammarskjold accused Belgium of violating the Security Council prohibition against direct military aid to the Congo. In reply, Brussels said her modest assistance was a response to a request from the legitimate head of state for what was, in principle, a relief operation. Brussels also rejected Hammarskjold's demand that Belgian authorities disarm and arrest the ANC troops while in the Trust Territory, insisting that such action would have been "a much more serious danger to international peace" than helping the ANC to get to Bukavu and that it would have violated the July 22 Resolution urging all

10 See Chap. 3.
11 See Appendix H, Incident 3.

states not to "impede the restoration of law and order and the exercise by the government of the Congo of its authority."[12]

The Bukavu operation failed, but Belgian support to the Kasavubu-Mobutu regime provided the basis for the reestablishment of informal diplomatic relations between the two governments on January 12, 1961.

By mid-September, 1960, Belgium had withdrawn its troops from Katanga,[13] but a number of Belgian officers and noncommissioned officers were placed at the disposal of the Katanga regime to serve as technical advisers and to rebuild the Katanga gendarmerie. Belgium also furnished military equipment to the Katanga forces. On September 7, a Sabena plane flew seven to nine tons of weapons into Elisabethville. Responding to Hammarskjold's protest, Brussels explained the deliveries resulted from the misunderstanding of an "ill-informed" official.[14] The shipment, however, occurred at the very time when the gendarmerie was faced with an ANC attack from the north just after the last Belgian troops had left Katanga territory.

The policy of simultaneously supporting the Leopoldville moderates and collaborating with Tshombe was intensely debated among Belgians. The *ultras* in Katanga opposed any aid to Leopoldville while the Belgian academicians who advised the Council-Mobutu government condemned aid to Tshombe. Within the Belgian government there was serious disagreement on where to place the primary emphasis.

HAMMARSKJOLD AND THE "BELGIAN FACTOR"

The difficult role of Belgium in the Congo was made more difficult by the opposition of Hammarskjold, Dayal, and other U.N. officials to the use of Belgian nationals who were prepared to help the new government succeed. The U.N. position reflected a widespread hostility against Belgium. The Communist states, many Afro-Asian leaders, and some Western spokesmen blamed Brussels for the mess in the Congo because she had failed to prepare the Africans for independence. After Belgian intervention to protect her nationals, Brussels was denounced as an

---

[12] U.N., *SCOR,* Supplement for Jan., Feb., March, 1961, S/4621 (January 11, 1961), p. 23. For the correspondence between Hammarskjold and the Belgian Representative on the Bukavu incident, see S/4606 and S/4606, Add. 1, pp. 1–15.

[13] On September 9, 1960, the Belgian Representative confirmed to the Secretary-General that all Belgian "operational troops" had left Katanga. U.N. *SCOR,* Supplement for July, Aug., Sept., 1960, S/4475, Add. 3 (September 9, 1960), p. 133.

[14] U.N., *SCOR,* Supplement for July, Aug., Sept., 1960, S/4482 (September 9, 1960), Add. 2, p. 140.

"aggressor" by many of these critics. This criticism was further intensified by Belgian military support of Tshombe.

Brussels found herself in a position of responsibility without authority. She was often unfairly held accountable for what went wrong, but she had no authority to correct the situation. For a period the Belgians were denied an opportunity to play a constructive role in the Congo because they allegedly had morally and politically disqualified themselves.

The failure to distinguish between a constructive and a disruptive role of Belgium in the Congo was expressed in Hammarskjold's attitude toward what he called the "Belgian factor." Since Belgian military aid to Katanga was a violation of the Council resolutions, he reasoned, any Belgian assistance to the Central Government or elsewhere in the Congo was likewise illicit and disruptive. In October, 1960, Hammarskjold declared that it was necessary to "fully circumscribe the Belgian factor and *eliminate it*" and requested Brussels to "withdraw all military, paramilitary or civilian personnel which it had placed at the disposal of the authorities in the Congo."[15] In the Congo itself, Dayal charged that the Belgians had "inhibited peaceful political activity . . . and the reestablishment of the unity and integrity of the country."[16] Hammarskjold and Dayal appeared intent on eliminating not only Belgian military personnel mentioned in the Council resolutions, but all Belgian *civilian* technicians, advisers, and administrators whose presence was essential to operate government services and the economy. The Congolese authorities in both Elisabethville and Leopoldville wanted the Belgian assistance.

The anti-Belgian views of high U.N. officials created consternation in Belgian circles. The Belgian representative in Katanga warned that the expulsion of the Belgians would result in chaos and the collapse of the Tshombe government.

Brussels insisted that Hammarskjold could not use the Council resolutions to compel her to channel all technical aid through the United Nations, especially when the Secretary-General steadfastly refused to use available Belgian specialists within the U.N. operation. Hammarskjold's demands violated the right of a sovereign state to re-

---

[15] U.N., *SCOR*, Supplement for Oct., Nov., Dec., 1960, S/4557 (November 2, 1960), pp. 44 and 48.

[16] *Ibid.*, para. 55. See also King Gordon, *The United Nations in the Congo*, (New York: Carnegie Endowment for International Peace, 1962), pp. 79–85. The author, chief U.N. information officer in the Congo in 1961, clearly portrays the anti-Belgian and pro-Lumumba orientation of Hammarskjold and Dayal in 1960 and early 1961.

quest foreign civilian aid from any friendly government, Brussels argued, and if given in to, would place the Congo under a U.N. trusteeship. The recall of Belgian technicans would deprive the Congo of "the services of officials who are under the direct authority of the Congolese government in order to replace them with international experts independent of that government." Further, the withdrawal of the approximately 2,000 key Belgians would "irreparably compromise the work being done in that country to reestablish order and restore prosperity" and the 200 U.N. civilian experts in the Congo could not begin to do the job.[17]

Brussels also pointed out that the U.N. presence was recent and primarily concerned with the maintenance of international peace and security. In contrast, Belgium's responsibility to help the new state was rooted in its eighty years of colonial rule. Further, Belgium had an obligation to protect its substantial interests there, and to do what it could to help prevent Communist subversion. Brussels held that Hammarskjold's rigid prohibition against all Belgians benefited no one, except perhaps Lumumba, and implied that it reflected pressures from the Communist and more militant African states.[18] Brussels tried to convince its Atlantic allies that Hammarskjold was wrong. London and Paris needed little convincing. After some friendly persuasion, the State Department issued a statement on November 4, 1960. "We have every confidence in the good faith of Belgium in its desire to be of assistance in the Congo" and reject Dayal's "implication to the contrary." The statement added: "It should be possible for the United Nations and the Belgian government to collaborate for the benefit of the peoples of all the Congo."[19]

At home and in the Congo, Belgian opinion was solidly against Hammarskjold's Congo "anti-Belgium" policies. Both the conservative and liberal press in Brussels accused him of appeasing Moscow and trying to make Belgium a "scapegoat" for his own failures."[20]

Fortunately, Hammarskjold's attempt to "eliminate the Belgian factor" failed. But the confusion caused by his unsuccessful effort to expel

[17] U.N., *SCOR*, Supplement for Oct., Nov., Dec., 1960, S/4557 (November 2, 1960), pp. 46–47.

[18] Institut royal des relations internationales, "Evolution de la crise congolaise," *Chronique de politique étrangère*, XIV (September–November, 1961), 821–22 and 981–99 *passim*.

[19] *New York Times*, November 5, 1960. The State Department statement was a comment on Dayal's second Congo report which condemned the return of Belgian administrators and advisers.

[20] *La Libre Belgique*, October 20, 1960; *Le Soir*, October 21, 1961.

the very technicians and advisers wanted by the Congolese intensified the problems of abrupt decolonization. The Belgians who stayed on or returned in face of U.N. opposition, proved to be indispensable in holding the Congo together during the Dayal period when the severe tensions between U.N. and Congolese officials threatened to tear it apart. It is difficult to assess the damage of the rigid anti-Belgian position, which was gradually superseded by a more responsible approach. One critical observer said the U.N. policy of erecting "every possible obstacle against the return of the Belgians either as private citizens or as government employees" made "a difficult job almost impossible and delayed perhaps by years the recovery of the Congo." He added: "The U.N. was unable to provide the Congo with the doctors, teachers, technicians, or administrators in anything like the number or quality necessary."[21] His comment is essentially correct.

REPATRIATION OF PROHIBITED BELGIANS

The "Belgian factor" persisted as a major though diminishing source of friction between Hammarskjold and Brussels until September, 1961. When the February 21, 1961 Resolution called for the evacuation of "all Belgian and other foreign military and para-military personnel and advisers" not under U.N. command, Brussels promised its support, pointing out that only a small group of its nationals were affected. The Belgian government made a distinction between personnel assigned to the Congo by Brussels, and Belgians chosen and employed by Congolese authorities on their own initiative, though in practice this distinction was sometimes blurred. It advised Hammarskjold to deal directly with the Congolese concerning the latter group.

Asserting that a precipitous withdrawal of military personnel would endanger public order and trigger the exodus of badly needed technicians and administrators, particularly in Katanga where the Belgian presence was substantial, Brussels nevertheless promised to phase out the prohibited personnel for whom it had direct responsibility. These included the cadres stationed at the Kamina and Kitona bases "by agreement with the United Nations," to be withdrawn by March 15, 1961, and former *Force publique* officers placed at the disposal of Congolese authorities, to be withdrawn as soon as the UNF could perform their task "with equal effectiveness." Brussels also promised

21 Smith Hempstone, *Rebels, Mercenaries, and Dividends* (New York: Praeger, 1962), pp. 235–36.

to recall former members of the Belgian army serving as training officers, to take steps to prevent further mercenary recruiting in Belgium, and to reinforce existing controls over the export of military equipment to the Congo.[22]

Leopoldville protested Hammarskjold's "over-simplified and completely utopian form of simply ejecting the Belgian military personnel," and insisted on retaining the services of the fourteen Belgian officers under General Mobutu's command.[23] This protest helped Brussels prevent the abrupt eviction of advisers and cadres.

Seen against this background, the contradiction between Brussels' promise to support the February 21 Resolution, and the revived recruitment of mercenaries in Belgium by the Marissal Mission to replace the cadres withdrawn from Katanga, can be understood. The private Marissal Mission, named after the colonel who headed it, worked closely with the Belgian military *Sûreté,* and succeeded in maintaining a force of some 250 Belgians in Katanga during the first six months of 1961.

A thaw in United Nations-Belgian relations developed in early May, reflecting changes in Brussels, New York, and the Congo. The new Belgian administration, with Théo Lefèvre as Prime Minister and Paul-Henri Spaak as Minister of Foreign Affairs, tended to favor Leopoldville in its conflict with the Katanga secessionists. On the U.N. side, Hammarskjold finally recalled Dayal, much to the relief of Brussels, her Western allies, and Leopoldville. Robert Gardiner, Chief of U.N. Civilian Operations, concluded the April 17, 1961 agreement with Kasavubu that permitted Kasavubu to decide whether or not he wished to retain his Belgian advisers, and thus represented the first formal retreat from the rigid U.N. position. In internal Congolese politics, the anti-Katangan sentiment in Leopoldville had deepened, symbolized by Tshombe's arrest in Coquihatville on April 26.

Against this backdrop, Brussels undertook a gradual disengagement from Katanga. By July, 1961, seventeen military and nineteen political advisers had been recalled from Katanga, including the influential Major Guy Weber. Spaak agreed to compile a complete list of political advisers who were to be withdrawn from Leopoldville, and Hammarskjold agreed to seek Kasavubu's consent for their release. A similar list was to be drawn up for Katanga. Spaak hoped that the publication

22 U.N., *SCOR,* Supplement for Jan., Feb., March, 1961, S/4752, Annex 2 (February 27, 1961), pp. 180–81. *Ibid.,* S/4752, Add. 2 (March 6, 1961), pp. 197–98.

23 U.N., *SCOR,* Supplement for Jan., Feb., March, 1961, S/4752, Add. 3 (March 6, 1961), pp. 199–201.

of this list would reassure those who were not involved, including the 10,000 Europeans in Elisabethville who would then be free of the fear of repatriation.

According to the agreement, General Mobutu would be permitted to retain the fourteen military advisers already in his service. Six of the nine Belgian military advisers in South Kasai had already been withdrawn; the others would presumably follow.

Spaak also agreed to assist in the phased recall of Belgian military forces from Katanga. Like his predecessor, Pierre Wigny, Spaak wanted to avoid any serious disturbance in Katanga which would open the door to chaos and extremism. He feared that the *ultras,* including some Belgians, would start an open war against the UNF. Consequently, Spaak accepted the so-called *Egge Plan*[24] which projected the phased withdrawal of 208 Belgian officers and others ranks and 304 mercenaries of various nationalities at intervals of eight to ninety days.[25]

Hammarskjold agreed in principle, according to Spaak, to the gradual recall of the Belgian military cadres from Katanga.[26] The Belgian consul in Elisabethville accepted the Egge Plan as the basis for withdrawal.[27] But the possibility of an orderly, peaceful, and cooperative repatriation was preempted by Operation Rumpunch on August 28.[28] Spaak regarded this UNF roundup of Belgian officers and mercenaries as precipitous and unwarranted in light of his talks with Hammarskjold. The operation was halted on the afternoon of the same day on the promise of the Belgian consul, in behalf of the European consuls in Elisabethville, to be responsible for the "surrender and repatriation and travel of all personnel to be evacuated, irrespective

[24] The Egge Plan was formulated by Lt. Colonel Bjorn Egge, a Norwegian U.N. intelligence officer, after discussion with the Katanga authorities and the Belgian Colonel B. E. M. Crèvecoeur. (Egge intended to replace the Belgian and European cadres with European officers recruited by and serving under the UNF.) Col. Crèvecoeur apparently sought the adoption of his report, which called for the establishment of a Katanga armed force over a period of five to ten years. Part of the Egge Plan is published in the Katanga government's *White Paper on the Events of September and December, 1961,* pp. 105–08. Col. Egge later said that Belgian nationals would not categorically be excluded from the U.N. recruited officers if they were "politically acceptable." Interview with author in Oslo, Norway, June 5, 1965. See Appendix H, 8.

[25] Of the 304 mercenaries, 210 were Belgians, according to Institut Royal des Relations Internationales, "L'ONU et le Congo," *Chronique de politique étrangère,* XV (July–November 1962), 357.

[26] "L'ONU et le Congo," p. 719.

[27] Davister and Toussaint, *Croisettes et Casques Blues,* p. 151.

[28] See Chap. 3.

of their nationality."[29] By September 9, the deadline for the roundup of foreign military personnel, practically all regular Belgian cadres— the former *Force publique* and Belgian Army members, whom the Ministry of African Affairs had placed at the disposal of the Katanga authorities—had been repatriated or had reported to the Belgian consulate. Only 10 of the 187 Regulars were missing.[30] When the Belgian forces left, the Belgian consul honored them publicly: "You have fought for a just cause with an ideal of peace."[31] Upon arrival in Brussels, in contrast, they were loaded unceremoniously into an army truck driven by a corporal.

On the mercenary question, Brussels informed the Belgian Consul that he could only advise, and not order, Belgian mercenaries to depart. For mercenaries of other nationalities, the Consul could accept no responsibility at all. By September 9, 121 of the 175 Belgian mercenaries and 41 of the 81 volunteers of other nationalities had been rounded up. A number of mercenaries and settlers who had joined the gendarmerie, disguised themselves in civilian clothes and continued to assist the Katanga forces.

Operation Morthor,[32] the first armed clash between the UNF and the gendarmerie, started on September 13, and aroused intense protest in official and private circles in Belgium and Katanga. Spaak declared that politically it was "poorly executed and useless. As to its military aspects, it would be more charitable to say nothing."[33] Partly because of Hammarskjold's death, Spaak, like the press in Brussels and Elisabethville, singled out O'Brien for the major criticism.

In spite of operations Rumpunch and Morthor, Brussels fulfilled its obligation under the February 21 Resolution. The government announced on October 30, 1961, that it would withdraw the passports of Belgian nationals who continued to serve in the Katanga forces.[34] On November 15, Spaak was able to say that all Belgian regular forces had been withdrawn from Katanga.[35]

---

[29] U.N., *SCOR*, Supplement for July, Aug., Sept., 1961, S/4940 (September 14, 1961), p. 100. Créner actually spoke in the name of the European consuls; the American consul did not attend the meeting in the afternoon of August 28, and was not associated with the decisions taken at the meeting.

[30] *Ibid.*, p. 106.

[31] J. Gérard-Libois, *Sécession au Katanga*, p. 259.

[32] See Chap. 3.

[33] "L'ONU et le Congo," p. 721.

[34] U.N., *SCOR*, Supplement for Oct., Nov., Dec., 1961, S/4975 (November 8, 1961), p. 67.

[35] "L'ONU et le Congo," p. 720.

EFFORTS TO INTEGRATE KATANGA

The Lefèvre-Spaak regime, like its predecessor, wanted Katanga reintegrated by peaceful means. After Round One and the November 24, 1961 Resolution authorizing the UNF to use force to apprehend prohibited personnel, Spaak feared the reoccurrence of armed conflict in Katanga. In an attempt to facilitate a peaceful reconciliation between Elisabethville and Leopoldville, Spaak agreed with Lord Hume to request an influential African chief of state—Leopold Senghor of Senegal was the man they had in mind—to serve as a mediator between Tshombe and Adoula.[36] Before any progress was made, Round Two began on December 5.[37]

In Round Two the European population in Katanga bitterly accused the UNF of bombing hospitals and other civilian targets. Spaak charged the UNF with violating the Geneva Conventions on the Laws of War and rejected Thant's claim that U.N. troops had acted only in self-defense.[38] He also called for an immediate cease fire, along with London and Paris, and urged renewed efforts for peaceful conciliation.

Spaak's relations with the Secretary-General improved because of Brussels' co-operation in eliminating prohibited persons and in spite of Rounds One and Two in which, according to the Belgian leader, the UNF had discredited itself by waging "war." Thant no longer singled out Belgium as the chief obstacle to the achievement of U.N. objectives, even though some Belgian mercenaries remained in Katanga, some Belgian civilians assisted in providing military equipment for Tshombe, and some Belgian residents served as advisers to Katanga officials. The central point was that the Belgian government could no longer be rightly accused of violating the U.N. resolutions.

Brussels supported U.S. and U.N. efforts to get Adoula and Tshombe together at Kitona and resumed formal diplomatic relations with Leopoldville on December 27, 1961. The unproductive conciliation efforts dragged on, and Spaak finally agreed to the Thant Plan for National Reconciliation. After an unsuccessful effort to get *Union Minière* officials to discuss the question of taxes and other obligations with Leopoldville, he said he would co-operate with economic sanctions against Katanga though he doubted their effectiveness.

When Round Three broke out on December 28, 1962, Belgium made restrained comments on the UNF's military action and recom-

---

[36] J. Gérard-Libois, *Sécession au Katanga*, p. 245.
[37] See Chap. 3.
[38] U.N., *SCOR*, Supplement for Oct., Nov., Dec., 1961, S/5025 (December 15, 1961), pp. 190–99, *passim.*

mended a cease-fire and a resumption of negotiations between Tshombe and the UNF. Through its representatives in Katanga, Brussels sought to persuade Tshombe to renounce his threatened scorched earth policy. Thanks to special financial contributions, which amounted to bribes, to foreign mercenaries by Belgian companies and the efforts of the European consuls and certain Belgian advisers close to Tshombe, there was no serious deliberate damage to Katanga's industrial infrastructure. Though Belgian authorities regretted the UNF's military action, they acknowledged that industrial interests in Katanga were far less adversely affected than they would have been by a thoroughly carried out scorched earth policy.

ASSISTANCE TO THE ANC

As the founder of the effective *Force publique* of colonial days, Brussels expected to have a major role in building a responsible Congolese army for the new state. The abrupt dismissal of the 1,100-man Belgian officer corps was a severe blow to this hope. In the first months of independence, Belgian military aid was provided mainly to Katanga and in the form of administrative and staff cadres. Primarily because of political constraints, military assistance to Leopoldville was severely limited. Nonetheless, a small group of Belgian officers never left Leopoldville. After the ouster of Lumumba, Mobutu recalled a number of military advisers. Belgian aid included occasional assistance with military operations, such as in the Bukavu move in January, 1961, and some financial and material aid.

Political conditions prevented any serious effort to train or reorganize the ANC until after Katanga was reintegrated. In late 1962, the Western powers concluded that the U.N. mission could make no progress in helping the Congolese to build a viable army. Brussels supported the Greene Plan put forward by the United States.[39] This Plan provided for several bilateral military aid programs to the Congo to be coordinated by the UNF. Its purpose was to strengthen and streamline the ANC. Brussels was to furnish training officers and advisers. Washington was to provide the equipment. Several other states were to extend assistance. Although Adoula was reluctant to accept U.N. involvement, he was finally persuaded to accept U.N. sponsorship and presented his request for such military aid to the Secretary-General in December, 1962, and February, 1963.

[39] The Greene Plan is discussed in Chap. 3.

In compliance with Congolese wishes, the Greene Plan allocated to Belgium the responsibility for organizing ANC headquarters, the bases, the gendarmerie, and the military schools. At a meeting in Brussels on February 27, 1963, Spaak promised Adoula that he would participate in the Greene Plan and would send a hundred officers to the Congo on the condition that the request for this would come from the Secretary-General himself.[40] Brussels wanted to observe the prohibition against providing direct military assistance in accordance with the September 20, 1961 Resolution. Thant originally endorsed the Greene Plan, but because of the opposition of some Afro-Asian states and other reasons, he informed Adoula in April, 1963, that he could not support his request.

With the Greene Plan dead, Brussels and Leopoldville concluded a normal bilateral military assistance agreement on May 20, 1963. Spaak told Adoula he had informed Thant of the decision, but he urged Adoula to continue to search for a formula that would permit U.N. participation in the reorganization of the ANC. Thant took "due note of the contents" of Spaak's communication.[41] At no time did the Secretary-General protest Belgium's military aid, and in private conversations he indicated his approval. Spaak kept Thant up to date on the status of the program which got underway slowly.

IMPACT ON THE U.N. MISSION

The changing Belgian policy toward financing the UNF was a barometer of Belgian relations with the U.N. effort as a whole. The refusal of Brussels to pay its assessment during the first years reflected its dissatisfaction with Hammarskjold's and Dayal's policy toward the "Belgian factor." Foreign Minister Pierre Wigny once said that the Secretary-General was trying to get us to pay for an operation which was determined to "eliminate us from the Congo."[42]

The Belgian attitude toward financing was not improved by demands from some quarters that Brussels pay more than its normal quota on the grounds that it was responsible for the Congo crisis, that it would derive special benefit from the mission, or that it had sub-

[40] CRISP, *Congo: 1963*, p. 116.
[41] *Documents parlementaires du Senate belge*, No. 143 (February 25, 1965), 1964–65 Session, pp. 107–09.
[42] *Compte-rendu analytique* (C.R.A.), Proceedings of the Belgian Senate, January 26, 1961.

stantial investments in the Congo. These demands were rejected as unwarranted and punitive.

As the relationship with the U.N. Mission improved toward the end of 1961, Foreign Minister Spaak attempted unsuccessfully to persuade his Senate to authorize payment of the regular assessment. The Senate instead proposed that an equivalent sum be placed in a National Indemnity Fund for the victims of UNF military action in Katanga.[43]

The deadlock was finally broken after the General Assembly accepted the Advisory Opinion of the International Court in December, 1962, and after Brussels requested an extension of the U.N. Mission beyond December, 1963. In May, 1965, Belgium made a settlement with Thant which involved 581 Belgian claims against the United Nations for damage to persons and property in the Congo, excluding damage "solely due to military operations or military necessity." Over 900 Belgian claims were withdrawn.[44] The Organization paid Brussels $1.5 million to settle the valid claims, and Brussels agreed to pay its share of the four-year operation. By the end of 1965, the full assessment had been paid.

The net impact of Belgian policy, like that of France and Britain, had a restraining effect upon the UNF. The outlook of these three powers was similar, though both London and Brussels extended far more co-operation and support than Paris. Belgian policy moved from passive co-operation, to opposition, to collaboration in response to changing events inside and outside the Congo. There could have been much more partnership from the start if U.N. officials had had a greater appreciation for the necessary Belgian role and the courage to resist Communist and militant neutralist pressures.

The major problem was Katanga until it was integrated in January, 1963. While official Belgian support of the Tshombe regime violated the resolutions calling for the end of secession, this support could hardly have undermined the territorial integrity and political independence of the Congo. In fact, Brussels did a great deal to strengthen the Central Government and at no time accorded diplomatic recognition to Katanga or officially supported secession as such.

Belgium's modest military support to the moderates in Leopoldville was a formal violation of the September 20, 1960 Resolution, but the very presence of Belgian military advisers, supplemented by civilian administrators and technicians, contributed significantly to the main-

---

43 *La libre Belgique,* December 11, 1961.
44 U.N., *SCOR*, S/6597 (August 6, 1965), mimeographed, pp. 1 and 2.

tenance of law and order, the central U.N. objective. Further, Belgian diplomacy in Leopoldville and Elisabethville made a major contribution to what reconciliation did occur after Round Three.

It is important to recall that in the early years these constructive Belgian efforts were undertaken in the face of serious obstacles raised by Hammarskjold's rigid policy against the use of Belgian military and civilian personnel. Brussels could never understand why the U.N. Mission insisted on a monopoly of civilian and military assistance to the exclusion of those who were best qualified by experience to provide it, especially when the Congolese themselves preferred Belgian nationals above all others. The full utilization of Belgians able and willing to serve by the United Nations from the beginning would have strengthened the mission and benefited the Congo. The damage of this short-sighted policy was considerable, but fortunately it was corrected under the pressure of realities in the Congo.

During the unhappy months of U.N. efforts to eliminate the "Belgian factor," Belgian and Congolese interests suffered. But in the long run the fundamental objectives of stability and a moderate central government were served by the UNF. Brussels had a special and legitimate interest in her substantial financial investment. This more tangible interest was protected by the reintegration of Katanga and the preservation of the Congo's territorial integrity. In so far as the U.N. effort contributed to these objectives, it served Belgian interests. And these interests were not incompatible with the interests of the Western and moderate neutralist states, including the Congo itself.

8.

The Smaller Western States

For the most part, the smaller Western states took a position toward the Congo crisis similar to that of the United States and were passive or active members of the Washington-led coalition supporting the U.N. peacekeeping operation. There were occasional minor differences in interpretation and emphasis among these governments, but as a group they were certainly closer to the United States than to Britain, to say nothing of France.

Unlike the Big Powers, none of the small Western states, with the notable exception of Belgium, had a deep interest in the Congo. All of them wanted the new state to succeed, and believed that a U.N. mission could contribute toward this end. A number of them had a desire to participate in a U.N. effort to dampen down small-scale conflict by using military personnel under the "pacific settlement" provisions of Chapter VI of the Charter.[1] Among the states actively interested in providing men and officers for a Congo mission were Canada, Denmark, Ireland, Italy, Norway, and Sweden, each of which made available more than four thousand man-months to the U.N. Force. Each was motivated by several considerations, including an interest in peacekeeping, the desire to respond favorably to a specific request from the Secretary-General, the opportunity to receive free or inexpensive overseas training and experience for soldiers and officers, and the belief that their participation in the UNF would confer a certain international prestige upon them. These same motivations operated among the Afro-Asian states that contributed troops. In the case of Italy, with the background of Mussolini's conquest of Ethiopia and his alliance with Hitler, there was the additional motivation of showing the world that Italian troops could go to Africa for constructive purposes. There were also about 3,000 Italians living in the Congo.[2]

[1] See Chap. 1 for the distinction between "peaceful settlement" and enforcement action.

[2] Author interview with Italian Foreign Ministry officials in Rome, June 21, 1965.

Seven additional Western states made smaller manpower contributions to the UNF: Brazil, Austria, Argentina, the Netherlands, Greece, New Zealand, and Ecuador. Though located in Asia, in political terms New Zealand may be considered a Western state. The motivation of these governments was not unlike that of those whose participation was more substantial.[3] In terms of man-months the contribution of the Western states was as follows:[4]

1.	Sweden	37,109
2.	Ireland	35,654
3.	Canada	13,322
4.	Norway	7,023
5.	Denmark	4,542
6.	Italy	4,020
7.	Brazil	1,563
8.	Austria	1,334
9.	Argentina	747
10.	Netherlands	435
11.	Greece	188
12.	New Zealand	10
13.	Ecuador	8

Hammarskjold wanted to rely primarily on African and Asian states for troop support, but he had to turn to the more developed states for specialized military units and qualified headquarters staff officers. The Big Powers were ruled out for political reasons. Of the thirteen Western states that responded to Hammarskjold's request for specific forms of assistance, ten were allied militarily with the United States. Only Sweden, Ireland, and Austria were neutral, though Western-orientated. In most cases, Washington supported the request of the Secretary-General for assistance from a particular state, and in some instances U.S. officials advised him where to turn for needed units. Incidentally, troops from the great majority of Western countries were politically acceptable to the Leopoldville government, though Lumumba at least once and on his own called for the expulsion of all non-African personnel in the UNF.

Of the Western states, only Sweden and Ireland sent regular combat battalions to the Congo. Canada manned the entire UNF communications system and provided Military Police for the Command head-

---

[3] The financial arrangements between the United Nations and the states providing troops or specialized military personnel are discussed in Chap. 11.

[4] The manpower contributions of all states are indicated in Appendix E.

quarters. The three Scandinavian countries sent movement control teams. Denmark and Norway send a composite electrical and mechanical engineering unit and several smaller detachments, including personnel, veterinary, and public health units. Norway sent an anti-aircraft unit. Italy, Brazil, and Argentina provided air transport units. Austria and the Netherlands sent medical personnel. This incomplete listing indicates the great dependence of the UNF on the Western military contribution.

Yugoslavia was the only Communist state to provide personnel. Its team of pilots and supporting technicians, a total of twenty men, were withdrawn from the Congo in December, 1960, after only four months in protest against Hammarskjold's alleged anti-Lumumba policies.

CANADA AS AN EXAMPLE

Among the significant donor states, Canada was both typical and unique. Her motivation and the problems she faced in a multinational force were similar, but her special interest and experience in U.N. peacekeeping was unique. (Sweden also had considerable peacekeeping experience and could be used as an example of a neutral-Western state.) Canada was one of the very few politically acceptable states that could make qualified communications personnel available on short notice. She could supply troops proficient in both English, the working language of the U.N. operation, and French. For these reasons Ottawa readily agreed to provide the communications unit which remained throughout the four years. It also sent the Military Police for the Leopoldville headquarters and a generous quota of headquarters officers. In addition, Ottawa provided $650,000 worth of initial airlift against U.N. reimbursement and made a voluntary contribution to the UNF of $263,000 above her regular assessment.[5]

Before 1960, Canada participated in all the major U.N. peacekeeping efforts and in most of the minor ones. Ottawa favored the eventual creation of a permanent U.N. peacekeeping force, but in the meantime it provided diplomatic and material support to *ad hoc* missions. Since the Congo crisis erupted, Canada has earmarked an Army Special Service Force for possible U.N. use. Certain other army units have been also listed as available for such an assignment. All units of the Canadian armed forces are given regular instructions on problems and procedures for U.N. peacekeeping or observation missions.

[5] See Appendix I.

Though there is wide public support for Canada's involvement in peacekeeping operations, the government sends only volunteers abroad. The number of military personnel made available for U.N. service is limited by Canada's NATO and other defense commitments. A force ceiling of 500 officers and men was established for the Congo. As matters developed, the Canadian contingent there averaged about 275 for the four years. Ottawa also insisted that its troops in the Congo be assigned to strictly noncombatant functions.

In political terms, Canada took a position somewhere between that of Washington and London. It had a limited view of the U.N. Mission, and opposed a solution of internal problems by force. To preserve a discreet impartiality, Canada even refrained from voting for or against the seating of the Kasavubu delegation in the General Assembly on November 22, 1960. Sweden and Ireland also abstained, but all the other Western donor states voted with Washington, London, and Paris to accredit the Kasavubu delegation. Ottawa was generally silent on the public Congo debate, and in the Congo Advisory Committee it was reluctant to express an opinion, preferring to transmit its views privately and directly to the Secretary-General. Canada recognized that the Committee's polyglot composition severely limited its advisory role.

CONTRIBUTION OF THE CANADIAN CONTINGENT

Immediately after the July 14, 1960 Resolution, Canada sent six officers to help receive U.N. troops arriving in the Congo. Hurried negotiations between Ottawa and New York and the Canadian and American military establishments led to a prompt agreement to provide the communications squadron and the airlift assistance. At its height, the communications unit included some 40 officers and 250 other ranks. Like other contributed contingents, it was operationally under the U.N. Command, but unlike most other national units it remained under the administrative control of Canadian Army headquarters in Ottawa. All Canadian detachments were commanded by Canadian officers. This practice was customary in the UNF.

The initial deployment of Canadian troops was marred by two incidents. On August 18 at the Leopoldville airport, Congolese soldiers disarmed and manhandled fourteen Canadians.[6] They were eventually rescued by members of a Ghanian unit. On August 27, eight U.S. air-

---

[6] This incident is discussed in Chap. 3.

lift crewmen and two Canadians were arrested and beaten by ANC soldiers at the Stanleyville airport. Later that day, eight other Canadians attached to U.N. headquarters in Stanleyville underwent similar treatment at the hands of Congolese troops. Ethiopian soldiers secured their release. On both occasions the Canadians were accused of being Belgian paratroopers, and on both occasions they kept their heads in the face of considerable provocation.

The sixteen Canadian Military Police attached to the UNF Command headquarters in Leopoldville worked closely with other M.P. units. Each Canadian was a professional soldier with an average of six years provost experience; each spoke English and French. Unit members provided on-the-job instruction for other Military Police, and occasionally gave assistance to their Congolese counterparts. M.P. responsibilities in Leopoldville were complicated because there was no uniform miiltary code agreed upon by the donor states and disciplinary action against any U.N. soldier or officer remained the responsibility of his national contingent commander. Under the Regulations for the United Nations Force in the Congo,[7] the rights, duties, privileges, and immunities were clearly spelled out and Military Police had the authority to bring any indiscipline or violation of a soldier or officer to the attention of his unit commander. Despite these limitations, the Canadian M.P.s made a significant contribution to the morale and discipline of U.N. troops by their competent and correct behavior.

Whatever the U.N. Command headquarters may have attained in the way of efficiency was due in a large measure to the disproportionately heavy share of Canadian officers assigned to it. In the early months, July through October, 1961, of the 171 officers attached to the Leopoldville staff, 31 were Canadians. Although Canada ranked twelfth in its total manpower contribution, it ranked first in the average number of officers at the U.N. headquarters.[8] There were several reasons for this. The Secretary-General could be certain that Ottawa would respond promptly to his requests. Canadian officers were in demand because of their professional military experience and their knowledge of Commonwealth military procedures which served as the general pattern for the UNF. Officers sent to the Congo had an aver-

---

[7] The UNF Regulations were circulated by Secretary-General Thant on July 15, 1963, as U.N. document ST/SGB/ONUC/1, and were "intended to continue in effect the policies and practices" of the Force since the beginning.

[8] See Appendix E.

age of sixteen years in the armed forces. Many of them were bilingual and several had served in UNEF and UNTSO.

The Canadians did not fill the top headquarters slots, but were assigned to the middle level where most of the daily work was done. Here they provided the essential continuity for the operation. This was especially important because of the multinational character of the headquarters staff, the rapid rotation of officers, and the fact that there were five Force commanders of five nationalities in four years.[9] For these reasons, the Canadians contributed mainly to the efficiency and integrity of the operation, and had only a modest influence on general military policies.

The limited character of Canada's influence became particularly apparent in 1960 when, under General Carl von Horn's tenure as Force Commander, Brigadier General I. J. Rikhye succeeded in forcing the dismissal of Canadian Chief of Staff Lieutenant Colonel John Berthiaume. Rikhye did this partly because he felt it was unwise to have a Canadian in that position. Canada did not protest and Lieutenant Colonel Berthiaume was replaced by an African officer. Thereafter no Canadian became Chief of Staff, but the Force commander thought enough of Berthiaume's abilities to retain him as his military adviser. He remained in this advisory post until April, 1961, when the position was assigned to an Irish officer on the insistence of the new Force Commander, Lieutenant General Sean McKeown of Ireland.

Accustomed to orderly military procedures, and in an excellent position to observe the U.N. Headquarters, the Canadians were appalled by the inefficiency and confusion around them and did what they could to correct it.[10] The Canadians, for example, were critical of radio links which some governments had established with their national contingents in the Congo. This was a violation of U.N. regulations designed to prevent unauthorized UNF information from falling into hostile hands and to encourage contingent commanders to submit all their complaints, comments, and suggestions through U.N. rather than national channels. Hammarskjold feared that too much direct communication with donor governments about details of the operation would subject him to unnecessary and unproductive pressures. India, Nigeria, Ghana, and several other governments had direct

[9] See Appendix D.
[10] Author interview with officers who had served in the Congo, at the Canadian Department of Defense, in Ottawa, December 17, 1964.

radio links with their unit commanders. This practice seems to have been virtually inevitable because of the sensitive political implication of the operation. On balance it may have been desirable. Nevertheless, Canada adopted what it regarded as a responsible middle course by establishing an "administrative" communications link between Ottawa and Leopoldville, using it for purely "administrative traffic of low priority and high volume which otherwise would crowd U.N. channels." This compromise is evidence of Canada's desire to be loyal to the U.N. command without overlooking its national interests.

IMPACT OF THE WESTERN DONOR STATES
ON THE U.N. MISSION

The Canadian military contribution to the UNF was significant and in some respects unique. The work of the communications unit has won high praise. The constant presence of approximately ten Canadian officers on the headquarters staff provided continuity and added to the efficiency and integrity of the whole operation. The headquarters M.P. unit was a good example for the entire force.

To say that the Canadian contribution was great, is not to say that the other Western donor states did not play significant roles in their respective spheres. The UNF simply could not have operated without the vital services of the specialized units. Major General Carl von Horn, who served as the first Force Commander, emphasized the Western contribution in his characteristic hyperbole: "our success in saving thousands of lives had rested exclusively on Western military discipline, training, technique, and know-how or on those same qualities the new National units had inherited from the old colonial armies."[11]

As far as general U.N. policy was concerned, neither Canada nor any of the other donor states had a great impact. The general strategy was determined by the Security Council resolutions as interpreted by Hammarskjold and Thant and by the interplay of the interests of the major actors—the United States, Britain, France, the Soviet Union, Belgium, and the Afro-Asian "bloc"—as these interests pressed in upon the Secretary-General.[12] There is no evidence that any of these Western contingents sought to subvert the U.N. effort or to support

---

[11] Major General Carl von Horn, *Soldiering for Peace* (New York: David McKay Company, 1967), p. 238.

[12] The role of the Secretary-General is discussed in Chap. 2.

any of the secessionist or rival political movements. As far as can be determined, they were loyal to the U.N. command.

In terms of their interests, the Western states profited from their direct participation in the U.N. Mission. Their soldiers and officers gained valuable experience at little or no financial cost to their governments. A measure of prestige came with serving in an international peacekeeping effort. More important than these specific benefits, these states and the West generally gained by the contribution of the UNF to a unified Congo with a moderate central government.

9.

The Afro–Asian States: Militants and Moderates

Most of the African and Asian states, many having received their independence since World War II, were active supporters of the U.N. peacekeeping mission in the Congo. The common element of their interest appeared to be a political and psychological identification with a new fledgling state whose independence, in their view, was being threatened by the intervention of the former colonial power and by related European economic interests. But there was considerable diversity among them on internal Congolese politics and on what the U.N. Force should do. They also differed in their interpretations of the significance of the crisis in its relation to the larger East-West struggle.

Among Asian states, India was the most active member of the supporting coalition, making available 142,704 man-months to the UNF. New Delhi as the largest contributor of manpower and Washington as the largest contributor of dollars and airlift became the two most important allies of the operation, though in the early months their views of the unfolding drama sometimes clashed. Japan quietly supported the effort. It provided no manpower but made a voluntary contribution of $115,352 in addition to its regular quota, the fifth largest such gift after the United States, Britain, Canada, and Australia. Nationalist China voted for the operation in the Security Council, but it provided no troops and as of December 31, 1965, it was $6,687,206 in arrears in its Congo assessment.[1] Communist China which was not a U.N. member, condemned the operation as a tool of Western imperialism.[2] A majority of the smaller Asian states provided manpower and paid their peacekeeping quotas.

Most of the independent states of Africa in 1960 became interested in the Congo crisis and supported the U.N. effort, though several of them later withdrew their troops in protest against Hammarskjold's

[1] U.N., *GAOR*, Supplement No. 6, A/6306 (December 31, 1965), p. 166.
[2] The role of Communist China is discussed in Chap. 5.

policies. As the African member of the Security Council in the early period, Tunisia provided the most active and consistent diplomatic support from the continent. Ethiopia, Nigeria, Tunisia, and Ghana were the largest manpower contributors. No African government made a voluntary financial contribution, but most of those providing troops have paid their assessment. The Republic of South Africa opposed the operation, has not paid its peacekeeping assessment, and in general took a position similar to that of France. A small number of mercenaries recruited in South Africa fought with secessionist Katanga.

A total of nineteen Afro-Asian governments provided troops or specialized personnel for the U.N. Force. The man-months made available and the approximate percentage of the armed forces of each state sent to the Congo were as follows:[3]

	Man-Months	*Percentage of Force*
India	142,704	1 or less
Ethiopia	119,226	8.9
Nigeria	63,617	26.7
Tunisia	48,368	15.8
Ghana	39,203	32.7
Malaya	37,044	10.8
Indonesia	28,460	1 or less
Pakistan	27,904	1 or less
Morocco	23,668	9.6
Liberia	9,558	12.8
Guinea	4,475	15.6
Sudan	3,652	4.4
U.A.R.	3,059	1 or less
Mali	2,292	18.6
Sierra Leone	1,610	6.9
Philippines	278	1 or less
Ceylon	206	1 or less
Iran	198	1 or less
Burma	54	1 or less

All the Asian governments made available less than one per cent of their armed forces. All the African states, except the U.A.R., provided more than four per cent. At the top were Ghana with 32.7 per cent, and Nigeria with 26.7 per cent. The combined Afro-Asian manpower

[3] The manpower statistics are drawn from Appendix G, charts B and H. This rough percentage of the armed forces in the Congo was calculated by comparing the maximum number of troops each state had at any one time in the Congo with the total manpower in their army at that time. Manpower figures were based on data in *Africa Report,* Vol. 9 (January, 1964), *Britannica Book of the Year,* 1965, and the *Statesman's Yearbook,* 1965.

contribution to the UNF was 82.4 per cent, the first five providing 61.2 per cent. This large troop contribution was essential to the success of the effort.

MILITANTS AND MODERATES

Support of the UNF by the Afro-Asian states was motivated primarily by their interest in successful decolonization in the Congo, though they differed on what was required to achieve this objective. The maintenance of internal stability was an occasionally expressed concern, but subsequent events indicate that it enjoyed a low priority compared with the expulsion of the Belgian military and "colonial" presence. Speaking for these states generally, Mongi Slim, the Tunisian Foreign Minister, characterized deployment of Belgian paratroopers as "aggression," but he did not insist on such a condemnation in the July 14, 1960 Resolution.

Some of these states regarded the United Nations as a special vehicle for advancing their interests in decolonization. It was considered a protector of the weak against the ambitions of the strong, a view held by Secretary-General Hammarskjold himself.

These states varied widely in their relations to the United States and the Soviet Union. None was primarily concerned with the Cold War, but neither was it adverse to exploiting East-West rivalries for its own purposes. They were united in their fear that a Big Power confrontation in the Congo would hurt the Congo and Africa. Jomo Kenyatta of Kenya once said: "When two elephants fight, it is the grass that suffers."

As far as the internal crisis was concerned, the Afro-Asian states shared the goal of a strong central government as opposed to a loose confederation. With their own problems of tribal or regional separation, they felt that firm authority at the center was essential to prevent fragmentation and chaos. A strong government in Leopoldville, they believed, would undergird the struggle to eliminate the remaining white regimes to the south, which represented to them the final barrier to the emancipation of Africa.

On the Congo issue the unaligned states fell into two general groups—the militants and the moderates. Ghana, Guinea, Mali, Morocco, the U.A.R., and Ceylon formed the more militant wing. They advocated rapid decolonization, were highly critical of manifestations of Western influence they regarded as "neo-colonial," and in general presented a more strident and militant stance. These states were not necessarily pro-Communist, but they were certainly more anti-West than the moderates. The militant states, typified by Ghana and Guinea, were generally ruled by men committed to strong nationalist governments and eager to assert leadership in the so-called Pan-African movement. They tended to see the Congo as an opportunity to exercise leadership which would win attention throughout the continent. Moroccan leaders became increasingly identified with the militant faction as they saw a dangerous parallel between separatist Mauritania and secessionist Katanga. By working with the militants, Morocco hoped to enlist their support for its claim to Mauritania.

The other Afro-Asian states were more moderate in their approach to the Congo drama. Ethiopia, Nigeria, Liberia, Malaya, Iran, Pakistan, the Philippines, and Sierra Leone did not regard the Congo's economic ties with the West as a threat to its independence as did the militants. These states tended to have good relations with the Western powers. Some of them received direct military aid from the West. Tunisia, India, Indonesia, Sudan, and Burma were more "neutralist"; their apprehensions were directed to both the East and the West. To a considerable extent, the views of the entire moderate group stemmed from their lack of any direct or immediate interest in the Congo. Indonesia was an example. On other international issues, Sukarno was anything but a moderate. But distance from the Congo, plus the fact that Indonesia was seeking at that time to enlist U.N. support for its claim on Western New Guinea against the Dutch, led to moderation on the Congo question.

From the outset, Foreign Minister Slim of Tunisia was the unofficial spokesman for the Afro-Asian bloc.[4] In terms of formulating a workable Congo resolution and getting the operation off the ground, it was a fortunate accident that the African seat on the Security Council was held by a moderate government and that Slim enjoyed the respect of most unaligned leaders. In the beginning, Slim's views satisfied the minimum requirements of the militants. At the first Council meeting he argued that Army mutiny was not a sufficient threat to the European population in the Congo to justify the dispatch of Belgian troops. On the contrary, he said, Brussels' action abetted disorder and was an act of aggression. Slim introduced the initial resolution calling upon the Belgian troops to withdraw and authorizing the Secretary-General

[4] The concept of the caucusing group has been elaborated by Thomas Hovet, Jr. See *Bloc Politics in the United Nations* (Cambridge: Harvard University Press, 1960) and *Africa in the United Nations* (Evanston: Northwestern University Press, 1963).

to take necessary steps to provide military aid to the Congolese government. He also declared that the African states were prepared to assist in the U.N. effort.[5]

On July 21, 1960, Tunisia commended Hammarskjold for his forthright implementation of the resolution and urged the "immediate" withdrawal of Belgian metropolitan troops. Tunisia also insisted that the purpose of Brussels' intervention was not to protect its nationals but support Katanga's secession which would undermine the unity and territorial integrity of the Congo. This charge was echoed by other Afro-Asian spokesmen and was spelled out in subsequent Council resolutions.

These nonaligned states entertained great expectations for the U.N. effort, expectations which were soon to be dashed in the eyes of the militants. They felt that the peacekeeping mission could rescue the Congo from a reassertion of "Belgian imperialism" and insulate it from the Cold War. They quickly responded to Hammarskjold's call for troops. They were motivated not only by the cause, but by the opportunity for their men and officers to gain free or inexpensive training and experience, and by the chance to acquire international prestige and status.[6] By October 7, 1960, fifteen of the nineteen Afro-Asian contributing governments already had military personnel in the Congo. Ethiopia, Ghana, Morocco, and Tunisia each had sent more than 2,000 troops by that date.

LUMUMBA'S DIVISIVE INFLUENCE

It was the Lumumba issue more than anything else that disenchanted the militant states with the U.N. Mission. Generally, the moderate Afro-Asians supported Hammarskjold's middle-of-the-road policies, partly because he took into account their arguments. The militants also criticized Hammarskjold's Katanga policy, especially his unwillingness to commit U.N. force against Tshombe.

In 1960, most Afro-Asian leaders regarded Lumumba as a promising nationalist leader and were committed to his support. The militants were more pro-Lumumba than the moderates, and they clung to him and his cause long after the moderates had shifted their support to Kasavubu. In June, 1960, Ghana established an office in Leopoldville

[5] U.N., *SCOR,* S/PV 873 (July 13, 1960), pp. 12–14.
[6] In author interviews with officials of most of the Afro-Asian states that made troops available to the UNF, the benefits of prestige and status were frequently mentioned.

headed by Andrew Djin who served as a link between Lumumba and President Kwame Nkrumah. Mr. A. N. Welbeck, the Minister in charge of Ghana's embassy, and other Ghanian diplomats and agents acted as instruments of Nkrumah's "stream of instructions" to Leopoldville during the summer of 1960.[7] President Nkrumah regarded Lumumba as his disciple and protégé.

Ghana and Guinea were the two African states most active in internal Congolese affairs and reflected the views of the less active militants. They repeatedly accused Hammarskjold of complicity with the colonial powers because he refused to use force against Katanga. Guinean agents apparently encouraged Lumumba to attack the secessionist regimes of Katanga and South Kasai, and to accept Soviet planes and trucks for this purpose. The Ghanians, however, expressed concern that this would invite a Russian-American confrontation in the Congo.

Guinea even threatened to provide Lumumba with direct military support to move against Tshombe if the UNF failed to take military action. But at the Pan-African Conference held in Leopoldville August 25–30, 1960,[8] only Guinea endorsed Lumumba's call for action independent of the UNF and with Soviet aid against the secessionist regimes. The other African states, almost without exception, advised against this course and insisted that the only way to save the Congo was to co-operate with the UNF. Ghana, Ethiopia, and Tunisia warned that their troops were already committed to the UNF and would not be withdrawn. The Africans hoped to bring about a reconciliation between U.N. officials and the Lumumba government by convincing Hammarskjold of the seriousness of the Katanga situation, and persuading Lumumba to arrive at a negotiated settlement with Tshombe. They feared Lumumba's use of Russian planes and trucks would compromise the Congo's neutrality. Most Asian donor states also wanted to avoid unilateral intervention.[9] The ouster of Lumumba on September 5, 1960, and the Mobutu coup nine days later frustrated African efforts to achieve an understanding between Lumumba and Hammarskjold. The militants strongly opposed the actions and policy of the U.N. representatives during the ensuing conflict between the Kasavubu and Lumumba forces. They were particularly critical of

---

[7] See "The Welbeck Affair," in Alexander, *African Tightrope,* pp. 50–60.

[8] The Conference was attended by delegates from the Cameroon, the two Congos, Ethiopia, Ghana, Guinea, Liberia, Mali, Morocco, the Somali Republic, Sudan, Togo, Tunisia, and the United Arab Republic.

[9] See, for example, Prime Minister Jawaharlal Nehru's speech on August 31, 1960, in *Nehru and Africa—Extracts from Jawaharlal Nehru's Speeches on Africa, 1946–1963* (New Delhi: Indian Council for Africa, 1964), p. 58.

Cordier's closing of the Leopoldville radio station which denied Lumumba access to the air, while Kasavubu was able to use Radio Brazzaville. They felt that the U.N. had deliberately sided with Kasavubu against Lumumba.

The African diplomats also tried to bring Kasavubu and Lumumba together. In his private letters to Lumumba, Nkrumah solidly backed Lumumba but argued that a temporary reconciliation with Kasavubu and U.N. officials was necessary until Lumumba's position could be firmly reestablished.[10] The Guineans saw a "reconciliation" primarily as a way to bring Lumumba back to power. Others, typified by the Tunisians, regarded a reconciliation as necessary for Congolese stability. The Ghanian and Guinean agents remained active in Leopoldville until Kasavubu felt strong enough to expel them from the Congo in October 1960.[11]

At the September, 1960, Security Council and General Assembly meetings, the militant states protested bitterly against the U.N. failure to intervene on behalf of Lumumba. They recognized Kasavubu as head of state, but they insisted that his dismissal of Lumumba was illegal. They demanded that the UNF support the Lumumba regime as the only legitimate government and refuse any kind of recognition to Mobutu's Council of Commissioners. Ghana, Guinea, and the U.A.R. threatened to withdraw their contingents from the UNF and place them at the disposal of Lumumba if the U.N. Command did not support Lumumba. Guinea insisted that UNF contingents from NATO members[12] be replaced by troops from African countries.[13] Ghana urged that the U.N. Command and the Force be entirely manned by troops from independent African states.[14] Among the more moderate states, India and Indonesia placed themselves squarely in the Lumumba camp. Other moderates, though critical of U.N. policy toward Katanga, were more reserved on the Lumumba question.

The sharp attack of the Soviet Union on Hammarksjold and on the U.N. operation united the moderates. They felt it was essential for the future of the Organization to uphold the Secretary-General's authority. They feared the withdrawal of the UNF would open the door to a

---

[10] For Nkrumah's letters to Lumumba, see CRISP, *Congo: 1960*, II, 909–13.

[11] Although the Ghanian representatives were declared *personae non gratae* in early October, they did not leave the Congo until November 22, 1960.

[12] As of September 2, 1960, Canada, Norway, and Denmark had a total of 326 men serving with the UNF. (See Appendix E.)

[13] U.N., *SCOR*, S/PV 905 (September 16, 1960), p. 28.

[14] U.N., *GAOR*, A/PV 869 (September 23, 1960), p. 68.

Spanish-type civil war in the Congo. They rallied to Hammarskjold's defense and reaffirmed their support of the U.N. effort. Both the moderate and militant states blamed the continued Belgian military presence for the tension between U.N. and Congolese officials, the increased friction among Congolese factions, and the Congolese requests for direct military aid.

The Soviet campaign against Hammarskjold also forced some of the militants to come to his support. In the debate preceding the September 20, 1960 Assembly Resolution, sponsored by the Afro-Asians and reaffirming all previous Council actions, Ghana argued that the issue was not the Congo, but rather the integrity and independence of the office of the Secretary-General and pleaded for the support of Hammarskjold to save the United Nations. The resolution was adopted by a vote of 70–0, with the Soviet bloc, France, and South Africa abstaining.

The resolution did not mean that the Afro-Asians had forsaken Lumumba. Their statements implied that U.N. officials should not accord legitimacy to the Mobutu regime.

This temporary Afro-Asian front was soon broken by the arrival, in September, of two rival Congolese delegations to the United Nations, one representing Kasavubu and the other Lumumba. Guinea, Ceylon, India, and Indonesia argued for seating the Lumumba delegates. Most moderates favored Kasavubu. The November 22 vote in the Assembly which accepted Kasavubu split the moderates and militants wide open, though some moderates, notably Ethiopia, Nigeria, and Tunisia, abstained. Ghana, Guinea, India, Indonesia, Mali, and Morocco voted with the Soviet bloc against seating the Kasavubu delegation. The vote was 53 for, 24 against, and 19 abstentions.[15]

The failure of the UNF to prevent the arrest of Lumumba on December 1, 1960, further deepened the disillusionment of the militant states with the U.N. Mission. Guinea, the U.A.R., and Indonesia announced in December their intention to recall their troops from the Congo. Mali's forces had already left because they were needed at home as a result of the disintegration of the Mali Federation and the subsequent tensions between Mali and Senegal.

At the Casablanca conference of the six militant donor states and Libya in early January, 1961, Guinea, Mali, and the U.A.R. maintained that the U.N. operation was now too compromised for any of them to co-operate further. The Conference communiqué called for

---

[15] For an interpretation of this vote from a U.N. official at the time, see Gordon, *The United Nations in the Congo*, 82–85.

the disarmament of Mobutu's troops, the release of political prisoners, and the reconvening of Parliament. It was assumed that Parliament would support Lumumba. The communiqué also asserted that the Casablanca conferees would withdraw their troops. Ghana still argued against the troop recall and urged that the UNF be given one more chance. Accra's argument did not prevail and four governments staged the Casablanca pullout. Indonesia withdrew its 1,152 troops, but by March 1963, some 1,700 Indonesians were again serving in the UNF.

The contingents from Morocco (3,259), Guinea (749), and the U.A.R. (519) left, and did not return. Mali had already withdrawn its 577 men.

With this sudden pullout of over 6,000 men, Hammarskjold was confronted by a manpower crisis. He succeeded in persuading Prime Minister Nehru, who still had serious reservations about U.N. policy, to provide an Indian brigade to take up the slack. By this time, India had come to Ghana's view that the survival of the United Nations was more important than the survival of Lumumba.

The situation was brought to a boil with the announcement of Lumumba's death on February 13, 1961. Guinea and Mali joined Moscow in demanding the resignation of Hammarskjold whom they blamed for Lumumba's "murder."[16] The militants increased their opposition to the U.N. mission and to Leopoldville, and strengthened their ties with the rival Stanleyville regime headed by Antoine Gizenga. On February 14 and 15, the U.A.R. and Guinea recognized the Gizenga government. Ghana, Mali, Indonesia, and Morocco did not extend formal recognition, but assigned agents to Stanleyville.

Hammarskjold was caught in the middle. Under conflicting pressures from moderate and militant Afro-Asians and from the more conservative European powers, he felt the U.N. mandate needed reaffirmation and clarification. The result was the February 21, 1961 Council Resolution, actually a compromise worked out behind the scenes by the moderates and the less militant militants, which strengthened his hand and for the first time gave the UNF the authority to use force to prevent civil war. With the solid support of the majority of Afro-Asians, Washington, and London behind it, the resolution recommended the reconvening of Parliament and the reorganization of the Congolese armed forces. It was a defeat for the Soviet Union and the militants.

16 U.N., *SCOR*, S/PV 936 (February 16, 1961), pp. 8 and 15.

By April the Indian brigade had arrived in the Congo. This large manpower contribution plus Nehru's support of Hammarskjold gave India considerable influence in U.N. circles. This influence was exercised in the disposition of the "Dayal problem."[17] Rajeshwar Dayal, an Indian, was Hammarskjold's Officer in Charge in Leopoldville from September, 1960 to May, 1961. He favored the Lumumba camp over the Mobutu regime. For this and other reasons, Leopoldville officials and Western diplomats began to exert mounting pressures on Hammarskjold to remove Dayal. He was finally recalled, but not until India was able to force an agreement calling for the withdrawal of the U.S. ambassador in Leopoldville in exchange for Dayal's departure.

Lumumba's disappearance from the scene decreased the influence of the militant African states in the Congo, though foreign African agents continued for some time to advise the Gizenga regime. The U.A.R. gave some financial, technical, and military assistance to Stanleyville, but when the Sudan closed its territory to non-United Nations arms shipments to the Congo, it became difficult for the U.A.R. to provide substantial material aid to Stanleyville. With the advent of the Adoula government in August, 1961, and Gizenga's return to Leopoldville as deputy prime minister, the militant African states again joined the moderates and switched their support to the Central Government.

THE KATANGA ISSUE

From the outset there was a broad concensus among the Afro-Asian states that Katanga secession was a threat to the political independence and territorial integrity of the Congo, and that it was engineered primarily by Belgian economic interests. Militants and moderates alike argued that Lumumba's acceptance of Soviet aid was understandable in the light of Belgian assistance to Tshombe. Repeated Afro-Asian demands that states refrain from direct military assistance were addressed to Belgium as well as to the great powers.

It was widely, though erroneously, assumed that the elimination of the Belgian military presence in Katanga would end secession. This assumption was implicit in the February 21 Resolution which demanded the "immediate withdrawal and evacuation" of all "Belgian and other foreign military and paramilitary personnel and advisers" not under the U.N. command. The Belgian response to the resolution

---

[17] The "Dayal problem" is also discussed in Chap. 3.

was too slow for the Afro-Asians, so they sponsored a strongly worded resolution directed explicitly against Belgium for her "noncompliance." It was adopted by the Assembly on April 15 by a vote of 61–5, with 33 abstentions. This is the only time Washington abstained on a Congo vote, joining with Paris and London.

After the inconclusive Round One, the moderate Afro-Asians, particularly Ethiopia, Nigeria, and India, each of which had the largest troop contingents in the UNF, called for action to end Katanga's secession. The Ethiopian delegate spoke for most of the nonaligned states when he said:

> The secession of Katanga, in our opinion, was never the result of genuine internal dispute, as it was clear from the beginning that the Katanga secession was engineered and maintained by foreign mercenaries and financial interests. The secession of Katanga is indeed a clear and unequivocal manifestation of Belgian and other interference in the domestic affairs of the Republic of the Congo . . . and should have been brought to an end promptly through the mandate of law and order given by the Security Council.[18]

The moderates were eager for the Adoula government to succeed and felt this was impossible unless Tshombe were brought to heel. Ceylon, Liberia, and the U.A.R., then members of the Security Council, introduced a draft which became the November 24 Resolution. It further strengthened the U.N. mandate by authorizing the use of force, if necessary, to apprehend prohibited personnel. The United States and the Soviet Union voted for the resolution; Britain and France abstained. After the equally inconclusive Round Two, Afro-Asian interest in the Katanga question tended to wane, mainly because the Kitona accord had seemed to transfer the dispute between Elisabethville and Leopoldville to the arena of negotiation.

After months of fruitless negotiation, the U.N. Plan for National Reconciliation was announced in August, 1962. It received the support of most Afro-Asian states, but its effective implementation depended upon the co-operation of the Big Powers. The economic sanctions of the Plan were never put into effect because of Round Three which ended Katangan secession in January, 1963. With the end of secession most of the Afro-Asians felt that the central objective of the UNF had been achieved and their interest in the U.N. effort fell rapidly. The size of the UNF, particularly in Katanga, decreased steadily until it was phased out completely on June 30, 1964, in accord the Assembly's decision to terminate the effort on that date.

[18] U.N., *SCOR*, S/PV 973 (November 13, 1961), pp. 8–9.

India initiated a rapid withdrawal of its brigade in Katanga at the end of Round Three, partly to meet the emergency at home occasioned by the violation of its northern border by Red China. The large units from Ethiopia and Nigeria remained in the Congo until the end.

IMPACT ON THE U.N. MISSION

The Afro-Asian governments provided 82.5 per cent of the manpower for the U.N. operation. Without this substantial support, the effort as it developed could not have succeeded. The threat of the Casablanca states to withdraw their troops and their eventual pullout failed to influence measurably the policies of Hammarskjold or to cripple the UNF. This material manifestation of militant displeasure was more than compensated for by the material and moral support of the moderates.

With no significant exceptions the contingents of the Afro-Asian states and their officers were loyal to the U.N. Command.[19] This may seem remarkable in light of the opposition of some militant governments to U.N. policies. But it was in the interest of the contributing state to observe the contract with the Secretary-General which specified that while in the Congo its troops were under his full authority. The expulsion of a disloyal officer or contingent by the U.N. command would have tarnished the reputation of the contributing government. On a few occasions diplomats or political agents from militant states threatened to issue direct instructions to their troops, but these threats were apparently never carried out. The Casablanca states withdrew their units rather than attempting to use them independently of the UNF.

Loyalty to the UNF is illustrated by the position of President Nkrumah in the fall of 1960 when he strongly was pro-Lumumba and anti-Hammarskjold. When Cordier closed Radio Leopoldville, it was guarded by U.N. troops from Ghana. These Ghanian soldiers prevented Lumumba from entering the station and he protested to Nkrumah. In reply Nkrumah acknowledged that it was "an unfortunate affair, but I think the troops behaved like that because they are for the moment under the orders of the United Nations."[20]

The financial contribution of the Afro-Asian states was modest be-

---

19 The control of the UNF is discussed in Chap. 10.
20 Cited in *Congo: 1960,* II, 909.

cause their assessments were small, but it is interesting to note the high correlation between the provision of troops and the full payment of the Congo peacekeeping quota. At the end of 1965, fifteen of the nineteen troop contributors had paid up their full assessment. The four exceptions were Guinea, which owed $9,938; Mali, which owed $24,259; the Sudan, which owed $5,860; and the U.A.R., which owed $48,387.[21] Three of these four participated in the Casablanca pullout. In contrast, about twenty Afro-Asian states not providing troops were in arrears at the end of 1965. This fact demonstrates the logical relationship between political, financial, and manpower support. It should be noted, however, that the United Nations was obligated to pay specified costs to governments sendings troops and the assessment often became a part of a negotiated settlement of these obligations and other claims.[22]

The political support of the Afro-Asian states was indispensable. Without it, no peacekeeping operation could have been authorized by the Security Council. The Soviet Union would have vetoed the effort were it not for the backing of most nonaligned governments. This broad support helped to shield the Secretary-General from Big Power pressures. By playing conflicting pressures against each other, Hammarskjold and Thant gained a degree of maneuver, but neither could wholly reject the views of the Afro-Asians, especially if they were united, or the views of significant Western supporters such as the United States and Britain. When the neutralists were split between moderates and militants, the Secretary-General's range of options widened. When they closed ranks after Lumumba's death, their influence as a bloc was correspondingly greater.

The U.N. Mission was greatly complicated by the intense involvement of some Afro-Asian states in internal Congolese affairs. Some of the militant leaders were more interested in the political fortunes of Lumumba than in the prospect for law and order in the Congo. They were more interested in expelling the "Belgian imperialists" than in saving the Congo. The simplistic love of Lumumba and hatred of Tshombe, attitudes constantly promoted by Communist propaganda, were hardly an adequate approach to the complexities of the Congo. The Secretary-General had to do battle with "anti-imperialist" slogans and demands to use force to overthrow Tshombe and, at the same time, meet the criticism of the Western states counseling restraint.

[21] U.N., *GAOR*, Supplement No. 6, A/6306 (December 31, 1965), pp. 166–167.
[22] The financial problem is discussed in Chap. 11.

As the story unfolded, it was the militants who were responsible for creating reasonably firm and consistent Afro-Asian support for the U.N. effort. The stridency of the militants in attacking Hammarskjold, in staging the Casablanca pullout, and in supporting the Lumumba delegation during the credentials fight, pushed the majority of the governments into the moderate camp. After that the road was smoother. As members of the American-led coalition, the moderates were prepared, if reluctantly, to take the measured steps dictated by the interplay of political forces inside and outside the Congo.

Even the moderate Afro-Asian states appeared to be more interested in using the United Nations to insure decolonization in the Congo than in initiating measures to advance law and order. Three facts point to this conclusion: (1) the interest in peacekeeping fell off sharply when the secession of Katanga was ended, though the minimal conditions of internal security had by no means been achieved; (2) the Afro-Asians showed virtually no understanding of or interest in realistic measures to retrain and reorganize the Congolese Army. What was most needed for an interim period was a European, preferably Belgian, officer corps, and the neutralists, along with top U.N. officials were stoutly opposed to the use of Belgian military technicians and advisers. Their position relaxed somewhat with the passage of time. They also opposed the Greene Plan, which was designed to streamline and strengthen the ANC by bilateral aid programs under a U.N. umbrella; (3) the Afro-Asian governments showed little or no interest in the Congolese rebel movements which got underway in 1963 and seriously challenged the authority of the Central Government and the territorial integrity of the country in 1964. During that year from 50,000 to 100,000 Congolese were killed by Congolese. These movements were probably a greater threat to the survival of a unified and independent Congo than secessionist Katanga ever was. Like Katanga, the rebels received some support from outside, but unlike Katanga, the support was from Communist states and their African allies. If European-backed Katangan secession was bad for the Congo, was not a bloody insurgency movement backed by Red China equally bad? The failure of some African leaders to appreciate the rebel danger was rooted in their sympathy with the rebels who were sometimes regarded as the legitimate heirs of Lumumba. The extent to which some African leaders were uninterested in the preservation of a moderate and united central government in the Congo was dramatically illustrated by their outcry against the Belgian-American mission to rescue foreign hostages held by the Stanleyville rebels in November, 1964, which was criticized primarily because it strengthened the Leopoldville government against the Chinese-supported rebels.

Despite the ambiguities and confusion in Afro-Asian attitudes and behavior toward the Congo crisis, it is fair to conclude that the interests of a majority of these states were served by the U.N. Mission, since most of them, at least in the long run, wanted a degree of stability in central Africa. The UNF made a modest contribution to that objective.

10.

The U.N. Force: Political and Military Control

The United Nations Force in the Congo was an army approximating a division in strength. It had combat battalions and specialized units. It had a small air force which included jet fighters. More than 93,000 officers and men from 35 countries served in the UNF during its four-year existence. Each man wore his national military uniform along with a U.N. arm insignia and a blue beret.

Like a national army, the UNF was commanded by a general and was the instrument of political purposes, but unlike a national army, its political directives were based upon resolutions of the Security Council and its civilian chief was the Secretary-General.

The UNF was a hobbled army, operating under unusual political constraints. It lacked the authority to initiate military action. It even lacked the full powers of a police establishment. Yet it had a mandate no less comprehensive than that of maintaining law and order in a chaotic country the size of Western Europe. As the instrument of an international coalition, its behavior was of more than usual interest to politicians and journalists around the world.

The command and control problems of a hastily created multinational force are in many respects more complex than those of a traditional military establishment engaged in a similar mission. The governments contributing military personnel for the Congo were not wholly disinterested in the outcome of the crisis. Many of them tried to influence the Secretary-General on the diplomatic level in New York, and some of them tried to influence the operation in the Congo directly. This chapter is concerned with the responsiveness of national contingents and the Force as a whole to the authority of the Secretary-General. Was the military or political control of the UNF compromised by its multilateral character?

THE SECRETARY-GENERAL AND CIVILIAN CONTROL

In its command structure the UNF adhered to the familiar principle of civilian supremacy. The Secretary-General was Commander in Chief under the authority granted him by the initial Security Council resolution. Politically he was accountable to the Council and the General Assembly.[1] Operationally the UNF was under his executive authority.

The simple chain of command between the Secretary-General and the Force Commander was complicated by the interposition of a civilian Officer in Charge located in Leopoldville. He was the Secretary-General's representative for both the civilian and military operations in the Congo. The authority of the Force Commander was strictly limited. He was "operationally responsible to the Secretary-General through the Officer in Charge for the performance of all functions assigned to the Force by the United Nations, and for the deployment and assignment of troops placed at the disposal of the Force"; the orders issued by the Commander were "subject to review by the Secretary-General and by the Officer in Charge."[2]

Civilian supremacy in the context of the U.N. operation meant that the goals and constraints embodied in the Security Council resolutions took precedence over strictly military considerations. A major constraint was the necessary consent of the Congolese government for any significant UNF operation. It was precisely this constraint that was violated in the first month of the operation by Major General H. T. Alexander when he disarmed units of the ANC. The controversial incident occurred when Ralph J. Bunche was acting as Hammarskjold's Officer in Charge and before the arrival of Major General Carl von Horn of Sweden, the first Force Commander. The absence of the Force Commander was complicated by the presence of General Alexander, a vigorous British officer who was Chief of the Defense Staff in Ghana. He had arrived on July 14, 1960, with a small group of Ghanian soldiers, in response to Lumumba's request for assistance from Ghana. The Ghanian troops were shortly thereafter placed under the U.N. Command.

In this confused situation, Alexander filled the command vacuum by exercising authority in behalf of the United Nations. On July 15, he made an agreement with General Gheysen, commander of the Belgian

---

[1] The role of the Secretary-General is discussed in Chap. 2.
[2] Paragraphs 4 and 11 from *Regulations for the United Nations Force in the Congo*, U.N. Document St/SGB/ONUC/1 (July 15, 1963).

forces in the Congo, and Maurice Mpolo, acting chief of staff of the ANC, for the peaceful disarmament of the ANC.[3] With this agreement and with Mpolo's assistance, he disarmed peacefully Leopoldville units of the ANC. Bunche says this disarmament was not authorized by the United Nations but Alexander maintains that Bunche said he would "back me completely in my attempt to persuade the Congolese soldiers to hand in their weapons" and "that something had to be done to restore peace, at least in Leopoldville."[4]

This successful disarmament of ANC units, coupled with persistent but erroneous references in the press to Alexander as the U.N. Force Commander, lent credence to his authority. In fact, he was never a member of the U.N. Command.[5] Within a few days, Alexander's initiative, which would have been commendable under more normal circumstances, had a serious effect on the relations between U.N. authorities and Prime Minister Lumumba. Alexander's perhaps justified initiative, though not clearly authorized by top U.N. or Congolese authorities, contributed to a lasting friction between the UNF and the ANC. Thereafter the complete disarmament of the ANC was virtually impossible. It also had a negative effect upon subsequent efforts of the U.N. Command to reorganize the ANC or train officers for it.

Alexander's initiative in the face of chaos led to the loss of civilian control over the military for a short but crucial period at the very outset of the operation. Civilian authority was reasserted when Hammarskjold named Bunche as the Acting Force Commander, pending von Horn's arrival, in addition to Bunche's position as the civilian Officer in Charge. This peculiar arrangement of appointing a civilian as the Force Commander was done at Bunche's suggestion, but it resolved the confusion over Alexander's position. At the same time, it led to some confusion because of Bunche's inadequate understanding of military matters.

The one other celebrated case where civilian control was challenged was the Lufira River incident during Round Three in Katanga. The UNF was moving outward from Elisabethville to exercise "freedom of movement" in the province. The U.N. Commander in Katanga, Major General D. Prem Chand, was under specific instructions from New York not to go beyond the Lufira River. Brigadier Reginald S. Noronha, commander of the Indian Brigade, was leading a column

---

[3] CRISP, *Congo: 1960*, II, 623.
[4] Alexander, *African Tightrope*, p. 38.
[5] See Hoskyns, *Congo Since Independence*, p. 136.

on the road to Jadotville and was stopped temporarily at the Lufira because the road and rail bridges were out. Since the column was encountering little resistance, though under sporadic sniper fire at the Lufira, Noronha ordered his troops across. When they arrived in Jadotville, they were warmly welcomed by the Congolese population.

Bunche was sent from New York to investigate this "serious breakdown in effective communication and coordination," but concluded that there had been no insubordination.[6] Later Secretary-General Thant said that Noronha's on-the-spot decision was "in accordance with good military practice" and contributed to the "remarkable success" and "low cost" of the operation.[7] This judgment is sustained by the evidence. The U.N. field commander had simply made a prudent tactical decision compatible with the larger UNF objectives in Round Three.

On the other side of the civilian-military problem, two examples of the unwise intrusion of civilian authority into military policy may be noted. One concerns the plan of Lieutenant Colonel Bjorn Egge of Norway, a U.N. intelligence officer, for the gradual Africanization of the Katanga gendarmerie by temporarily using European officers recruited by the United Nations.[8] This plan appeared to be the only practical way to make the Katanga gendarmerie more responsible and thus contribute to order in the province. But Hammarskjold turned it down because he was more concerned with expelling Tshombe's mercenaries than in improving the quality of the Katanga security forces. Apparently he did not realize that the abrupt Africanization of the Katanga officer corps would have had the same disruptive effects that were suffered elsewhere in the Congo when the Belgian officer was summarily dismissed by Lumumba in 1960. Even without Africanization of Tshombe's officers, the situation deteriorated when Belgian officers, at Hammarskjold's insistence, were removed without replacing them with other competent Europeans. To take up the slack, Tshombe hired French mercenaries who were considerably more hostile toward the U.N. Mission than the Belgians.

The other example of a potentially disastrous interference of civilian authority took place in connection with the Congolese attack on the

6 U.N., *SCOR*, Supplement for Jan., Feb., March, 1963, S/5053, Add. 14 (January 10, 1963), pp. 156 and 157.

7 *Annual Report of the Secretary-General on the Work of the Organization* (June 16, 1962–June 15, 1963), U.N. Document A/5501, p. 7.

8 The Egge Plan is described in Appendix H, 8.

U.N. Sudanese garrison in Matadi in March, 1961.[9] A civilian member of the Leopoldville headquarters staff attempted to order a U.N. counterattack involving the use of the Matadi landing strip, which at the time was under Congolese control and obstructed by trucks, barrels, and other materials. Fortunately, the Force Commander was briefed on the plan before it was implemented. He immediately canceled it. Had it gone through, the UNF might well have sustained losses greater than those of the three rounds in Katanga combined.

Perhaps the best civilian-military relationship was developed in Kasai province between the Nigerian contingent, largely staffed by British officers, and the U.N. civilian representative there. *Operation Union,* a co-ordinated civilian-military effort involving the Nigerian Brigade, under the command of a competent British officer, Brigadier Edward R. Lewis, succeeded in establishing an effective U.N. presence throughout the province. The operation involved helicopter lifts of small civilian-military teams to outlying areas. The province was brought under control and civilian functions were reestablished without diverting combat troops from their essential security duties along the Port Francqui-Kamina railroad.

THE MULTINATIONAL HEADQUARTERS STAFF

The Congo operation was initially directed in a highly informal, *ad hoc* manner. After Bunche settled the Alexander problem, he assumed personal control of the military operation until General von Horn's arrival. He directed his attention to the first and most important task, establishing a visible U.N. presence at key points throughout the Congo, except for Katanga. There was no military headquarters staff during the first few days and Bunche issued orders orally.[10]

The first Leopoldville headquarters staff consisted of twenty officers brought by General von Horn on a temporary basis from the U.N. Truce Supervision Organization in Palestine (UNTSO). They arrived

[9] Donald R. Gordon, *The Canadian Contribution to the U.N. Peacekeeping Operation in the Congo* (Washington: Brookings Institution [unpublished manuscript], 1965), p. 64.

[10] Author interview with General Iyassu Mengesha, in Addis Ababa, February 15, 1965. (Iyassu was in command of the Ethiopian contingent in 1960.) Major General Carl von Horn has criticized Bunche's role in the Congo during this period. He said Bunche had no "firm or definite policy," interfered in or bypassed the military command, and simply did not understand military realities. "His passion for involving himself in the minutiae of administrative detail was a nightmare." See von Horn, *Soldiering For Peace,* pp. 175–76.

with him on July 18, 1960. It was almost immediately apparent that these officers lacked the requisite training and experience for directing and planning the complex Congo operation. Toward the end of July, Brigadier Indar Jit Rikhye, Hammarskjold's military adviser, was sent to the Congo to examine the confused situation, make recommendations on the size and character of the UNF, and develop an appropriate headquarters organization. His recommendations were presented to the Secretary-General on August 11, 1960, and shortly thereafter, steps were taken to regularize the organization at the top. By late September, 162 officers, other ranks, and civilians, were assigned to the military headquarters in Leopoldville. This total was only twenty less than the permanent headquarters strength formally authorized on November 20, 1961.

The staff organization was a compromise between the United States and British staff systems. Some modifications were made to deal with problems peculiar to the Congo effort. The most serious and persistent problem was to reconcile the demands of political necessity with the need for competent performance. Hammarskjold insisted that all significant national contingents be represented at the headquarters level. At the same time there was the practical requirement that the officers had to be qualified and of an appropriate rank. The problem was made still more difficult by the political unacceptability of officers from permanent members of the Security Council and certain other countries. In the beginning, Canada, Pakistan, and India were the only politically acceptable states that could provide a sufficient number of officers of the required rank who were properly trained for general staff duties.

In the first expansion of the Leopoldville headquarters, the top positions in the two key branches—Intelligence[11] and Operations—were given to the Scandinavian countries and India respectively. India retained the Chief of Operations position for the first two years, but in November, 1962, it was turned over to an Ethiopian. An Indian retained the Deputy position until mid-1963. At lower levels in this section, Pakistan was represented until the beginning of 1964, and Canada until mid-1963. Ireland, Liberia, and Denmark rotated officers through the lowest officer position in Operations until the end of 1963.

[11] The intelligence section (corresponding to G–2 in U.S. military organization), was always designated as the Military Information Branch in the UNF, because of political sensitivity to military intelligence operations.

Sweden and Norway, whose armies had sent officers to Intelligence staff schools in the United States and Britain for years, shared the top Intelligence assignment throughout the operation. Other countries represented in the lower officer positions in the intelligence branch, in descending order of numbers, were: India, Canada, Ireland, Ethiopia, Pakistan, and Nigeria.

Assignments to the other staff sections were apportioned to give adequate headquarters representation for the states providing troops. (See Chart A below.) There was no direct correlation between the size of the national contingent and the number of officer spaces allocated.[12] Canada, for example, maintained the highest average officer representation in the headquarters, yet ranked twelfth in its manpower contribution. India, whose total troop contribution was greater than any other

A. *National Officer Representation at U.N. Force Headquarters**

Country	Nov., 1961	Nov., 1962	Nov., 1963	Nov., 1964	Average
1. Canada	11	13	9	8	10¼
2. India	10	15	7	6	9½
3. Pakistan	8	10	6	4	7
4. Sweden	5	11	7	5	7
5. Ireland	7	6	3	5	5¼
6. Norway	5	7	4	4	5
7. Denmark	4	3	3	3	3¼
8. Ethiopia	4	5	1	2	3
9. Nigeria	1	0	1	2	1
10. Netherlands	1	1	0	0	½
11. Malaya	1	1	0	0	½
12. Indonesia	0	0	2	0	½
13. Ceylon	2	0	0	0	½
14. Liberia	0	1	0	0	¼

* This chart was prepared from official U.N. records.

state ranked second with an average of nine to ten officers. Ethiopia, whose total contribution was exceeded only by India and was almost twice that of third-ranking Nigeria, had an average of only three officers, but they held senior positions.[13]

[12] This can be demonstrated by a comparison of Chart A with Appendix E.

[13] On the November, 1962 and January, 1963 rosters, Ethiopia held both the position of Commander and that of the Chief of Operations Branch. Ethiopia also provided a Deputy Commander.

The manning of the Special Staff[14] and the Technical Staff sections presented no particular difficulties. Personnel for these sections and branches, such as communications, provost, logistics, movement control, ordnance, electrical and mechanical engineers, transportation, and medical, were almost always drawn from the contingent which supplied the associated or specialized technical unit. Thus in the headquarters, Pakistan and India were represented heavily in the supply and transportation,[15] the Scandinavian countries in electrical and mechanical engineering and movement control, and the Canadians in communications ("signals," in UNF parlance). The disproportionately heavy Canadian representation in the headquarters is in part attributable to the high professional qualifications of the Canadian officer corps, and in part to the linguistic requirements of the headquarters. A liberal sprinkling of officers who spoke English and French was essential. Of the politically acceptable countries, Canada was best equipped to meet this need.

The "staff officer's nightmare" of the early days in Leopoldville, occasioned primarily by the multinational character of the headquarters, was largely corrected by filling the key staff positions with officers from states that followed the British Commonwealth military traditions. There is considerable truth in the comment that "a whiskey and Sandhurst set" had emerged.[16] Without this unifying Commonwealth factor, it would have been far more difficult for the headquarters to function effectively.

Neither the organization of the headquarters nor the allocation of positions to participating governments provides any evidence that any state or group of states was able to capture the key policy-making positions. The informal organization which developed outside the formal

[14] The Special Staff is composed of sections specifically concerned with supporting operations as opposed to the General Staff sections which are responsible for general plans, policy, and operations.

[15] Frequent allegations that the Indians and the Pakistanis had monopolized supply posts in order to favor their own contingents and to profit from black market operations appear to be unfounded. Their representatives held these positions for the administrative and military reasons indicated above. In these fields, however, they were in a better position to engage in black market activities than in the other sections. All observers agree that there was considerable black market activity in cigarettes, liquor, and other U.N.–P.X. items.

[16] Both quotations are from William Gutteridge, *Armed Forces in New States* (London: Oxford University Press, 1962), pp. 62 and 65. General von Horn called the situation "bizarre" and attributed this to the "hodgepodge" character of the "polyglot force" and the "hopeless mandate that made us everybody's enemy." See von Horn, *Soldiering For Peace*, pp. 187 and 237–39.

structure of the headquarters, however, does suggest that such a danger existed.

INFORMAL ORGANIZATION OF THE HEADQUARTERS

There is probably no military headquarters or staff without an informal organization or chain of command outside the formal structure. These informal lines of information and authority may or may not coincide with the formal channels. Most senior commanders attempt to man their headquarters with officers of their choosing. They exercise the greatest possible care in the selection of personnel to fill the critical policy positions. When a senior commander's freedom of choice is limited by factors beyond his control, it is an exceptional officer who does not occasionally bypass the formal hierarchy, or find some other means of dealing directly with officers he knows and trusts.

The Leopoldville headquarters was no exception to this general practice. Formal command lines were often bypassed, particularly in the early days.[17] This was dramatically true when Brigadier Rikhye of India intruded into the line of command, apparently with the Secretary-General's consent. Shortly after his initial survey trip to the Congo in August, 1960, Hammarskjold's military adviser was sent back to Leopoldville to help establish a working headquarters staff. The basic problem was the inadequacy of the Force Commander and the twenty officers he brought with him from UNTSO. Although of impressive personal mien, General von Horn simply lacked the experience and training necessary to cope with the complex Congo situation. His staff was likewise unqualified. There was confusion and bungling on the U.N. civilian side as well. Bunche's instructions were vague and uncertain. By mid-August, with the approval of Hammarskjold and the governments concerned, the UNTSO group had returned to Palestine and was replaced by an equal number of better qualified officers from the UNEF staff which Rikhye had headed from April, 1958 to February, 1960. These officers, selected by Rikhye, formed the nucleus for the reorganized staff. General von Horn remained as Force Commander until December, 1960.

While he was in Leopoldville helping to organize the headquarters staff, Rikhye became deeply involved in the line of command, which

[17] The account in this section is based upon author interviews with knowledgeable U.N. officials and military officers of various nationalities who served in the Leopoldville headquarters.

was clearly outside his normal duty as an adviser. Recognizing the command vacuum, Rikhye held regular but informal meetings with von Horn, and presented his own plans and suggestions. In most instances, von Horn indicated his concurrence. Rikhye would later write up general orders and give them to the operations branch with oral instructions to translate them into specific orders. When these specific orders were later submitted to the Force Commander, he would be reminded of his prior approval and would authenticate them. This system worked for about four months, apparently without von Horn's being fully aware that Rikhye had assumed a considerable degree of command.

The fact that Rikhye—sometimes in co-operation with two fellow Indians, Rajeshwar Dayal, the controversial officer in charge, and a Colonel Mitra, the operations officer—made plans over von Horn's head was well known in UNF circles. For this reason von Horn's successor as Force commander, Major General Sean McKeown of Ireland, made his acceptance of the position conditional upon the clarification of Rikhye's role. He did not want his authority diluted by interference from Hammarskjold's military adviser.

Rikhye's role was further complicated by his appointment by Hammarskjold as the Acting Officer in Charge from November 3 to November 23, 1960. This was a civilian post. In addition, he made frequent troubleshooting trips to the Congo at the request of Hammarskjold. As military adviser, Rikhye was not authorized to run operations, or even to act as a military adviser to the Officer in Charge. The Force Commander was supposed to take his orders from the Secretary-General, and act as the military adviser to the officer in charge.[18]

Under General McKeown the Leopoldville headquarters had a staff within a staff. This development was based upon a precedent started under General von Horn. For unclear reasons, Rikhye succeeded in having dismissed von Horn's capable but somewhat forceful chief of staff, a Canadian. Rikhye also arranged for his replacement by an African officer with the approval of the Congo Club.[19] General von Horn accepted the change on condition that the Canadian officer be retained as his "Military Assistant." Following suit, succeeding commanders also demanded one or more assistants. When General

[18] For General von Horn's view of Rikhye's role, see his *Soldiering for Peace*, pp. 222–23, and 241. This problem is also discussed in Chap. 2, above.

[19] The Congo Club was an informal, but influential, group within the Secretariat that advised the Secretary-General. Its function and "membership" are discussed in Chap. 2.

McKeown took over, he insisted on having Irish aides. The headquarters roster shows that a number of Irish officers were assigned during McKeown's tenure. Just as Rikhye earlier had encroached on the authority of the Force Commander, these staff assistants tended to encroach on the authority of the Chief of Staff.

While these informal and irregular headquarters staff relationships doubtless resulted in some friction, there is no evidence that they compromised the integrity of the U.N. operation. In a multinational staff it is quite understandable that General McKeown should want to have as his intimate staff aides fellow Irishmen. Potentially more serious was Rikhye's intrusion into command. But even here his extraordinary exercise of authority was a response to a recognized command vacuum. Something needed to be done. Rikhye did undercut von Horn, but he did so to make the operation work, not to pursue policies contrary to what a disinterested and competent commander would have done under the circumstances. This interference probably helped to ensure more effective control of the UNF. There were better ways to deal with the command problem, and Hammarskjold, not Rikhye, is responsible for misusing his Military Adviser in this unfortunate way.

UNITY OF COMMAND PROBLEMS

The problem of achieving unity of command was complicated by the multinational character of the UNF and the vast territory over which it was deployed. Generally the UNF was organized along provincial lines. With the exception of Katanga, the provincial command headquarters did not have multinational staffs. Each had at its core the headquarters staff of a major national contingent.

The principal difficulty of this arrangement was that the implementation of U.N. policies in the provinces were subject to differing interpretation by the different national commands, each of which tended to see its task in terms of its own military tradition and experience. This permitted a considerable degree of initiative to the provincial commanders, especially in the early months when the Leopoldville headquarters was not effectively organized and instructions were broad and vague.

In July, 1960, when the first commander of the Ethiopian Brigade in Orientale province attempted to get specific instructions from Bunche, the officer in charge, he was simply told that his task was to maintain order. Our biggest problem, the Commander later reported, was the "unclearness of our mission."[20] Under the circumstances he concluded that his Force was expected to serve as a "substitute government," so it behaved like a military government. The Tunisians in lower Leopoldville province made a similar interpretation of their mission.[21]

The absence of precise instructions from Leopoldville and the relative autonomy of the provincial commanders created a situation in which a field commander could have pursued policies or undertaken operations contrary to the general mandate. As it turned out, there were no serious problems of this sort. The Tunisians succeeded in accomplishing the voluntary disarmament of ANC units in the lower Congo. Though this went beyond the guidelines laid down by the Leopoldville headquarters, no harm resulted.

Reflecting the special character of the Katanga problem, the composition and command of the UNF in that province was unique. For political and psychological reasons the first U.N. troops to enter were white. Two Swedish companies, escorted by Hammarskjold, arrived in Katanga on August 12, 1960. Shortly thereafter, combat units from Sweden, Ethiopia, Morocco, Mali, and Ireland were deployed in the province.

As the situation in Katanga approach a climax in August, 1961, the command structure was modified in anticipation of military action. Brigadier K. A. S. Raja of India was given command over the entire UNF in Katanga with his headquarters in Elisabethville. This arrangement remained virtually unchanged until preparations for Round Two got under way. These involved organizing the forces in Katanga into two operational brigades, one including the Swedish and Irish battalions and the other the Indian battalions and an Ethiopian battalion that arrived on December 6, 1961.

During 1962, the Elisabethville headquarters evolved into a formally organized counterpart of the Leopoldville command, though fewer nations were represented on its staff. The commander and operations chief were Indians. It had a Swedish chief of staff, an Ethiopian personnel officer, and an Irish intelligence (Information) chief. Pakistani officers predominated in supply and transportation. The predominance

---

[20] Author interview with General Iyassu Mengesha in Addis Ababa, February 15, 1965. General von Horn also complained of the "ill-defined" mandate. *Soldiering for Peace*, p. 187.

[21] Lincoln P. Bloomfield, "Headquarters–Field Relations: Some Notes on the Beginning and End of ONUC," *International Organization*, XVII, No. 2 (Spring, 1963), 381.

of the Indians at the Command level before and during Round Three was due to the fact that there were as many Indian troops in Katanga as all other national units combined, and the Indian Brigade head-quarters was in Elisabethville. This resulted in a more unified and efficient operation in Round Three than in the two previous clashes in Katanga.

Though each soldier and all national units in the UNF were en-joined to act always "with the best interests of the United Nations *only* in view," as the UNF Regulations put it, men and officers naturally did not forget their national loyalties. Their U.N. service was tem-porary, but their relation to their own government was permanent. Career officers and men tended to be more concerned about their long-range professional advancement than their brief service in the Congo, if there appeared to be a conflict between the two. While the problem of dual loyalty is inherent in a multinational operation, the question here is whether the national allegiance of any officer or unit ever compromised the integrity of the U.N. Command. Such compromises have been alleged.

Ghana provides two examples. Dissatisfied with Hammarskjold's policies, Ghana on August 11, 1960, informed the Secretary-General it would "be justified in taking independent action" with its contingent "in agreement with the government of the Congo and, if necessary, in concert with other African states."[22] Guinea and the U.A.R. made similar threats to employ their troops independently of the U.N. Command in behalf of Lumumba. To these threats, Hammarskjold gave a forthright reply:

> Were a national contingent to leave the United Nations Force, they would have to be regarded as foreign troops introduced into the Congo, and the Security Council would have to consider their continued presence in the Congo, as well as its consequences for the United Nations Operation, in this light.[23]

The Ghanian threat never materialized. The contingent was not withdrawn, but in September, 1960, President Kasavubu accused Ghanian troops of supporting Lumumba to the detriment of the Central Government. There is no evidence to support this charge. Ghanian troops actually took part in the UNF action on September 12, 1960, to deny Lumumba entry into the Leopoldville radio station which

---

22 U.N., *SCOR*, Supplement for July, Aug., and Sept., 1960, A/4427, (August 11, 1960), p. 93.
23 U.N., *SCOR*, S/PV 896 (September 9–10, 1960), p. 20.

was closed by U.N. authorities. Dayal, the officer in charge at the time, insists that the Ghanian contingent was loyal to the U.N. Command.[24] Major General Rikhye also supports this view, and has said the Ghanian contingent should be especially commended because of its loyalty to the U.N. Command in view of the strong pressure its officers were under from Ghanian diplomats and agents in Leopoldville.[25] After waiting a respectable length of time so as not to appear to be taking orders from Kasavubu, the U.N. Command moved the Ghanian unit out of Leopoldville to quiet down the controversy and to protect the unit from the political pressure of its own government.

Throughout the four years, there was only one major conflict between governments providing troops and the Secretary-General serious enough to result in the threat and subsequent withdrawal of national contingents for political reasons. That was the Casablanca pullout of more than 6,000 troops in early 1961.[26] While this situation confronted Hammarskjold with a manpower crisis, the withdrawal actually strengthened the political reliability of the UNF by removing a potentially serious problem of dual loyalty. Thereafter, there was sufficient agreement between the contributing states and the U.N. Command to operate without serious conflict.

The contributing governments continued to criticize or offer advice on the operation at the political level in New York, a practice Hammarskjold found wholly legitimate. In the Congo many of the national contingents communicated directly and frequently with their home governments.[27] These reports from the Congo were used by diplomats in their dealings with the Secretariat and in public debates. By January, 1962, national radio links had been established between the contingents and home governments of India, Malaya, Ethiopia, Brazil, Nigeria, Ghana, and Canada.[28] The Secretary-General took a dim view of this direct communication, but was powerless to prevent it.[29]

The primary function of the national liaison officers in the Leopold-ville headquarters was to handle administrative matters connected with their contingents. They were not a part of the command structure, but their presence helped serve the political purpose of having virtually

---

[24] Author interview with Dayal in New Delhi, February 22, 1965.
[25] Author interview with General Rikhye in New York, April 27, 1965.
[26] The Casablanca pullout is discussed in Chap. 9.
[27] Author interview with Col. Knut H. Raudstein, U.S.A., in Washington, March 25, 1966. He was the U.S. Military Attaché in Leopoldville from June, 1962–August, 1965.
[28] Donald R. Gordon, *The Canadian Contribution*, p. 76.
[29] Canada's approach to this problem is discussed in Chap. 8.

B. *Strength of African and Other Troops in the U.N. Force**

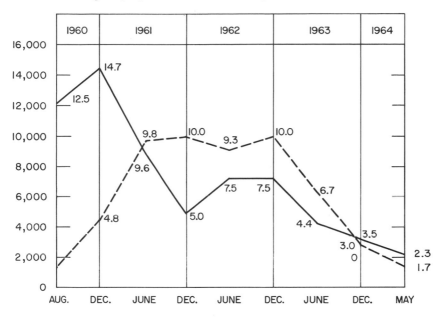

——————— Strength level of African contingents

— — — — Strength level of non-African contingents

* This chart was prepared from official U.N. records.

all contributing states represented in the headquarters staff. These officers, according to some observers, usually acted as channels of communication to their governments, a function which compromised to some extent the integrity of the staff.[30]

In connection with the Matadi incident,[31] a national liaison officer became involved in the chain of command between Leopoldville and a field unit. After the Sudanese U.N. unit had been withdrawn from Matadi, the U.N. movement control detachment located there attempted to resume operations. On March 7, 1961, the Danish movement control officer in charge of the detachment sent a report on the situation to the Leopoldville headquarters, *not* to the movement control section, but to the Danish liaison officer there. Later that day, the

[30] Author interview with Lt. Col. D. A. Ejoor, acting chief of staff of the Nigerian Army in Lagos, February 3, 1965. He served in the Congo, November, 1960–July, 1961. Also, Raudstein, interview with author, March 25, 1966.

[31] See Appendix H, 6.

Danish liaison officer ordered the Matadi movement control officer to prepare to evacuate the post on short notice. On the following day, the detachment received orders to move out of Matadi and back to Leopoldville, not through military channels, but from the Danish consul general in Matadi, J. Paludan, who relayed the order he had received from the Danish liaison officer in Leopoldville.[32]

This unusual case of a national liaison officer exceeding his terms of reference illustrates both the ambiguity of that position and the confusion which so often characterized the Congo. The Matadi incident was unexpected and placed a strain on U.N. communications. In fairness to the officers concerned, it may be noted that no one was criticized for acting improperly. In fact, there appears to have been a sense of relief that the messages got through in time, though transmitted by unorthodox channels, and that the endangered unit was successfully evacuated.

In the area of discipline, the national contingent commander played the key role. The UNF had no body of military law or code of discipline. Each soldier and officer was under the code of his own national military establishment. Crimes, willful failure to obey orders, and lesser infractions of discipline could not be dealt with directly by the U.N. Command. Any formal disciplinary action was the sole responsibility of the national contingent commander of the offender. A Canadian M.P. in Leopoldville could arrest a U.N. soldier for drunkenness, but he had to be returned to his national unit for discipline. Theoretically, the U.N. command's lack of authority to exercise discipline in serious matters was a great handicap, but in practice, according to the testimony of several Force commanders, discipline was handled reasonably well. General Rikhye has said, however, there were a "few cases, including major crimes, in which the governments concerned were not disposed to make the necessary investigations and to take suitable disciplinary action against the culprits. The impact of this attitude on the reputation, discipline, and morale" of the UNF and on the host government was a serious matter.[33]

INTELLIGENCE AND COMMUNICATION

Good intelligence and communication are essential components in any military command and control system. Intelligence provides infor-

---

[32] This information is based on two U.N. reports: "Ledger of Events at Hotel Metropole, Matadi, March 4, 1961," and "Events in Matadi, March 4–9, 1961."
[33] Indar Jit Rikhye, *Preparation and Training of United Nations Peacekeeping Forces*, Adelphi Paper No. 9 (London: Institute for Strategic Studies, 1964), p. 7.

mation about the operational environment, the movements and activities of hostile or potentially hostile forces. The U.N. Command recognized the need for intelligence, but was sensitive about using the word. Consequently, the UNF intelligence branch was euphemistically called "Military Information." In the Leopoldville headquarters, Military Information had a larger staff and more commissioned officers than any other branch. All operating units at the brigade and battalion level also had intelligence elements.

A number of means were exploited to secure intelligence, especially in Katanga. They included radio interception, air reconnaissance, combat and other types of patrol (including helicopter), and a system of provincial or field liaison officers, as they were called, whose specific function was to keep Leopoldville informed of the local situation.

Many observers believe that the U.N. intelligence system in the Congo was considerably less than adequate. The UNF was hampered by too few qualified specialists and too little equipment, especially for aerial photography and for recording Katanga broadcasts. A major problem was the lack of money to buy information.[34] In spite of these limitations, the UNF was able to secure, mainly by aerial reconnaissance, sufficient information on the location of all Katangan aircraft which they were able to destroy on the ground at the beginning of Round Three.[35] During that Round, the UNF also secured valuable intelligence by improvised interception of radio traffic in Katanga.

The absence of an effective UNF communications system in the Congo was very serious until the arrival and deployment of the Fifty-seventh Signal Squadron of the Canadian army, a bilingual unit organized especially for the Congo operation. This unit was in operation by August 28, 1960, and thereafter provided the backbone of the entire U.N. communications network.

Before the Canadian squadron arrived, the communication between Leopoldville and the field was handled by an improvised mixture of Congolese and U.N. facilities, personnel, and equipment, including voice telephone, teletype, and hand-operated Morse code radios.[36]

---

[34] Author interviews with Indian officers in Elisabethville, September 25–27, 1962.

[35] According to the U.N. air commander at the time, Tshombe's air force consisted of two jet *Vampires*, six or seven *Harvards* with machine guns, as well as some other small planes and transport craft. Because of good U.N. aerial reconnaissance, most Katangan aircraft were destroyed or disabled on the ground, "without loss of life," by ten Swedish J-29 jets. "We are very proud of that—it is the best memory I take away from the Congo." (Author interview with Maj. Gen. Christian R. Kaldager in Oslo, Norway, June 5, 1965.) After serving as air commander, Gen. Kaldager served as U.N. force commander, August–December, 1963.

[36] Comdt. E. D. Doyle, "Signals in Katanga and Kivu, 1960," *An Consantoir, The Irish Defense Journal*, XXI, No. 10 (October, 1961), 489.

The full U.N. communications system was not completed until the end of October, 1960. By that time the Canadians had staffed the Leopoldville center and stations in Coquilhatville, Gemena, Luluabourg, Stanleyville, Kamina, and Elisabethville. These facilities were able to operate on a 24-hour-a-day and seven-day-a-week basis. Within the various national contingents in the provinces, communication was facilitated by the use of compatible equipment and the same language. The multinational composition of the Katanga command presented some language difficulties.

The efficiency of the Canadian signals unit was widely acknowledged and in general, military communications were satisfactory. Some difficulties were caused by the fact that both the UNF and U.N. civilian operations used the same system. When the traffic was unusually heavy, important messages were sometimes delayed due to the failure to develop an adequate priority system. During Round One the reply to a simple code message from Leopoldville to Elisabethville sometimes took four hours.[37] During Round Three, the system was overburdened by an unnecessary number of classified messages. Usually, however, all traffic was cleared within twenty-four hours after it originated.

ROUNDS ONE, TWO, AND THREE

The U.N. command and control system was most severely tested during the three armed clashes between the UNF and Katangan forces. The key military command questions about these operations are: (1) did the Force Commander have cognizance of the plans for all operations and the opportunity to influence operations after they were under way? (2) did field commanders disobey specific orders or established military policy, or otherwise act improperly? (3) did U.N. civilian representatives in Katanga assume command responsibilities which properly belonged in Leopoldville or to the U.N. Katanga commander?

Operation Rumpunch, the peaceful roundup of 338 mercenaries in Katanga on August 28, 1960, which served as a prelude to Round One, appears to have been properly planned, directed, and executed until it was terminated by Conor Cruise O'Brien, the U.N. civilian representative in Elisabethville. All appropriate military echelons had knowledge of the plan and had taken the necessary preparatory mea-

---

[37] Author interview with Sture Linner, the U.N. officer in charge at that time, in London, September 27, 1966.

sures prior to the actual start of the operation. Hammarskjold praised the efficiency and bloodless character of Operation Rumpunch.[38] Under pressure from the European consuls in Elisabethville who promised to co-operate with him, O'Brien decided to halt the operation before all mercenaries on the U.N. list had been apprehended. Since he had the concurrence of Sture Linner, his civilian chief in Leopoldville, O'Brien had the necessary authority to make this decision, even if Brigadier Raja, who commanded the military forces involved, objected to it, which he did. Therefore, O'Brien did not exceed his terms of reference in halting a military operation, nor was military control lost.

In Round One, the Secretary-General temporarily lost control of the UNF, but there was no loss of *military* command and control as such.[39] The abortive attempt of O'Brien to end Katanga's secession on September 31, 1961, dramatized a failure of full communication among all the relevant U.N. civilian and military officers, and illustrates the confusion that can arise when strong-willed men take specific initiatives without fully informing all concerned parties. As far as can be ascertained, both the U.N. Command in Elisabethville and in Leopoldville approved the O'Brien-Khiary plan, including the significant details.

Perhaps the most serious military control problem in Round One was the alleged failure of the Swedish component of the Katanga command to seal off President Tshombe's palace, immobilize him, and hold him if a decision to detain him were made.[40] O'Brien ascribes the failure to inadequate communication, possibly a language problem between the Indian headquarters officers and the Swedes. The official written orders for Round One, however, contain no reference to this mission, which O'Brien regarded as crucial. There must have been a serious misunderstanding if such a key element was not included in the written orders. It could hardly have been a deliberate omission from the orders which were subject to later examination by superiors. Apparently control was lost through a staff error, probably a breakdown in oral communication between staff officers and the Katanga commander.

The primary command and control issue in Round Two was the undue use of force, principally by the Ethiopian contingent. The Ethiopian unit involved in this operation had moved into Elisabethville in

[38] O'Brien, *To Katanga and Back,* pp. 207 and 216–20.
[39] Round One is discussed in Chap. 3 as a problem in United Nations–host-state relations.
[40] O'Brien, *To Katanga and Back,* p. 249.

December, 1961, and was almost immediately assigned a key role in the operation, suffering five killed and about twenty wounded in its first encounter. Given the violence of the Katanga response to the U.N. action, the intensity of the firing, and the involvement of local civilians, a vigorous response by the Ethiopians is understandable. While questions of discipline may have been involved, there was apparently no breakdown in command and control.

All accounts of Round Three, which resulted in the termination of Katanga secession, suggest that a highly effective and unified command structure had been achieved. The only point at which some possible breakdown in control might have was during the crossing of the Lufira River. As discussed earlier in this chapter, evidence indicates that the unauthorized crossing resulted not from the breakdown of military control, but from a deliberate military decision which was subsequently justified by U.N. civilian authorities.

It was also during the three Rounds in Katanga that the U.N. constraints against the use of force were most severely tried. Throughout the four years, the UNF was restricted largely to the use of force in self-defense.[41] At the outset, the troops were denied "any initiative in the use of armed force." The February 21, 1961 Resolution broadened the permissible use of force to that necessary to prevent civil war, and the November 24, 1961 Resolution extended it to that necessary to apprehend prohibited foreigners.

It has been alleged that in Katanga the U.N. Command exceeded these constraints on the use of force. During the three clashes, the UNF killed approximately 350 Katangan soldiers and civilians and lost 42, a ratio of about eight-to-one.[42] This fact in itself does not mean the UNF violated the Security Council constraints. It must be remembered that the Force also had the right to "freedom of movement" throughout the Congo,[43] a right conspicuously denied in Katanga by Tshombe's regime until it was forcibly exercised by the U.N. Command in Round Three.

With the possible exception of Round One, the UNF did not initiate the use of force, though it was clearly prepared to do so in early 1963, had not Round Three started prematurely on December 28 in response

---

[41] The limitation on the use of force is discussed in Chap. 1.

[42] The three Rounds are summarized in Chap. 3.

[43] Paragraph one of the Basic Agreement Between the Secretary-General and the Congo Government (initialed on July 29, 1960), ensures "freedom of movement of the Force." See Appendix C for the text. (Freedom of movement is discussed in Chap. 1.)

to harassment from Katanga positions. U.N. military action to defend its existing positions in Elisabethville during Round Two and the first phase of Round Three was well within the limits of the permissible use of force. In the second phase of Round Three, units of the UNF moved out from Elisabethville and occupied Jadotville, Kolwezi, and other towns in Katanga. This may have involved a somewhat greater exercise of initiative than was originally contemplated under the freedom of movement doctrine. Speaking of this action, Secretary-General Thant said that the U.N. mandate to maintain law and order, prevent civil war, and eliminate mercenaries could never have been discharged without freedom of movement in Katanga. For this reason, he said, this right was reaffirmed in the U.N. Plan of National Reconciliation announced on August 20, 1962.[44] In this light, Round Three was a reasonable and restrained exercise of force, especially in view of Tshombe's repeated promises of freedom of movement for the UNF.

To conclude that the UNF, with the possible exception of Round One, did not exceed its legal authority to use force and did exercise freedom of movement with restraint is not to say that the U.N. operation, especially in Katanga, was above reproach. It is virtually certain that some U.N. troops in Rounds One and Two were guilty of brutal and unnecessary force and that some Katangans were killed by U.N. soldiers in cold blood. The Katanga side was also responsible for a small number of atrocities. The Secretary-General has been rightfully criticized for his reluctance to acknowledge at the time, and in more specific terms, the violations by U.N. troops of the Geneva Conventions on the laws of war, the treatment of prisoners, and the protection of civilians which were affirmed in Paragraph 43 of the *Regulations for the U.N. Congo Operation.*

EFFECTIVENESS AND EFFICIENCY

A meaningful evaluation of the effectiveness of the UNF is difficult because of its unique mission, its multinational composition, and the political constraints under which it operated. The UNF should not be expected to perform as efficiently as an integrated force of the same size under the command of a single government. With most of its troops drawn from underdeveloped states, its performance should not be expected to match that of forces from militarily competent countries, such as Britain, France, and the United States.

[44] U.N., *SCOR,* Supplement for Jan., Feb., March, 1963 S/5240 (February 4, 1963), p. 94.

Keeping these limitations in mind, how well did the UNF fulfill the missions assigned to it? From the beginning until mid-1963, it succeeded in maintaining a minimum degree of internal law and order. Comparing the internal security situation in July, 1960, and July, 1963, there was a significant improvement. Its effectiveness in preventing civil conflict ranged from poor to good.[45] No major civil war broke out while the UNF was in the Congo. Tribal warfare was usually contained. It should also be said that any improvement in the internal situation must be credited to several factors other than UNF military operations, including the diplomatic efforts of friendly governments and U.N. civilian officials to effect national reconciliation and get the civil administration moving after the initial breakdown.

The UNF made a significant contribution to the elimination of prohibited personnel in Katanga and to the ending of secession there, thus helping to assure the territorial integrity of the Congo. The closing of the airports in September, 1960, frustrated direct Soviet military intervention in behalf of Lumumba.

During the phase-out of the UNF after Round Three, the internal security situation deteriorated. Various rebel movements got under way in late 1963, and became a major threat to the authority of the Central Government. In 1964, they created an internal security crisis as serious, and perhaps more serious than that in July, 1960. At its height in mid-1964, about one-third of the country was in the hands of, or harrassed by, rebels. The rebels were to some extent encouraged, supplied, and directed by Communist China and states working with Peking. The rebels also received political and material support, including arms, from the Soviet bloc. The internal danger and threat of foreign intervention posed by the rebel movements cannot be ascribed to a *military* failure of the UNF. The fact that it got under way as the U.N. troops were leaving and reached its high point after the Force had left is evidence of the stabilizing effect of the U.N. military presence. This effect stemmed largely from political and psychological factors since the actual number of troops in February, 1964, was only 5,000. The decision to withdraw the UNF by June 30, 1964, was a political decision.

At the same time, the seriousness of the rebel movements was not wholly unrelated to one failure of the United Nations—a failure that

---

[45] It was ineffective in dealing with the abortive invasion of Bukavu by Leopoldville ANC in late December, 1960, and in the invasion of Katanga by Stanleyville ANC in January 1961. (See Appendix H, 3 and 4.) It was successful in Orientale and Equateur provinces in February, 1961. (See Appendix H, 5.)

had little bearing on the effectiveness of the UNF as such. This was the incapacity of the U.N. Mission to make any progress toward re-molding the ANC into a reliable internal security establishment. This problem which was ultimately, and for largely political reasons, approached on a bilateral basis rather than under U.N. sponsorship. Rooted in the absence of a reliable and competent officer corps, the ANC problem persisted into the post-UNF period, though some modest improvements were made through the bilateral assistance from Belgium, Italy, Israel, and the United States.

On the question of protecting U.N. personnel and installations in the face of isolated provocations or deliberate attack, the principal weakness of the UNF was made clear on a number of occasions—especially in the Port Francqui, Matadi, Kindu, and Niemba incidents in which at least seventy-two U.N. troops were killed, thirty more than the combined fatalities of the three Rounds in Katanga.[46] In some cases, such as Matadi, lack of adequate combat power was mainly responsible for the failures, but more often the cause was confusion over the rules of engagement on the part of the U.N. contingent officers concerned. This was particularly true of the Niemba incident.

A distinction should be made between effectiveness and efficiency. In terms of its broad mission, the UNF was reasonably effective politically, though its technical efficiency ranged from fair to poor compared to what could be expected of an integrated force of a significant military power. Taking into account the extraordinary political constraints and the multinational character of the UNF, its efficiency was good. Its inefficiency was due primarily to the lack of an adequate number of qualified personnel, which in turn was a product of its multinational character. The essential point is that this technical deficiency did not prevent the Force from being reasonably effective. The failure of the UNF to achieve more fully its political objectives was due primarily to powerful internal and external political factors over which the U.N. operation had very little control.

CONCLUDING OBSERVATIONS

The operational inefficiency and occasional blunders of the UNF led to tension and greater cost, but they did not adversely affect the course of the operation or lead to the loss of political or military control.

---

[46] See Appendix H, 2, 6, 7, and 9. In the Port Francqui incident, forty-seven Ghanian soldiers were killed according to U.N. records. General Alexander contests this figure and claims that "120 Ghanian soldiers with their British officers were murdered." See Alexander, *African Tightrope*, p. 66.

Implicit in the U.N. Command system was a dangerous potential for abuse, primarily because of its multinational character. The key aspects of this problem were: the development of small, informal groupings of headquarters staff officers from a single government; the essentially single-nation character of the organization and command structure in the field; and, especially during the early critical stages, the extremely vague and general nature of the orders and assignments given. These vulnerabilities could easily have been exploited by staff officers or national contingents for purposes contrary to the U.N. mandate. That they were not speaks well for the loyalty of the various contingents and for their understanding of the political constraints. Further, officers are naturally disposed to obey orders from superiors, and the Force commander was the supreme military authority while the national contingents were in the Congo. Governments providing troops were anxious to put their best foot forward and had a political stake in observing their contract with the Secretary-General.

At the Leopoldville headquarters there was never any serious loss of civilian or military control. No state or group of states captured key policy positions or exerted undue influence. Brigadier Rikhye was improperly interposed into the chain of command, but this situation was rectified before any lasting damage was done. Thereafter he remained only an irritant, not an obstacle, in the command system. The only incidents which challenged civilian control—General Alexander's disarming of ANC units and Brigadier Noronha's crossing of the Lufira River in Round Three—were temporary and did not erode civilian supremacy.

If control over the military operation was ever close to being lost, it was during the first hectic weeks in 1960. This was due mainly to the failure of the Leopoldville headquarters to give clear-cut orders to the contingents being deployed. National commanders were permitted too much leeway, both in terms of operational objectives and rules of engagement. If any donor state had entertained objectives incompatible with those of the U.N. effort, it would have been an easy matter to influence military policies of its contingent accordingly.

The principal weakness of the Leopoldville headquarters was in staff work and co-ordination which was generally conceded to have been poor. This weakness sprang from the alleged political necessity for donor state representation on the staff, and resulted in a wide range of competence, experience, and training, as well as in language problems and differences in staff procedures. The situation was exacerbated by the too frequent officer turnover, often at six-month intervals.

The problem was resolved in part by the allocation of key staff positions to countries which could supply qualified personnel.

Turning to the behavior of the national contingents, there is no evidence that any officer or unit deliberately attempted to support any Congolese faction or otherwise to violate the directives of the U.N. Command. The threat of Ghana, Guinea, and the U.A.R. to use their contingents independently of the UNF never materialized. The actual withdrawal of more than 6,000 troops from Morocco, Guinea, Indonesia, the U.A.R., and Mali, largely in protest against Hammarskjold's policies, contributed to the integrity and political reliability of the UNF because it eliminated the most militant African states which had specific political objectives in the Congo. In fact, the general effectiveness of the Force improved as the number of national contingents decreased and the size of contingents increased. The UNF was least effective when it most nearly reflected Hammarskjold's original concept that troops be drawn largely from Africa. It reached its maximum effectiveness during Round Three when its major components were drawn from non-African states, notably India, Sweden, and Ireland.

In conclusion, the Secretary-General never lost political control of the UNF. The Force Commander observed the directives from New York and remained in effective control. The command structure of the UNF, and its supporting communications and intelligence services, may have left a good deal to be desired, but the essential fact is that the system worked.

11.

The Politics of Financing the Force

When the United Nations Congo Mission was suddenly launched in July, 1960, without prior military, logistical, or financial planning, no one could foresee its eventual size, duration, or cost, all of which were determined by unpredictable political factors. As it turned out the operation was far larger than anticipated, with a total four-year cost of $411 million. This figure includes the air and sea transport of men and materiel to and from the Congo (a substantial portion of which was contributed), military supplies and equipment, rations, and the reimbursement of "extra costs" to states providing military personnel.

On the day the last U.N. soldier left the Congo, UNF bills of $104 million were still unpaid. By September 30, 1965, the debt had been reduced to $30.8 million.

The costly and controversial Congo effort precipitated a so-called financial crisis at the United Nations which was really a manifestation of a deep and persistent political cleavage among the member states over the operation and U.N. peacekeeping generally. This political conflict—dramatized by the announced refusal of France and the Soviet Union to pay a single cent for the UNF—led to a protracted debate over the application of Article 19 which specifies that a state may be deprived of its vote in the General Assembly if its U.N. assessments are in arrears.[1]

---

[1] This chapter does not deal with the Article 19 issue. For analyses of it, see Ruth B. Russell, "United Nations Financing and 'The Law of the Charter'," *Columbia Journal of Transnational Law*, Vol. 5, No. 1 (1966), pp. 68–95; H. G. Nicholas, "The United Nations in Crisis," *International Affairs*, Vol. 41, No. 3 (July, 1965), pp. 41–50; and Meg Greenfield, "The Lost Session at the U.N.," *The Reporter* (May 6, 1965), pp. 14–20.

CORRELATION BETWEEN FINANCIAL AND
POLITICAL SUPPORT

As might be expected, there was a high correlation between the material and political support of the UNF. Governments are not in the habit of paying for things they believe are not in their interest. Nor are they inclined to supply manpower or other forms of material assistance to operations they oppose on political grounds. In terms of their interest in the Congo effort, U.N. member states fell into three general categories: (1) active participants in the supporting coalition; (2) those with a marginal interest in the mission; (3) those opposed to the UNF.

1. The core of the supporting coalition led by Washington included about 25 states which provided most of the money and manpower for the operation. Of the total Congo costs, the United States has paid or will pay $170.7 million or 41.52 per cent, including the U.S. share of the bond issue repayment. Of this total, $127.3 was the share assessed by the General Assembly. The remaining $43.4 represents a voluntary contribution above the assessment and includes $10.3 for the U.S. airlift in 1960. By the end of 1964, thirteen governments had voluntarily contributed a total of slightly more than $46 million, as follows:[2]

United States		$43,396,648
Cash	$33,078,986	
Airlift	10,317,662	
Twelve Other Governments		$ 2,644,029
Cash from the 12 ...	$ 1,474,029	
Canada (airlift)	650,000	
U.K. (airlift)	520,000	

Of the twelve governments making voluntary contributions, eight (Australia, Denmark, Canada, Japan, Netherlands, New Zealand, Norway, and Britain) are military allies of the United States, and four (Austria, Ireland, Sweden, and Finland) are European and Western oriented. No African, Asian, or Latin American state made a voluntary contribution of money by the end of 1964. A number of these states, however, did buy U.N. bonds to pay for the Congo effort and UNEF.

If the UNF was sustained financially largely by Washington and its allies, it was supported by manpower largely from the nonaligned Afro-Asian states. India, Ethiopia, Nigeria, Tunisia, Ghana, Malaya, Indonesia, Pakistan, and Morocco were among the top twelve troop

---

[2] For details, see Appendix I.

contributors. Sweden, Ireland, and Canada, each of which made a voluntary financial contribution to the UNF, were also in this group of twelve.[3] There was a very high correlation between financial and manpower support among the Afro-Asian states. Virtually no government sending troops has failed to pay its full assessment. This is true in part because manpower contributors incurred costs the United Nations was obligated to pay, and in the negotiations over these costs the assessment was often settled at the same time.

As of September 30, 1965, a total of fifty-one member states had paid their full Congo quota. Most of the underdeveloped countries in this group have received some economic assistance from the United States since 1960 which increased their resources and made it easier for them to pay their relatively small Congo assessments.

2. There were about thirty-five states marginally interested in the Congo effort, of which about half had paid their full assessment. The other half are in arrears for a larger or smaller portion of their quotas. Among those that paid in full are Algeria, Burma, Ceylon, Colombia, Cyprus, Finland, Greece, Iran, Israel, Ivory Coast, Philippines, Sierra Leone, Tanzania, Thailand, Turkey, and Venezuela. Among those that still owe a portion of their assessment are Afghanistan, Argentina, Bolivia, Brazil, Nationalist China, Costa Rica, Guatemala, Guinea, Iraq, Mali, Paraguay, Senegal, Somalia, U.A.R., Upper Volta, and Yugoslavia. In general, the failure of this latter group to pay up can be attributed to lack of interest, though in the case of Mali, the U.A.R., and Yugoslavia, there was active political opposition to the Congo effort.

3. Of the thirty-two states that have paid none of their assessment, about half were politically opposed to the UNF.[4] This is clearly the case with the twelve that announced they would not pay—Paris, Moscow, and the Soviet bloc, including Cuba. Incidentally, the U.S.S.R., by its own testimony, contributed $1.5 million to the Congo effort when it waived its earlier claim for that amount for airlifting U.N. troops in 1960. Of the other twenty nonpaying governments, South Africa, Spain, and Portugal were politically motivated. It is more difficult to explain why Mexico, Chile, Jordan, and Togo have not paid.

---

[3] See Appendix E.
[4] The complete list of these states together with the amount of their unpaid assessments as of September 30, 1965, is found in Appendix J.

HOW THE UNF WAS FINANCED

At the outset, the Secretary-General and the supporting governments were more interested in fielding the UNF than in developing arrangements to pay for it. Hammarskjold was preoccupied with securing acceptable national contingents. Fortunately, he did not have to worry about transporting the troops to the Congo because Washington promised to provide any necessary airlift. (The U.S. Air Force took care of approximately four-fifths of the original airlift. The Soviet Union, Canada, and Britain together provided the other fifth.) The early financial decisions were made in an act-now, pay-later atmosphere.

The difficulties of financing the operation were not primarily economic or legal, but political. Had there been a solid political concensus among the great powers, there would have been no serious financial problem, though there would doubtless have been a debate over how to apportion the costs.

The financial problem embraced two basic and sometimes incompatible values—the ideal of collective responsibility and the necessity for respecting the interests of sovereign states. The principle of collective responsibility for peacekeeping is central to the U.N. system. But the Charter also respects the right of member states to protect their interests. The debate over financing the Congo reflected the struggle between these two values. Predictably, the assertion of national interest prevailed over the ideal of collective responsibility.

The political decisions on the Congo were made by the Security Council and the financial decisions by the General Assembly. From the beginning it was assumed that the collective obligation formula developed for UNEF would apply to the Congo. On December 20, 1960, the General Assembly adopted its first and most controversial financing resolution by a vote of 46–17, with 24 abstentions.[5] It established the apportionment pattern, stating that the Congo costs for 1960 "constitute 'expenses of the Organization' within the meaning of Article 17, paragraph 2," and that "the assessment thereof against Member States creates binding legal obligations."[6] The resolution established an *ad hoc* Congo account and apportioned $48.5 million among member states according to "the regular scale of assessment." At the same time, the Assembly authorized $8 million a month for the

---

[5] The negative votes were cast by the Soviet bloc, several Middle Eastern states, and Portugal. Among the abstainers were Belgium, France, India, Mexico, Indonesia, and Yugoslavia.

[6] U.N., *GAOR*, A/4676 (December 19, 1960), Annexes, Agenda items 49/50, pp. 11 and 12.

first quarter of 1961. Additional authorizations were made as required until June 30, 1962.

By mid-1961, the United Nations was confronted with an acute deficit because of the failure of France, the Soviet Union, and other members to pay their assessments. To meet the immediate crisis, the Assembly in December authorized a $200 million bond issue to be re-paid over twenty-five years out of the regular U.N. budget. It also re-quested an advisory opinion from the International Court of Justice on the legal issues in the financial dispute.

The United States agreed to buy $100 million in bonds on a match-ing basis with other states. From July, 1962, through June, 1963, the total Congo costs of $120 million were underwritten by bond pur-chases, and no assessments were levied against members. Though suc-cessful in liquidating a substantial portion of the peacekeeping deficit, the bond issue was only a stopgap.

In July, 1962, the Court, by a vote of nine–five, advised that the costs of UNEF and the Congo operation were "expenses of the Orga-nization" according to Article 17. The advisory opinion was endowed with greater force when the Assembly "accepted" it by a vote of 76–17, with 8 abstentions. To the majority, this apparently meant that peace-keeping arrears of a member state could properly contribute to a de-ficit by which it could be stripped of its right to vote under Article 19. Neither the Assembly action nor diplomatic pressure by Washington succeeded in inducing the Soviet Union, France, and the thirty other nonpaying states to pay their assessments as of mid-1967.

CONTRACTS WITH STATES PROVIDING TROOPS

Following the UNEF pattern, the United Nations never undertook to pay the total costs of troops in the Congo. The General Assembly agreed that the U.N. obligation covered only the "extra and extra-ordinary costs" incurred by governments providing military personnel. Each such government had to pay the normal and regular costs, such as salaries, it would have paid if it had sent no troops to the Congo.

The United Nations was obligated to pay every man and officer the overseas allowance established by the existing laws of his government. In addition, to equalize spending money in the field, the United Nations paid every man and officer regardless of nationality a daily allowance of $1.30.

Each donor government was entitled to compensation to cover the purchase of any special equipment for U.N. service, and for the loss or depreciation of any supplies of equipment taken to the Congo. It was also entitled to compensation for injury or loss of life of its nationals for any cause while in U.N. service.

The United Nations was obligated to pay all logistical expenses, including transportation of units to and from the Congo, and their full maintenance while they were abroad.

There were wide variations in the remuneration of military personnel of the same rank and doing the same job in the Congo, reflecting the disparity in salary scales in the contributing states. This was inevitable in a U.N. force composed of national contingents. The average monthly salary of a member of the Swedish contingent, for example, was about $270, and his average monthly overseas allowance was approximately $120, or a total monthly income of $390. In contrast, the average monthly salary of a member of the Indian contingent was about $25 and his overseas allowance was about $8, or a total of $33. This wide discrepancy between $390 and $33 sometimes had an adverse effect upon morale.

There was an even greater disparity in the direct cost to the United Nations for Swedish and Indian men and officers. For the average Swedish Force member, the organization paid $390 and for the Indian $8, since India, like virtually all of the contributing states, paid the salaries of *all* its men and officers. Sweden, Norway, and Denmark, on the other hand, paid the salaries of only a few of the officers and NCOs they sent to the Congo. The United Nations paid the full salaries and overseas allowances of the great majority of all the Scandinavian military personnel because they were recruited especially for UNF service.

While not paying the salaries of Indians in the Congo, the United Nations had to reimburse the Indian government for the salaries and equipment of reserve units called up in India to replace some of the regular Indian troops in the Congo.

The U.N. obligation to reimburse contributing states for lost or depreciated equipment has led to protracted negotiations. The negotiation process can be illustrated by a claim for more than $1 million from the government of India for the depreciation of armored cars and trucks taken to the Congo. Some of these vehicles were quite worn upon arrival, but there was no adequate U.N. inspection or record of their condition at the time. The U.N. controller's office was confronted by conflicting testimony from UNF officials. After a series of conferences between U.N. and Indian officials, which took into account economic and political factors, including the financial plight of the United Nations and U.S. economic assistance to India, New Delhi readily agreed to an outright purchase of the vehicles by the United Nations for less than half of its original claim.

The United Nations reimbursed the donor states for personal injury or death of nationals in the Congo, in accordance with the laws of each state. The actual death claims made under this provision ranged from a few hundred dollars to $40,000, depending upon the circumstances. The unusual $40,000 claim was settled at a much lower figure.

A number of governments provided services for the UNF under contract. The most substantial contracts were with the United States for airlift, sealift, and military equipment. As of June 30, 1965, the United Nations still owed Washington $4,577,000 for reimbursable services and equipment.

FINANCING AS AN INSTRUMENT OF POLITICAL CONTROL

The old adage, "He who pays the fiddler calls the tune," is not wholly applicable to the Congo operation where the fiddler, whether Hammarskjold or Thant, was accountable not to one government, but a coalition of states. If the collective payer had been of one mind, he might have called the tune, but this was never the case. There was enough diversity within the coalition to give the Secretary General considerable maneuverability, but not a free hand. If the payer could not call the tune, he could and did call it off on June 30, 1964. And at any earlier point a financial veto by a half dozen of the chief supporters could have stopped the music.

To say that the United States and the other major financial contributors did not exercise full control over the UNF is not to say that they were without influence. There was no mechanistic one-to-one ratio between financial support and influence. But the extent of financial support among the Big Powers was a barometer of influence because financial participation and influence are both functions of political interest. Washington was the most influential government, but not primarily because it provided the greatest financial support. It bore a large share of the cost and was the most influential because it was the strongest and most consistent political supporter of the mission. And it gave such support because there was a high concurrence between the objectives of the United States and the objectives of the UNF.

The Soviet Union and France, the chief nonsupporting states, had an ambiguous impact on the operation. Their relative lack of influence was a reflection of their political aloofness or opposition, and constituted a restraint on the operation. The Secretary-General could not wholly ignore their financial nonsupport, but he could move ahead as long as he had a working coalition which provided the necessary diplomatic and material backing.

The financial participation or nonparticipation of the smaller states, while important psychologically and diplomatically, had little influence on the operation. The Afro-Asian states exerted pressure directly and through their political influence with major powers. Their willingness or unwillingness to provide troops and their capacity to withdraw troops already in the field also had a marginal impact on the operation.

In short, financial nonsupport was a qualifying factor, but not a controlling force. The nonpayment of thirty-two states and the delayed payment of many more did not prevent the authorizing and fielding of the UNF or alter substantially its course or duration. Ultimately it was the decision of the chief financial and political backers that determined the character and length of mission.

Whether recognized as a fundamental right, an excusable exception, or an unfortunate breach of collective responsibility, the refusal of a member state to pay for a U.N. operation it believes is against its interests is in fact an important safeguard against collective encroachments on the accepted prerogatives of statehood.

12.

The Limits of U.N. Intervention: Conclusions

United Nations intervention in the Congo internationalized a local crisis and intensified the political conflict there. Paradoxically, the U.N. Mission also helped to contain the crisis and mute the conflict. When the Security Council authorized the Congo mission in 1960, it endowed that troubled state with a special political significance by focusing international attention upon it. In U.N. debates, the governments of the world—large and small, concerned and unconcerned, interested and disinterested—were obliged to occupy themselves with the Congo's internal conflict and even to choose between rival political factions there. In the General Assembly, for example, they had to vote whether to seat the Kasavubu or the Lumumba delegation, and all this under the white glare of world-wide publicity. The moderates and the militants in the Congo had their defenders and detractors in the larger world.

The U.N. peacekeeping effort did not suspend internal or international politics or keep the Cold War out of the Congo. On the contrary, it further politicized the crisis and assured that the Cold War would be waged in that chaotic arena. The UNF was an instrument of international politics. It was authorized under the rules of the U.N. system and managed by the Secretary-General, who in turn was largely the instrument of a coalition of states led by Washington. This temporary and loosely knit alliance included governments with widely differing interpretations of the Congo crisis. They were united only in their belief that something should be done and that support of the U.N. Mission was preferable to opposition.

While U.N. intervention may have exacerbated the Congo problem and delayed the restoration of order, it also helped to contain tribal and factional violence and to limit the permissible means available to the Cold War adversaries. Such were the contradictions in this controversial experiment. The net impact of the U.N. mission on the Congo, on interested states, on the prospects for peace, and on the future of the United Nations as a peacekeeping instrument, was ambiguous. The limitations and liabilities of the U.N. effort can be seen most clearly when measured against the probable consequences of alternative ways of managing the crisis.[1]

As a supplement to, and not a substitute for, conventional political efforts to influence events in the Congo, the U.N. Mission did not preclude diplomatic representation or covert activity by interested states. The normal struggle of power and interest, pressure and persuasion, assistance and advice, persisted, but it was slightly qualified by the legal constraints imposed by the Security Council and the large and obvious U.N. presence in the Congo. During the early part of the mission, for example, the U.N. Command prohibited bilateral military assistance to the Central Government or competing political factions in the Congo. The UNF also curbed certain political and military activities of the Congolese leaders.

The UNF was only one of many actors in the unfolding Congo drama, and it was certainly not the most important one. There were powerful internal and external forces at work. After the abrupt withdrawal of Belgian authority—the only source of cohesion and coherence in the Congo as a whole—the fledgling state was torn apart by tribalism, regionalism, and the rival ambitions of inexperienced political leaders. The endemic chaos was intensified by the summary dismissal of the Belgian officer corps of the Congolese army. These internal centrifugal forces were exploited by Communist and other militant governments bent on gaining an economic or political foothold in the Congo.

As the instrument of a multistate coalition and as the largest peacekeeping operation ever authorized by an international organization, the U.N. effort was unique. Three major questions may be asked about its character, performance, and significance: (1) did the operation maintain its integrity?; (2) what did it accomplish and fail to accomplish?; (3) were there viable alternatives to U.N. intervention? These questions will be examined primarily in terms of the objectives and expectations of the interested governments.

POLITICAL INTEGRITY OF THE U.N. MISSION

Throughout the four turbulent years, the integrity of the UNF was threatened by factions within the Congo and governments outside

[1] Possible alternatives to U.N. intervention are discussed later in this chapter.

which attempted to enlist it in the service of their special interests. Against these pressures the Secretary-General sought to keep the operation true to the changing mandate of the Security Council as interpreted by the supporting coalition. The Secretary-General was authorized to pursue broad security objectives in the Congo, but the means he was permitted were severely limited. This lopsided relation between ends and means was both a cause and a symptom of the U.N. dilemma. The Council placed three severe constraints on the UNF—a blanket prohibition against interfering in internal affairs, the necessity for cooperation with the government without becoming its instrument, and restrictions on the use of military force. The Secretary-General was more successful in observing the legal constraints than in achieving the objectives of the peacekeeping mission.[2]

Given the chaos of the Congo, the Secretary-General could not avoid taking sides in the internal conflict. Both Hammarskjold and Thant tried to remain aloof from political factions or to support the more legitimate of two contending elements, but the mandate itself was not impartial. Nor were the supporting states. The resolutions were explicitly against Tshombe and implicitly for a strong central government. The Lumumba-Kasavubu struggle was very confused. The imperatives of maintaining order compelled actions which, whether intended or not, favored one group over another. With the benefit of conflicting political pressures, both men succeeded in being more impartial than the Council resolutions. In spite of the necessary breach in the strict noninterference rule, the operation retained its essential integrity.

In its relations with Leopoldville, the UNF succeeded in co-operating with the government when there was a government to work with, without becoming its instrument or losing its independence. Formal consent for specific UNF operations was seldom requested and never denied, with one important exception—the U.N. authorities never secured Leopoldville's consent for reorganizing or streamlining the ANC. The U.N. Force never became the instrument of the government or any Congolese faction. There was never a joint operation of the UNF and the ANC.

The limitations on the use of force specified by the Security Council were partially offset by the right of "freedom of movement" for the UNF. The only possibly significant violation of these limitations was

---

[2] An assessment of how well the UNF succeeded in achieving its goals follows this section. The operation of the Security Council constraints is discussed primarily in Chap. 3.

O'Brien's use of military action to end secession in Katanga in September, 1961. There was an occasional overuse of force and even some brutality by U.N. troops in Rounds One and Two, but as a whole the UNF operated well within the limits of permissible force.

In the larger political arena the Secretary-General was constantly assailed by critics and advised by supporters. The critics had a restraining effect upon the mission, but did not force the mission to deviate from its course. The supporters were more influential because the operation depended upon their political and material backing. Yet there was sufficient diversity in the coalition to permit the Secretary-General considerable latitude in interpreting the mandate. The United States was the most influential government in the coalition, but its influence fell short of domination. Its advice tended to reinforce the prior disposition of the Secretary-General, rather than to alter it. Neither the Secretary-General nor Washington exploited the other, but they enjoyed a kind of symbiotic relation rooted in a common understanding of how the conflict should be contained.

In spite of the vague mandate, the lack of adequate legal precedents, and continuous political pressures, the Secretary-General largely succeeded in adhering to the fundamental intent and constraints of the resolutions. While neither Hammarskjold nor Thant exceeded or misused his legal authority, each made errors in political analysis and judgment. How serious and frequent these errors were depends upon one's perspective. There is no evidence, however, that either sought consciously to serve the special interests of particular governments, international blocs, or Congolese factions.

Many of the charges of illegality made by critics against the Secretary-General appear to spring from disagreements with his political judgments. During most of the operation there was only a fragile political concensus in the Security Council sufficient to sustain the U.N. effort. Dissenting members, particularly the Soviet Union and France, were often critical of the Secretary-General's policies. Nevertheless, neither Hammarskjold nor Thant was ever censured by the Council, and none of its members felt strongly enough to veto or nullify the enabling resolutions. If the Secretary-General pursued a course in the Congo contrary to the collective intent of the Council, it was the obligation of the Council to call him to account. If the resolutions were so ambiguous that he could not act under one paragraph without violating another, the Council should have cleared up the ambiguity. In any event, if the Secretary-General misused his authority, the Council was ultimately accountable for failing to exercise its basic responsibility for political control.

Turning to executive and military control, as distinguished from political control, the record clearly indicates that the Secretary-General maintained reasonably effective executive control throughout the Congo operation. Though the integrity of this control was challenged by political pressures, administrative inefficiency, unqualified personnel, and several specific incidents involving unauthorized initiative in the Congo, it was never seriously eroded.

The widespread and persistent administrative inefficiency in the Congo operation can be attributed largely to inherent factors such as the vague mandate, the large number of different national units in the Force, some incompetent civilian and military officers, and the fact that the Secretariat was not equipped to handle a field operation of that size and complexity. This inefficiency led to waste, delay, and unnecessary expense, but it did not seriously compromise the control of the Secretary-General.

The few top-ranking U.N. civilian and military officers who failed to perform their functions properly constituted perhaps the most serious threat to the integrity of the operation. Dayal, General von Horn, O'Brien, Khiary, and Linner created or permitted problems which their replacements, confronting virtually the same situation, were able to avoid. Each of these controversial officers was appointed by Hammarskjold whose judgment of character and competence left something to be desired. This weakness was also illustrated by Hammarskjold's asking or permitting his Military Adviser, Brigadier Rikhye, to intrude into the line of command in the Congo when General von Horn was the Force Commander. In all these situations the question of dual loyalty was apparently not present. As far as can be ascertained, none of these men was taking instructions from his own or any other government.

Just as the Congo operation as a whole did not escape the executive control of the Secretary-General, there was never any significant loss of control of the UNF by the Force Commander or the lower command echelons. (Brigadier Rikhye's informal intrusion into command undercut General von Horn, but under the unusual circumstances it had the effect of maintaining military control.) Civilian supremacy was maintained. The integrity of the command and control system was challenged but never breached.

The most significant weakness of the command system was the potential for abuse it offered, primarily because of the large number of national units in the Force and the multinational character of the command headquarters. The headquarters was overstaffed and had too many unqualified officers. Informal lines of communication tended to supercede the formal command structure. This made for confusion and general inefficiency, particularly in the early months, but no contributing state or group of states took advantage of the situation, and control was maintained in spite of multinational feather bedding.

In the field, where most provisional headquarters were under single-nation command, it would not have been difficult for national units to have pursued objectives contrary to those of the U.N. Command. This did not happen. Nor did any single government represented in the Leopoldville headquarters gain the upper hand. The national contingent commanders remained loyal to the U.N. Mission. There were several instances when a unit commander was subjected to pressure from political agents of his government to act unilaterally. In each case he refused. The political reliability and military integrity of the UNF was enhanced by the withdrawal of more than 6,000 troops by five governments in early 1961 in protest against Hammarskjold's policies.

ACCOMPLISHMENTS AND FAILURES

The extravagant expectations for the peacekeeping mission in 1960 in some quarters, particularly in the United States, appear to be rooted in a profound misunderstanding of inherent limits of the U.N. Mission, or in a serious misreading of the Congo problem, or both. The UNF was severely limited politically, legally, and militarily. The U.N. presence was a marginal actor in the drama. It was in the Congo with the consent of the government. More important, its existence depended upon the consent and active co-operation of a voluntary coalition of states. The Secretary-General had to serve, or at least not seriously offend, many masters. The Congo was not a U.N. trust territory. The UNF did not have the authority of an occupying power. It was not a substitute government.

The Congo had a certificate saying it was a state, but the certificate bore little relation to reality. The Congo had no effective central government. It had no reliable state-wide army or police force. The United Nations was not equipped to provide, even temporarily, these fundamental requirements of statehood. In fact, no external assistance short of the substantial help from one or two competent and friendly states could have compensated for the weakness of the Congo government and the fragmentation of the country. At best the UNF was a stopgap until the basic structure of central authority and internal security could be established. At worst the UNF postponed effective assistance from interested states and the resolution of major internal political conflicts.

After the mission was over, Secretary-General Thant soberly acknowledged the limited state-building capacity of the organization: "The United Nations cannot permanently protect the Congo, or any other country, from the internal tensions and disturbances created by its own organic growth toward unity and nationhood." The main problem, he added, is the "absence of a genuine and sufficiently wide-spread sense of national identity among the various ethnic groups" and this is an essentially internal problem for which the further extension of the UNF would "provide no solution."[3] The movement from tribalism to national consciousness and loyalty is a gradual process that may take generations.

Against this realistic backdrop, a fair appraisal of the UNF may be made. No one should have expected the mission to transform the Congo into a viable state. Given the limitations of the UNF and the magnitude of the problem, its modest accomplishments are noteworthy. A State Department publication in August, 1966, accurately summarized the contribution of the UNF: it "helped the Central Government to restore law and order and preserve the territorial integrity of the Congo."[4]

Along with diplomatic and other efforts working in the same direction, the UNF advanced specific objectives called for by the Security Council. It was the chief factor in maintaining minimal order. No major civil war erupted. Tribal strife was largely contained. In short, the UNF succeeded in holding down the lid, but it failed to make any provisions for the maintenance of internal security after it left. The law and order problem was just about as serious the day the last U.N. soldier left the Congo as it was when the first U.N. troops arrived four years earlier. Some observers believe the situation in mid-1964 was considerably worse—at that point Communist supported and encouraged rebels controlled or harassed one-third of the country.

The internal security picture did not substantially improve, partly because the United Nations made no progress in transforming the

---

[3] Secretary-General's last Congo report, S/5784 (June 29, 1964), p. 42.

[4] *The U.N.: Action Agency for Peace and Progress,* Department of State Publication No. 7733 (Washington: U.S. Government Printing Office, August, 1962), p. 5.

faction-ridden and irresponsible Congolese army into a reliable force, and because it temporarily blocked efforts by Brussels, Washington, and other friendly states to pursue the same objective. The major ANC problem was the absence of an effective officer corps, a problem that could be corrected in the short run only by filling the great majority of officer and NCO posts with Europeans. Under the circumstances, virtually the only qualified Europeans acceptable to the Congolese were Belgians. And Hammarskjold was strongly opposed to the use of Belgian military personnel whom he regarded as morally disqualified. The Secretary-General made several abortive attempts to install officer training programs staffed largely by Afro-Asians, but this offended General Mobutu who wanted European officers, advisers, and technicians of his own choosing. The net effect of U.N. policy was to delay, perhaps by three years, effective bilateral military aid programs desperately needed and wanted by the government. This delay has had serious consequences.

On the deeper psychological and political level, it should have been clear from the outset that a multinational effort serving as the instrument of a voluntary coalition of states with different interests was a singularly inappropriate agency for helping a weak and divided government to deal with the highly sensitive problem of national security. When governments are in serious trouble, they almost always turn to a close ally or another friendly state. In fact, this is exactly what the Congo Cabinet (in the absence of Kasavubu and Lumumba) did on July 12, 1960, when it asked Washington for 3,000 American troops to restore order. The deployment of Belgian paratroopers, though there was virtually no bloodshed, and the announcement of Katanga's secession, of course, changed the character of the crisis, and Lumumba promptly rejected the idea of American assistance. These developments also ruled out the most obvious and immediate source of aid—the former metropolitan power. Since military assistance is always sensitive, the relation between the donor and recipient governments must be intimate and confidential. No multinational U.N. operation with a multinational staff could meet the minimal requirements of security and confidence. For this basic reason, it was unrealistic to expect the U.N. Mission to make any real progress in helping the government build a reliable army.

The clearest accomplishment of the UNF was to end the secession of Katanga and thus contribute to the territorial integrity of the country. It also contributed to the political integrity of the Congo by closing the airports in September, 1960, which frustrated direct Soviet military assistance to the deposed Lumumba. But the UNF did nothing to protect the government from the rising rebel movements of late 1963 and 1964. Reflecting the general view of its Afro-Asian supporters, the U.N. Mission was far less concerned about the Peking and Moscow-backed rebels who threatened to overthrow the Adoula government in 1964 than about secessionist Katanga in 1962, which sought only an unspecified degree of autonomy from the Adoula government. This differential in concern was due primarily to the mistaken beliefs that Tshombe was simply the puppet of European economic interests and that the ambiguous Belgian support of Tshombe in 1960 was a stra-tegem to reassert Belgian authority in the Congo. Further, some of the Afro-Asians accorded more legitimacy to the rebels who were receiving military aid from the Soviet bloc and China through Algeria and the U.A.R. than to the moderate Adoula government.

The net internal political impact of the U.N. mission, perhaps not explicitly intended by the Secretary-General, was to support the con cept of a strong central government as opposed to a loose confedera-tion, and to support a moderate government as opposed to a militant one.

EFFECT ON INTERESTED STATES

The United Nations is a creature of the multistate system and not a substitute for it. It was established to serve legitimate national inter-ests and the larger though not inconsistent interests of international peace and security. It is, therefore, entirely appropriate to ask what impact the U.N. Congo operation had upon the interests of the states most directly concerned, insofar as this impact can be distinguished from that of other forces moving in substantially the same direction.

In the Congo itself, as noted above, the UNF helped to maintain order and territorial integrity. It reinforced efforts moving toward a unified and moderate central government, thus helping to block the political militants and the territorial secessionists. On the other hand, Hammarskjold's anti-Belgian policies delayed the restoration of essen-tial administrative and internal security services, though the amount of damage resulting from these policies is impossible to ascertain. In his final report, Thant implied that the UNF had remained in the Congo too long. He may have been right. The internal security situation in mid-1963 was better than it was a year later, but this deterioration can-not be laid to the door of the UNF. It should be recalled that the rebel movements reached their highest pitch after the U.N. troops left.

Given the situation in mid-1964, the complete withdrawal of the UNF at that point doubtless helped the rebels.

As a holding operation, the UNF contributed to the security interests of the Congo, but it fell far short of what was required. In a certain sense it was always an obstacle, perhaps a necessary one, to the free give-and-take between developed and underdeveloped states that is so essential to the strengthening of the weaker partners. Had the U.N. not intervened, however, the Congo might have become an arena of Cold War rivalry to the detriment of the Congolese people. On the other hand, rivalry between Washington and Moscow might have benefited the Congo as it has in some other countries of the Third World such as India.

Long-range Belgian interests were served by the UNF, though this does not mean they might not have been served equally well or better by alternative ways of dealing with the 1960 crisis. The same can be said of Western interests generally. The United States, its allies, and the European neutralists all wanted a stable Congo with a moderate government capable of sustaining mutually beneficial relations with other states. The total U.N. presence contributed toward this end.

The force of some arguments heard in Washington for providing military assistance through U.N. channels rather than giving it directly eroded with unfolding events. Adlai Stevenson's hope that U.N. intervention would keep the Cold War out of the Congo went unfulfilled. Harlan Cleveland spoke of the risk of "a confrontation of nuclear powers in the center of Africa." This fear was hardly credible in light of earlier Soviet threats to intervene by direct military means in distant disputes. Ambassador Edmund Gullion compared the U.N. presence to a lightning rod which was expected to absorb charges of neo-colonialism that might otherwise be directed against the United States, presumably from the Afro-Asians. The lightning rod was not effective. U.N. troops were called "American mercenaries," and Washington was frequently charged with carrying a neo-colonial dagger under the U.N. cloak. Moscow never made a political or moral distinction between direct U.S. military assistance, which started quietly in October, 1962, and U.S. support through the United Nations.

The U.N. operation did not prevent a political confrontation between the West and the Communist states in the Congo, but it did impose legal and political constraints which lent support to the efforts of Washington and other capitals working for a unified state and a moderate government. Conversely, the mission reinforced those elements inside and outside the Congo that resisted the designs of Russia,

Red China, and the militant African states in Central Africa. The effect of the UNF was a net gain for the United States and a net loss for the Soviet Union. In the Afro-Asian world the interests of the moderates were served and the objectives of the militants were frustrated.

From its sudden birth to its demise the UNF was a novel and controversial experiment. It was assailed on all sides. In many respects it was inefficient, wasteful, and confused. But, measured against its primary political goal—international stability—it made a modest but constructive contribution.

WAS THERE A BETTER OPTION?

Was there a politically feasible alternative in July, 1960, that would have served the interests of the Congo and the more inclusive interests of peace as well or better than U.N. intervention? There can be no conclusive answer to this question because there are too many contingent factors. Nevertheless, speculation, while risky, may be of some value.

The Tanganyika crisis in January, 1964, which bears some resemblance to the earlier Congo crisis, throws some light on the problem. On January 21 and 22, two battalions of Tanganyika army mutinied against their British officers and demanded higher pay and total Africanization of the officer corps. This led to rioting in the streets of Dar es Salaam. President Julius Nyerere called for emergency military assistance from Britain, from whom his country had received independence just two years before, to halt the mutiny. About 500 Royal Marine commandos were brought in from Aden and they quickly restored order. The Tanganyika mutiny was followed by similar but smaller disorders in Uganda and Kenya. They, too, requested and received British military aid. In each case the British were invited, did their job with almost no bloodshed (one man was killed and two were injured in Tanganyika), and left promptly at the request of the host state. Eventually Ethiopian and Nigerian troops replaced the British in Tanganyika and stayed about a year.

In the Tanganyika crisis, which was complicated by the Zanzibar coup on January 12, there is no evidence that Nyerere ever contemplated turning to the United Nations for military assistance. He wanted quick and reliable action, and he felt the former metropole could best provide the help. In fact, he probably saw the U.N. Congo operation as a negative precedent. He knew that the UNF had made no progress in solving the mutinous ANC problem in three-and-one-half years.

Considerable evidence indicates that many African leaders in 1964 and since, generally oppose U.N. intervention in disputes among themselves. Many, perhaps most, African leaders were not fully satisfied with the accomplishments of the Congo mission and regard a similar experience in their countries as one to be avoided. These same men, however, generally favor U.N. action against "European regimes" in Africa. For their purpose, Tshombe was labeled a "European stooge" and his regime was lumped together with the governments of Angola, Rhodesia, and the Republic of South Africa as an appropriate target for U.N. condemnation and action. This African posture, particularly pronounced among the militant leaders, demonstrates that these leaders are more interested in using the United Nations as an instrument for accomplishing their goal of "decolonization," rather than as an instrument for containing conflict and keeping peace. The Afro-Asian states made no move to secure U.N. action to stop the bloodbath in the Congo in 1964 or in Nigeria in 1966. They did not recommend censure of the oppressive regime of Nkrumah in Ghana. In short, there has developed a kind of double ethic which, unchecked, can lead to further turmoil in Africa.[5]

There were many political differences between the Congo and Tanganyika situations, especially in the relation of the new states to their former colonial powers, but in the first few days there was a great similarity in the two crises. In both cases, the mutineers demanded better pay and some prospect for professional advancement. But in Dar es Salaam, the demands for Africanization of the officer corps were more specific and insistent, and the crisis was related, at least psychologically, to political events in Zanzibar, including the involvement of Red China and Cuba. In Leopoldville, the initial army protest was mild and apparently unrelated to outside political interests. This suggests that prompt and decisive disciplinary action against the mutinous soldiers at Camp Leopold II by their Belgian officers at the *first stage* of the crisis might have nipped it in the bud and without bloodshed. The Belgian officers of the then *Force Publique* had the authority to discipline their troops without special permission from the government. Their indecisiveness and panic doubtless encouraged the spread of the mutiny throughout the Force.

[5] See Thomas J. Hamilton, "U.N. and New Africa," *New York Times,* February 2, 1964, p. E–9.

The *second stage* of the crisis was characterized by panic in the European population. As a precaution, Brussels flew in paratroopers, but did not deploy them for several days while Belgian officials pleaded with the government for permission to intervene to restore order. Lumumba refused. Finally, in desperation, the Belgians started to deploy paratroopers without permission on July 10. Though already late, this action, along with the efforts then underway to meet some of the soldiers' demands, would probably have restored order were it not for two fateful events on July 11 which transformed the crisis into its *third* and most critical stage. The first event was Tshombe's proclamation of independence and the other was the Matadi incident in which about a dozen Congolese were killed in a clash with Belgian forces. From then on, an official request for Belgian military assistance was precluded as long as Lumumba was Prime Minister.

In retrospect, it appears that decisive Belgian action at the first or second stage of the crisis, with the quiet diplomatic support of Britain, France, and the United States, as suggested by President de Gaulle, might have been the best and least costly alternative for containing the original mutiny.

After the Matadi incident and Tshombe's secession, the only feasible sources of external aid were Moscow, Washington, or the joint action of Britain, France, and the United States. From a Western perspective, we can rule out Moscow because aid from this source would hardly have enhanced stability in Central Africa. Washington could have done the job, and was invited to do so on July 12, but refused to assist directly mainly because she overestimated the political cost of such assistance. This miscalculation resulted in part from exaggerated reports of the disorder and oversensitivity on the part of Washington to charges of "neo-colonialism." Some observers believe that a quickly dispatched U.S. military presence in mid-July could have stopped the mutiny without firing a shot; this study has encountered no evidence to contradict this view. If this were the case, the political backlash of U.S. aid in 1960 probably would have been considerably smaller and less intense than the criticism of the Belgian-American rescue mission to Stanleyville in November, 1964. In the Stanleyville mission Washington was accused of backing "reactionary" Tshombe as Prime Minister against the Communist-supported rebels. In 1960, Washington would have had the propaganda advantage of helping to guarantee the independence of the Congo whose Prime Minister was Lumumba, the "great African nationalist."

It is probable, though not provable, that earlier Belgian action or later U.S. aid would have been less costly and more effective than U.N. intervention. But given the clouded reading of the Congo situation in Washington and the prevailing political assumptions at the time, including the fear that America's anti-colonial image may be tarnished, the State Department felt that Washington should not move directly, even with a legitimate invitation. The vague fear of some kind of unspecified clash with the Soviet Union also contributed to the U.S. decision.

With the entire Congo drama, including the U.N. effort and the Stanleyville rescue mission, as a guide and warning, the President would probably be very reluctant to support a large U.N. peacekeeping force in any future crisis, especially if the threat to international peace was not clear and if there were a serious internal conflict in the host state or states. He would carefully weigh the comparative political costs and consequences of bilateral aid, joint action with several allies, action through a regional organization, and U.N. intervention. Given its inherent limitations, U.N. action should not be regarded as the first option for crisis management, but rather as a last resort. U.N. involvement should be considered when the more conventional means involve unacceptable costs or risks. This general guideline leaves plenty of room for disagreement over when U.N. action should be pressed in a particular crisis.

The Congo experience dramatizes the severely limited peace*making* capacity of a U.N. peace*keeping* force when the host state is torn by internal conflict. In this situation, a protracted U.N. presence may actually obstruct the normal processes of internal political adjustment and accommodation, thus freezing the situation and delaying a political settlement. *Peacekeeping,* by definition, is designed to stabilize a crisis, not to settle the conflict that caused it. In this sense, peacekeeping is similar to police action to restore order. *Peacemaking,* on the other hand, is essentially political and dynamic. It is concerned with the peaceful resolution of conflicting interests, and involves threats, bargaining, adjustment, and compromise. A settlement, peaceful or otherwise, can be achieved only by the conflicting parties themselves or be imposed from without by a strong third party. A third party may help the conflicting parties to get together, but the third party cannot *make* peace.

The Secretary-General was never given authority to impose a political solution on the Congo. The main function of the UNF was to stabilize the situation so that the internal conflicts might be resolved without violence. The U.N. civilian presence, however, was given the responsibility to help facilitate a settlement among the rival political claimants. This meant that the U.N. mission had both a *peacekeeping* and *peacemaking* function. It tried simultaneously to keep the peace and work for a political settlement. In this two-pronged task, it was forced to take sides, thus violating its strict peacekeeping and mediation role. It became involved in these confused and not wholly compatible functions not by deliberate design, but as the result of a series of Council and Assembly decisions over a period of time in response to unfolding events in the Congo and changes in the international climate. This inevitable, though regrettable, confusion could have been avoided only by giving the Secretary-General a mandate limited to peacekeeping or to peacemaking, not both.

Normally peacemaking should precede peacekeeping. The peacekeepers need a peace to keep, an agreed border to observe, or a neutral zone to police. Only when the conflicting parties have an interest in stabilizing the situation and when there is a specific agreement, can peacekeeping be effective. Such was the case in UNEF. But a U.N. presence cannot effectively keep the peace in a crucible of unresolved conflict like the Congo.

The U.N. Congo Mission points to the serious danger in overloading a fragile instrumentality that has to depend upon the voluntary support from a coalition of states for any positive action. The so-called U.N. financial crisis was only a symptom of the basic political disunity in the organization and the larger world, disunity which is likely to manifest itself in any serious future threat to the peace. On the other hand, there are smaller and more limited crises in which the United Nations might be employed to achieve or supervise a truce. UNEF is the best example of effective U.N. peace observation. It should be abundantly clear from the events of May, 1967, that UNEF was effective only as long as Israel *and* the U.A.R. wanted it to be. When President Nasser no longer wanted the U.N. observers, who were deployed only on Egyptian soil, he ordered them to leave. U Thant speedily complied.

Peace and stability in the Third World are not served by overlooking the inherent and inescapable limitations of the United Nations as an instrument for states that want to contain conflict or facilitate peaceful change. Secretary-General Thant, having seen the Congo experiment to its end, appears to recognize these limitations. Perhaps if Dag Hammarskjold had lived, he too would have more fully realized the implications of his own words in 1956, a few weeks after UNEF had been established. During those harried days he issued a "solid warning" to governments inclined to shift too much to the shoulders of the Secretary-General in "sheer escapism" from their own responsibilities.[6]

[6] Quoted in *The Reporter* (October 26, 1961), p. 22.

The U.N. Congo Mission was launched by a Security Council Resolution on July 14, 1960, with the strong support of the Eisenhower Administration. Here, U.S. Ambassador Henry Cabot Lodge confers with Secretary-General Dag Hammarskjold. (Chapters 1 and 4) *United Nations Photo*

The Soviet Union voted for the original Congo Resolution, but withdrew its support of the operation three months later in opposition to Hammarskjold's policies. Here the Soviet representative, A. A. Sobolev (right) confers with the Secretary-General during the July, 1960, Security Council debate. In the middle is José A. Correa of Ecuador, the Council President. (Chapters 1 and 5) *United Nations Photo*

The erratic behavior of Prime Minister Patrice Lumumba, seen here talking with Secretary-General Dag Hammarskjold in New York, was a major factor in precipitating the Congo crisis. It also led to trouble with Hammarskjold, Western diplomats, and top Congolese politicians. President Kasavubu dismissed him on September 5, 1960. (Chapter 3) *United Nations Photo*

Hammarskjold's executive assistant, Andrew W. Cordier (in the white shirt), attempted to calm down the Lumumba-Kasavubu dispute in September, 1960, by closing Radio Leopoldville and by closing all Congolese airports to Soviet planes. Here, he is talking with Major General Carl C. von Horn (Sweden), U.N. Force Commander, and Brigadier I. J. Rikhye (India), Hammarskjold's military advisor. (Chapter 3) *United Nations Photo*

Ralph Bunche (U.S.), U.N. Undersecretary, briefing Rajeshwar Dayal (India) for his assignment as U.N. Officer in Charge in the Congo. Dayal became a controversial figure for the alleged support of the Lumumba cause and other reasons and was removed by Hammarskjold in March, 1961. (Chapter 3) *United Nations Photo*

Robert A. K. Gardiner (Ghana), seen here with Ralph Bunche in front of the U.N. Headquarters in Leopoldville, was the highly regarded U.N. Officer in Charge who served in the Congo from February, 1962, to May, 1963. (Chapter 3) *United Nations Photo*

Conor Cruise O'Brien (Ireland), who launched the highly controversial U.N. military operation against Katanga on September 13, 1961, is seen here with officers of the Swedish battalion in Elisabethville. The O'Brien affair was a great embarrassment to Hammarskjold and was strongly criticized by Britain and France. (Chapters 3 and 10) *United Nations Photo*

Here, Indian U.N. troops are waiting to cross the Lufira River during Round Three, in which the U.N. Force ended the secession of Katanga. This crossing was made against explicit orders from New York. Subsequently, Brigadier Reginald S. Noronha, the officer responsible for the decision, was fully exonerated after an on-the-spot investigation by Ralph Bunche. (Chapters 3 and 10) *United Nations Photo*

The U.N. Force engaged in three military clashes with Katanga forces to end the secession of the province. Here two U.N. soldiers, protected by their disabled armored vehicle, attempt to flush out Katanga gendarmerie in Elisabethville during Round Two in December, 1961. Note the U.N. olive-branch symbol on the vehicle and the arm patch. (Chapters 3 and 10) *United Nations Photo*

During the four-year operation, there were five U.N. Force Commanders of five nationalities. The most respected one, who also saw the longest service in the Congo, was Lieutenant General Kebede Gebre of Ethiopia (in light uniform) shown inspecting troops of the Nigerian contingent. (Chapter 10) *United Nations Photo*

U.S. diplomatic representatives in the Congo worked actively to settle the political conflict between the General Government and Katanga. Pictured here is Ambassador Edmond Gullion with the two Congolese antagonists, Moise Tshombe (center) and Prime Minister Adoula, at the Kitona Conference in December, 1961. President Kennedy made available his presidential plane to transport Tshombe to the unsuccessful conference. (Chapter 4) *United Nations Photo*

Throughout the entire U.N. Mission, General Joseph Mobutu was the Commander in Chief of the Congolese National Army. Mobutu (seen here inspecting an honor guard at Williams Air Force Base in Arizona), consistently opposed U. N. efforts to train his officers and expressed a strong preference for Belgian assistance. Starting in 1963, the Adoula government accepted bilateral military aid from Belgium, the United States, Israel, and Italy. (Chapters 3, 4, and 7) *U.S. Air Force Photo*

Lieutenant General Louis Truman (far left) led an eight-man U.S. Mission to the Congo in December, 1962, to see what additional American military supplies were needed to support the U.N. effort to end secession in Katanga. Here, Colonel Knut H. Raudstein (next to Truman), U.S. Army attaché, escorts party at Leopoldville airport. (Chapters 3 and 4) *Courtesy of the author*

Washington airlifted 74,396 U.N. troops and 10,446 tons of cargo to or from the Congo. Along with its sealift, the U.S. transported 118,091 troops and 18,596 tons. The U.S. Air Force also provided substantial internal airlift. Here Pakistani troops are unloaded from a *Globemaster* at Leopoldville. (Chapter 4) *U.S. Air Force Photo*

During late 1963 and 1964, various rebel movements seriously threatened the Leopoldville government. The rebels were often armed with primitive weapons (left). "General" Nicholas Olenga (right), a major rebel leader in the Stanleyville area, had political contacts with militant African governments. (Chapter 12) (a) *Photo by Stig von Bayer* (b) *Courtesy of the author*

The Soviet Union and Red China provided weapons and ammunition for the Congolese rebels as well as political support. The smaller shell pictured above is a 12.7 mm. Chinese shell. The Chinese also provided anti-tank weapons. (Chapter 12) *Courtesy of the author*

Appendixes

APPENDIX A

<small>Concise Chronology of Congo Events: 1960–1964[1]</small>

Lumumba government, June 30–Sept. 5, 1960

July 5–14 . . . . Congolese Army mutiny, panic, and Belgian action.
July 11 . . . . . . Tshombe declares Katanga independent.
July 14 . . . . . . First U.N. resolution authorizes peacekeeping mission.
September 5 . . Kasavubu dismisses Lumumba; appoints Ileo.

Council of Commissioners, Sept. 14, 1960–Feb. 9, 1961

September 14 . Mobutu coup establishes Council of Commissioners.
November 22 . Kasavubu delegation seated at the United Nations.
December 12 . Gizenga establishes rival regime in Stanleyville.

Ileo government, Feb. 9–Aug. 2, 1961

February 13 . . Lumumba's death in Katanga announced.
February 21 . . U.N. authorizes military force to prevent civil war.
March 8–12 . . Tananarive conference (Confederation Plan).
Apr. 24–May 28 Coquilhatville conference (Federal Plan).
July 27–Aug. 2 Lovanium Parliament (Crisis ended by electing Adoula).

[1] President Kasavubu was in office during this entire period.

Adoula government, Aug. 2, 1961–June 30, 1964

August 5	Gizenga recognizes Adoula government.
Sept. 13–21 . .	*Round One* (inconclusive clash between UNF and Katanga).
December 5–19	*Round Two* (inconclusive clash between UNF and Katanga).
Dec. 20–21 . . .	Kitona Accord; Tshombe recognizes Adoula government.

1962

January 16 . . .	Adoula removes and arrests Deputy Prime Minister Gizenga.
March–June .	Adoula-Tshombe talks on Katanga inconclusive.
August 20	Thant Plan for National Reconciliation announced.
December 14 .	Thant requests economic sanctions against Katanga.

1963

Dec. 28–Jan. 21	*Round Three* (Katanga secession ended by UNF).
June 14	Tshombe leaves the country for self-imposed exile.
September 29 .	Parliament indefinitely adjourned.
October 2	National Liberation Committee formed in Brazzaville.

1964

January	Rebellion breaks out in Kwilu.
Feb.–June . . .	Rebellion spreads through one-third of Congo by June.
June 26	Tshombe returns to Leopoldville from self-imposed exile.
June 30	Last UNF troops leave Congo.
July 9	Tshombe becomes Prime Minister.

APPENDIX B

Cables from the Congo Requesting U.N. Military Aid[1]

I. Telegram dated July 12, 1960, from the President and the Prime Minister of the Republic of the Congo to the Secretary-General

The Government of the Republic of the Congo requests urgent dispatch by the United Nations of military assistance. This request is justified by the dispatch to the Congo of metropolitan Belgian troops in violation of the treaty of friendship signed between Belgium and the Republic of the Congo

[1] These two telegrams, dated July 12 and 13, 1960, were sent by the President and the Prime Minister of the Republic of the Congo to the Secretary-General and were circulated by him on July 13 as U.N. Document S/4382.

on 29 June 1960. Under the terms of that treaty, Belgian troops may only intervene on the express request of the Congolese Government. No such request was ever made by the Government of the Republic of the Congo and we therefore regard the unsolicited Belgian action as an act of aggression against our country.

The real cause of most of the disturbances can be found in colonialist machinations. We accuse the Belgian Government of having carefully prepared the secession of Katanga with a view to maintaining a hold on our country. The Government, supported by the Congolese people, refuses to accept a *fait accompli* resulting from a conspiracy between Belgian imperialists and a small group of Katanga leaders. The overwhelming majority of the Katanga population is opposed to secession, which means the disguised perpetuation of the colonialist régime. The essential purpose of the requested military aid is to protect the national territory of the Congo against the present external aggression which is a threat to international peace. We strongly stress the extremely urgent need for the dispatch of United Nations troops to the Congo.

(Signed) Joseph KASAVUBU
President of the Republic of the Congo and
Supreme Commander of the National Army
(Signed) Patrice LUMUMBA
Prime Minister and Minister of National Defence

II. TELEGRAM DATED JULY 13, 1960, FROM THE PRESIDENT AND THE PRIME MINISTER OF THE REPUBLIC OF THE CONGO TO THE SECRETARY-GENERAL

In connexion with military assistance requested of the United Nations by the Republic of the Congo, the Chief of State and the Prime Minister of the Congo make the following clarification: (1) the purpose of the aid requested is not to restore the internal situation in Congo but rather to protect the national territory against acts of aggression committed by Belgian metropolitan troops; (2) the request for assistance relates only to a United Nations force consisting of military personnel from neutral countries and not from the United States as reported by certain radio stations; (3) if the assistance requested is not received without delay the Republic of the Congo will be obliged to appeal to the Bandung Treaty Powers; (4) the aid has been requested by the Republic of the Congo in the exercise of its sovereign rights and not in agreement with Belgium as reported.

(Signed) Joesph KASAVUBU
President of the Republic of the Congo
(Signed) Patrice LUMUMBA
Prime Minister and Minister of National Defence

APPENDIX C

BASIC AGREEMENT BETWEEN THE SECRETARY-GENERAL AND THE CONGO GOVERNMENT[1]

1. The Government of the Republic of the Congo states that, in the exercise of its sovereign rights with respect to any question concerning the presence and functioning of the United Nations Force in the Congo, it will be guided, in good faith, by the fact that it has requested military assistance from the United Nations and by its acceptance of the resolutions of the Security Council of 14 and 22 July 1960; it likewise states that it will ensure the freedom of movement of the Force in the interior of the country and will accord the requisite privileges and immunities to all personnel associated with the activities of the Force.

2. The United Nations takes note of this statement of the Government of the Republic of the Congo and states that, with regard to the activities of the United Nations Force in the Congo, it will be guided, in good faith, by the task assigned to the Force in the aforementioned resolutions; in particular the United Nations reaffirms, considering it to be in accordance with the wishes of the Government of the Republic of the Congo, that it is prepared to maintain the United Nations Force in the Congo until such time as it deems the latter's task to have been fully accomplished.

3. The Government of the Republic of the Congo and the Secretary-General state their intention to proceed immediately, in the light of paragraphs 1 and 2 above, to explore jointly specific aspects of the functioning of the United Nations Force in the Congo, notably with respect to its deployment, the question of its lines of communication and supply, its lodging and its provisioning; the Government of the Republic of the Congo, confirming its intention to facilitate the functioning of the United Nations Force in the Congo, and the United Nations have agreed to work together to hasten the implementation of the guiding principles laid down in consequence of the work of joint exploration on the basis of the resolutions of the Security Council.

4. The foregoing provisions shall likewise be applicable, as appropriate, to the non-military aspects of the United Nations operation in the Congo.

---

[1] This "basic agreement" between Mr. Hammarskjold and Leopoldville was initialed on July 29, 1960. It was circulated as U.N. Document S/4389/Add. 5. This contract was superseded by a full Status Agreement, November 27, 1961.

APPENDIX D

U.N. Civilian and Military Representatives in the Congo
1960–1964

Officers in Charge[1]

1. Ralph J. Bunche (U.S.), July 13, 1960–August 27, 1960
2. Andrew W. Cordier (U.S.), August 27, 1960–September 6, 1960
3. Rajeshwar Dayal (India), September 8, 1960–May 25, 1961
4. Indar Jit Rikhye, Acting (India), November 3, 1960–November 23, 1960
5. Mekki Abbas, Acting (Sudan), March 10, 1961–May 20, 1961
6. Sture Linner (Sweden), May 20, 1961–February 10, 1962
7. Robert Gardiner (Ghana), February 10, 1962–May 1, 1963
8. Max H. Dorsinville (Haiti), May 1, 1963–April 30, 1964
9. Bibiano F. Osorio-Tafall, Acting (Mexico), April 30, 1964–June 30, 1964

Representatives in Elisabethville

1. Ian E. Berendsen (New Zealand), August, 1960–March, 1961
2. Georges Dumontet (France), March, 1961–May, 1961
3. Conor Cruise O'Brien (Ireland), June, 1961–November, 1961
4. Brain E. Urquhart (U.K.), November, 1961–January, 1962
5. George Ivan Smith, Acting (Australia), December, 1961
6. Georges Dumontet, Acting (France), December 27, 1961–January, 1962
7. Jose Rolz-Bennett (Guatemala), January, 1962–June, 1962
8. Jean Back (France), June, 1962
9. Eliud Mathu (Kenya), June, 1962–May, 1963
10. George L. Sherry, Acting (U.S.), January, 1963–February, 1963
11. A. Nashashibi (Jordan), May, 1963–June, 1964

Force Commanders

1. Major General Carl von Horn (Sweden), August, 1960–December, 1960
2. Lieutenant General Sean McKeown (Ireland), January, 1961–March, 1962
3. Lieutenant General Kebede Gebre (Ethiopia), April, 1962–July, 1963
4. Major General Christian R. Kaldager (Norway), August, 1963–December, 1963
5. Major General J. T. U. Aguiyu Ironsi (Nigeria), January, 1964–June, 1964

U.N. Commanders in Katanga

1. Colonel H. W. Byone (Ireland), August, 1960–December, 1960
2. Brigadier K. A. S. Raja (India), March, 1961–April, 1962
3. Major General D. Prem Chand (India), May, 1962–April, 1963
4. Colonel Worku Metaferia, Acting (Ethiopia), April, 1963–June, 1963
5. Brigadier General Abebe Teferra (Ethiopia), June, 1963–June, 1964

[1]Until May 25, 1961, this title was *Special Representative of the Secretary-General.*

APPENDIX E

MANPOWER CONTRIBUTION TO THE U.N. FORCE BY STATES [1]

(Expressed in Man-Months, August 2, 1960–June 20, 1964)

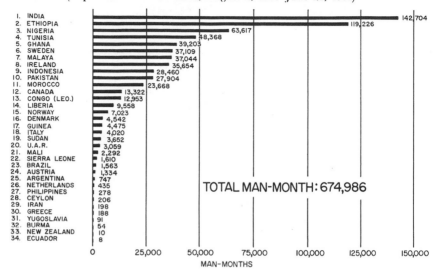

APPENDIX F

CHANGES IN U.N. FORCE COMPOSITION

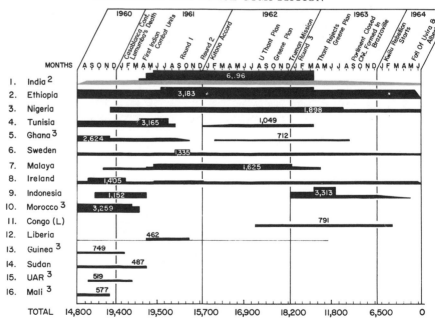

1. This chart was prepared from official U.N. records.
2. The gray bar represents Indian service units.
3. Participant in the Casablanca Conference, January 3-7, 1961.

APPENDIX G

MESSAGE FROM THE SECRETARY-GENERAL ON ORDINANCE 70[1]

We have studied with care the text of your telegrams 1981–82 and think that the letter that Adoula sent or directed to you represents an important first step which concerns the Katanga problem. I am nevertheless of the opinion that the first step must be followed, in the quickest and most energetic way, by other acts in the name of the Central Government. We must at all costs avoid pursuing long discussions, either with the Katangese authorities or with the Belgian authorities.

It seems to me, then, that the Adoula Government should immediately issue an order, the terms of which should declare as "undesirable" all the non-Congolese officers and mercenaries serving in the Katangese forces who have not accepted a contract obligation with the Central Government and demand that they leave the Congolese territory without delay. The Government should then inform us of this order in a new letter which refers to the last letter. [Emphasis added.]

In this new letter, the government should add that, the persons in question have been placed under the threat of an expulsion order, and it asks us for assistance to assure the execution of this order conforming to paragraph A–2 [of the February 21, 1961 Resolution] and taking into account security factors.

The forces of ONU to Katanga should have thus been led to act against the non-Congolese officers of the gendarmerie, not only by virtue of the paragraph A–2 but also in execution of the Central Government's orders. Then we could pay attention to, in the first place, the expulsion of those Belgian officers whose positions are enumerated in the Third Egge Report. If the Government would see the possibility of formally issuing an order of this nature, O'Brien and his collaborateurs could take immediate measures to take care that the report is fully executed.

It goes without saying that if the Government would take such measures, it would reinforce its position not only with regard to Katanga, but also with regard to the so-called Stanleyville group. I hope to receive here tomorrow a second letter from Adoula, of the sort that precious time will not be lost in vain.

By right of preliminary measures, I will enter a report with the Belgian delegation here to make known to them that a good many weeks have passed since the time when the Egge Report has been presented to them without them having made known any reaction. I will give notice that the question becomes more urgent from now on than it has ever been in the past and that I intend to furnish all assistance possible to the Central Government in solving the Katanga problem. With regard to the Belgian Government, I hope that it will order the withdrawal of its jurisdictions, enumerated in the Egge Report, in a way to not find itself in a new and embarrassing political situation.

[1] This cable from Mr. Hammarskjold to Mahmoud Khiary, the Chief of U.N. Civilian Operations in the Congo, was sent on August 23, 1961. It recommends that the Adoula government "should immediately issue an order" which would strengthen the hand of the United Nations in arresting prohibited foreigners. Ordinance 70 was the result.

APPENDIX H

BRIEF SKETCHES OF MILITARY INCIDENTS AND DEVELOPMENTS[1]

1. BELGIAN INTERVENTION IN MATADI: JULY 11, 1960

Background: On July 8 and 9, there was some disorder in the port city of Matadi at the mouth of the Congo River. Congolese soldiers and policemen attacked, beat, and imprisoned some Europeans. Fearing Belgian intervention, Kasavubu and Lumumba came to Matadi and released the captive Europeans and apologized for the mistreatment of Europeans by the Congolese.

Incident: On July 11, the Belgians intervened to prevent looting and to insure access to the port. The *S.S. Kamina,* four armed escort boats, and three armed smaller boats with about 100 Belgian marines occupied the town. Four *Harvard* planes flew overhead to impress the Congolese. Not a shot was fired.

Suddenly fighting started. The Belgians fired at least four 75 milimeter shells on the port. The cause of the fighting is obscure. A *Harvard* crashed and some observers believe that the Congolese thought it was the beginning of an air attack. One *Harvard* attacked a Congolese armored column on its way from Thysville to Matadi. All Belgian troops left Matadi on July 11.

Casualties: From 12 to 19 Congolese were killed, and 13 Belgians were wounded.

2. AMBUSH OF IRISH U.N. TROOPS AT NIEMBA: NOVEMBER 8, 1960

Background: There was a gradual buildup of Baluba irregular operations in northern Katanga from August through October, 1960. Troops of the Irish contingent, with headquarters in Albertville, were given the responsibility for maintaining law and order. To accomplish this, a number of small detachments were stationed in various key locations where they operated patrol bases. One of these was in Niemba. It was manned by an Irish platoon under the command of Lt. Kevin Gleason.

Incident: On November 8, Lt. Gleason left Niemba with a twelve-man patrol to open the road south of the town which had been blocked by Baluba irregulars. Despite warnings he had received from an experienced Swedish officer only the day before to be extremely careful in dealing with the Baluba, he permitted the patrol to be surrounded too closely by a group of Baluba a short distance from Niemba. The Baluba attacked unexpectedly splitting the patrol into two groups and massacred all but two men who were able to escape. One Irish soldier was recovered the day of the attack and the other, who was severely wounded, the day after by a relief patrol. A Baluba who had participated in the attack was later questioned to determine why a patrol which had operated in the same area a few days before had been left alone, and the November 8 patrol assaulted. He stated that the Baluba had "re-

---

[1] From the numerous military events during the first four years of the Congo's independence, the following nine have a special bearing on the analysis in this book. (Each is referred to in the text.)

ceived strong witchcraft" and that the earlier patrol had looked too aggressive to attack.

Casualties: Ten U.N. Irish personnel killed, two wounded. Number of Baluba casualties unknown.

3. ANC LEOPOLDVILLE ATTEMPT TO CAPTURE BUKAVU THROUGH RUANDA–URUNDI: DECEMBER 31, 1960–JANUARY 1, 1961

Background: By December, 1960, the Gizenga regime in Stanleyville had consolidated its influence in large parts of Kasai, Kivu, north Katanga, and western Leopoldville provinces. Gizenga announced on December 12, 1960, that Stanleyville would henceforth be the capital of the Congo. On December 25, some 60 Stanleyville ANC troops moved into Bukavu, capital of Kivu, and arrested the local ANC commander, accusing him of preparing to transfer allegiance to Leopoldville. They also arrested the provincial president and took them both to Stanleyville.

Incident: The Central Government reacted to the Bukavu arrests by moving approximately 100 Leopoldville ANC troops from Luluabourg into Ruanda–Urundi on December 31. These troops landed in Usumbura late New Year's eve and were moved by truck to the eastern end of the Ruzzi River bridge in Bukavu. About half of this number moved under the protection of a white flag across the bridge into Bukavu at dawn on January 1. The Stanleyville ANC garrison in Bukavu attacked the troops and forced them to surrender.

Concurrently a Belgian paratroop unit in Shangugu, Ruanda–Urundi, captured and disarmed the other 50 Leopoldville ANC troops on the Ruanda–Urundi side of the river. During this action, U.N. troops (Nigerian) were instructed to deploy in depth behind the Stanleyville ANC Bukavu garrison to avoid interfering with the ANC defenses, and to try to promote a cease-fire. U.N. troops did not become directly involved in the fighting, but provided their good offices to arrange a cease-fire. Although there was some sporadic firing across the border on January 3, 1961, the Leopoldville ANC made no attempts to cross the border after January 1.

Casualties: U.N.—none. Leopoldville ANC—two wounded. One Usumbura official was killed.

4. STANLEYVILLE ANC INTRUSION INTO NORTH KATANGA: JANUARY, 1961

Background: After the abortive attempt by Leopoldville ANC to enter Bukavu and establish control (see above incident), Gizenga appointed Anicet Kashamura as head of Kivu province on January 2, 1961, to consolidate Stanleyville control.

Incident: On the night of January 7, 1961, some 400 to 600 Stanleyville ANC troops, who had moved secretly through Kivu province and into northern Katanga, entered the town of Manono. They brought with them two Balubakat politicians, Prosper Mwamba Ilunga and André Shabani, who announced they were establishing the independent "Province of Lualaba." U.N. forces in Manono (Nigerian) were caught completely by surprise, despite the fact that the United Nations had agreed to exclude armed forces from this area in the Rikhye-Tshombe accord of October 17, 1960. As a result of this incident Tshombe abrogated the accord on January 12, 1961.

Casualties: U.N. forces—none. Stanleyville ANC casualties unknown, but presumed light, if any.

5. CONGOLESE MILITARY OPERATIONS ON THE EQUATEUR-ORIENTALE BORDER: FEBRUARY, 1961

Background: By the end of 1960, the Gizenga regime in Stanleyville had been established with an effective military force of 5,000 local ANC soldiers under General Victor Lundula. Gizenga also had 300 provincial gendarmerie who were personally loyal to him. Leopoldville's attempts to put down the rival regime had been limited to a partially successful economic blockade during the late fall of 1960. In late December and early January, the Stanleyville regime began operations which expanded into Kivu and north Katanga, and began to mass troops on the Orientale-Equateur border.

Operation: In order to counter the threat of a westward military expansion by the Stanleyville ANC, Leopoldville moved approximately 1,500 troops from Leopoldville into the Bumba area in Equateur province and concurrently redeployed elements of the twentieth ANC battalion from Coquilhatville eastward to Bumba. In Lisala, west of Bumba, the civilian population, in reaction to ANC plundering, attacked the ANC. The U.N. Commander met with General Mobutu on February 21, to discuss the establishment of a neutral zone between the regions occupied by Leopoldville and Stanleyville ANC.

On February 25, 1961, Stanleyville ANC bypassed Mobutu's forces to the south and crossed into Equateur province at Ikela where the local Leopoldville ANC surrendered. Leopoldville ANC reinforcements sent from Boende, west of Ikela, defected to the Stanleyville ANC. Concurrently, there were Leopoldville ANC movements from Coquilhatville to Boende and Ingende which involved no fighting. These movements culminated in the surrender of an additional company of the Leopoldville ANC. By the end of February, the U.N. Force Commander had secured the agreement of General Lundula in Stanleyville to withdraw his forces from Equateur province on the condition that the UNF occupy Ikela.

Casualties: No reports of casualties are available. They were extremely light, if any.

6. INCIDENTS BETWEEN ANC TROOPS AND U.N. TROOPS AT BANANA, MATADI, AND KITONA: MARCH 3–6, 1961

Background: Among the first U.N. facilities established in the lower Congo were the major base at Kitona, a small facility at the port of Matadi, and a small naval facility at Banana at the mouth of the Congo River. Previously under the control of the Moroccans, a Sudanese battalion of reduced strength had been made responsible for securing these three facilities in mid-February 1961. Total U.N. strength was only 350 in the lower Congo against a total of 1,000 ANC, of which about 600 were in Matadi.

Incident: On February 28, the U.N. civilian administrator at Kitona and a sergeant were arrested and the sergeant disarmed. About noon on March 3, a U.N. civilian radio operator arrived at the Moanda commercial airfield and was arrested because he had no U.N. identification. Released for dinner, he returned to the airport with the commander of the Sudanese contingent, escorted by a Sudanese security detachment. Halted by the ANC, the Sudanese fired overhead shots, causing four of the ANC troops to drop their arms and flee. Two Congolese surrendered.

After the Sudanese commander's departure the detachment attempted to return the two Congolese to the ANC camp in Banana. Fired on by a Congolese soldier from the rear, the Sudanese returned fire, killing a Congolese soldier. Late in the afternoon the ANC opened fire on the U.N. camp in Banana, ultimately causing the U.N. detachment to withdraw from the base to Kitona about midnight of March 3. During the same evening communications between the Sudanese outposts in Matadi and the company headquarters were cut. Civilians vacated the streets during the night and, in mid-morning of March 4, the Canadian signal detachment in the Hotel Metropole found itself surrounded. Sporadic firing was opened by the ANC and returned by the Sudanese guard detachment. Concurrently, the Sudanese camp was taken under small arms fire. The fire-fight continued with several interruptions during the rest of the day and into March 5 when a U.N. liaison officer, the Acting Chief of Staff of the ANC, and the Minister of the Interior (acting as Minister of Defense) opened negotiations for a cease-fire. At noon the Congolese again opened fire, apparently prearranged. Faced with a shortage of ammunition, and clearly overwhelming Congolese strength the local Sudanese commander agreed to a cease-fire on condition of Sudanese withdrawal from Matadi. The Sudanese were disarmed and moved out of Matadi on March 6 leaving the port unoccupied by the United Nations until June 19, 1961.

Casualties: ANC not reported and unknown. U.N.—two Sudanese soldiers killed.

7. Ghanian U.N. Troops Killed by ANC Troops at Port Francqui: April 28, 1961

Background: In accord with its policy of providing protection to high Congolese leaders, two officials from Luluabourg were flown to Port Francqui in a light U.N. aircraft on April 26 to elude ANC roadblocks set up in anticipation of their arrival. The officials asked for U.N. protection at the Hotel des Palmes in Port Francqui which the United Nations had taken over as a billet from the Bas Congo-Katanga railway. Friction between the ANC and the UNF had been exacerbated by the closing of the hotel bar to all ANC personnel and Congolese civilians. The ANC was further angered when the railroad flag was hung from a balcony, reportedly to dry, which they took to mean that the Belgians were in control of the hotel.

Incident: In the late afternoon of April 26, some 20 ANC troops came to the Hotel des Palmes to interview the Congolese officials in order to find out why they had sought protection from the United Nations rather than from the ANC. Receiving no satisfaction, the ANC the folowing morning began to disarm the scattered Ghanian troops in Port Francqui. Two British officers, commanding the Ghanian troops, were intercepted by the ANC as they were investigating the situation and three Swedish members of the local movement control unit were arrested at the hotel during the day. During the evening of April twenty-seventh, the Ghana Brigade in Luluabourg received a report of these events and sent two platoons and a reconnaissance detachment as a relief column to Port Francqui. Learning that the relief column engaged a roadblock south of Port Francqui at 8:00 A.M., April 28, the ANC in Port Francqui murdered a disputed number of Ghanian troops and officers. Only two bodies were recovered. Local investigations made it clear that the bodies of the others killed had been thrown into the river.

Casualties: In Port Francqui: 47 U.N. personnel killed, according to U.N. records. At the road block, one U.N.–Ghanian soldier killed, and three wounded. Two ANC soldiers killed. According to General Alexander, 120 Ghanians with their British officers were murdered. (See Major General H. T. Alexander, *African Tightrope: My Two Years as Nkrumah's Chief of Staff* [New York: Praeger, 1966], p. 66.)

8. THE EGGE PLAN: JUNE, 1961

Background: To implement the February 21, 1961 Security Council Resolution which called for the immediate withdrawal of Belgian and other foreign military personnel from the Congo, the U.N. Command requested Lt. Col. Bjørn Egge (Norway), a U.N. intelligence officer, to make a survey of the situation in Katanga. His study, which resulted in the so-called Egge Plan was completed on June 30, 1961, but it was never adopted by U.N. authorities, primarily because they were not interested in building a reliable gendarmerie which would be used to perpetuate Katanga's secession.

The Egge Plan: The Plan called for a phased withdrawal of prohibited foreign officers in Katanga, who were to be replaced by foreign officers recruited by the United Nations or qualified Congolese. Colonel Egge estimated that there were 512 foreigners of all ranks in the gendarmerie. To prevent disorder in the period of transition, Egge recommended that:

1. The Katangan forces should immediately designate a Congolese commander.

2. Fifty-two of the 512 foreigners who belonged to non-cadre personnel (i.e., officers and NCO's who were not integrated in command and similar positions with Katangan troops in the gendarmerie) should be removed immediately.

3. The remaining 460 non-Congolese cadres should be withdrawn according to a phased plan within 8 to 90 days. They should be replaced by U.N. recruited personnel. All U.N. recruited officers had to speak French and all officers and NCO's in direct contact with Katangan troops had to have a working knowledge of the dominant tribal language.

4. Simultaneously with the phasing-out of non-Congolese personnel in the gendarmerie, the Africanization of the gendarmerie should be implemented as quickly as possible.

9. ITALIAN AIRMEN KILLED BY ANC TROOPS AT KINDU: NOVEMBER 11, 1961

Background: During October, 1961, the Gizenga regime extended its military control from Orientale province into Kivu. Troops of the Twentieth ANC battalion of the Third Group (headquartered in Stanleyville), were stationed in the city of Kindu. U.N. forces in Kivu totalled slightly over 200 men stationed at the airfield. The total ANC strength approximated 1,000, divided between the airfield and the city of Kindu.

Incident: On November 11, a U.N. C–119 transport carrying two armored cars for the Malayan contingent arrived at the Kindu airfield. The thirteen Italian crew members left the field for the Malayan contingent's officers' mess in Kindu, about one-and-one-half miles away. Shortly after their arrival, the mess was surrounded by 260 ANC troops, some 60 of whom were from Stanleyville. The Italians were arrested on charges of being spies from Katanga, beaten and removed to the Kindu prison, where they were immediately shot, their bodies dismembered, and pieces of their bodies distributed to members of a crowd which had gathered. Parts of the bodies were thrown at non-Congolese in the crowd, and part of a hand was later thrown on the table of a U.N. civilian doctor. The bodies were never recovered.

Immediately after the arrest the Malayan battalion commander entered into negotiations with Colonel Pakassa for the release of the airmen and the removal of the besieging ANC troops from the airfield. Colonel Pakassa professed to have little control over his troops and asked General Lundula from Leopoldville to come to Kindu. On November 13, General Lundula sent two ANC officers, accompanied by two U.N. officers, to Kindu. Colonel Pakassa, however, refused to acknowledge the authority of the special Leopoldville mission, and on November 14 informed the U.N. officials that the Italian prisoners had escaped. That same day General Lundula and fourteen other officials flew to Kindu to join in the negotiations between Pakassa and the U.N. officials. General Lundula insisted that Pakassa meet all the U.N. demands and submit a report on the incident. On November, 15, Pakassa reported that he had no information on the "escape" of the thirteen men. ANC troops were finally withdrawn from the airfield, but no further action was taken.

Casualties: U.N. Italian contingent personnel, 13 killed; ANC, none.

APPENDIX I

Voluntary Financial Contributions to the U.N. Force

The following information on voluntary contributions to the Congo operation as of December 31, 1964, was compiled from U.N. financial reports. All twelve governments, in addition to the United States, were Western oriented and all but Austria, Ireland, Sweden, and Finland were allied militarily with Washington.

United States Contributions: 1960–1964

1960	$ 3,900,000
1961	15,305,596
1962	11,400,800
1963	1,768,479
1964	704,111
Total	$33,078,986

All Contributions: 1960–1964 (Only the U.S. contributed before 1963.)

		1963	1964	Total
1.	Australia	$ 92,000	$ 36,500	$ 128,500
2.	Austria	25,000	9,900	34,900
3.	Denmark	37,000	13,286	50,286
4.	Canada	173,000	90,000	263,000[1]
5.	Ireland	5,053	2,947	8,000
6.	Japan	81,927	33,425	115,352
7.	Netherlands	57,000	22,694	79,694
8.	New Zealand	22,916	9,002	31,918
9.	Norway	28,000	10,000	38,000
10.	Sweden	75,000	37,500	112,500
11.	Finland	18,635	8,244	26,879
12.	United Kingdom	410,000	175,000	585,000[1]
13.	United States	1,768,479	704,111	33,078,986[1,2]
	Total	$2,794,010	$1,152,609	$34,553,015

APPENDIX J

GOVERNMENTS MAKING NO PAYMENTS FOR THE U.N. FORCE

As of September 30, 1965, thirty-two U.N. member states had paid none of their assessed quota for the UNF. Of these, twelve—France and the Soviet bloc—have announced that they will not contribute. These figures are from the Report of the Ad Hoc Committee of Experts to Examine the Finances of the United Nations and the Specialized Agencies, *A/6289/Add. 1 (March 31, 1966), pages 39 and 40.*

States Announcing They Will Not Pay	Assessment
1. Albania	$ 43,602
2. Bulgaria	190,746
3. Byelorussian SSR	1,357,881
4. Cuba	260,259
5. Czechoslovakia	2,759,408
6. France	17,031,152
7. Hungary	995,024
8. Mongolia	17,215
9. Poland	2,466,010
10. Romania	641,015
11. Ukrainian SSR	5,185,697
12. USSR	39,223,085
Sub-Total:	$70,171,094

[1] Indicates countries providing initial airlift services amounting in total to $11,487,662 including the United States, $10,317,662; Canada, $650,000; and the United Kingdom, $520,000. These amounts were in addition to the total authorized for initial period.

[2] The total U.S. voluntary contribution, including the initial airlift of troops in 1960, which cost $10,317,662, was $43,396,648.

Other Nonpaying States   *Assessment*

13.	Burundi	$ 10,471
14.	Chile	224,847
15.	Dominican Republic	54,503
16.	Haiti	33,916
17.	Jordan	43,602
18.	Mauritania	17,215
19.	Mexico	786,193
20.	Nicaragua	33,916
21.	Panama	33,916
22.	Peru	89,184
23.	Portugal	201,673
24.	Rwanda	10,471
25.	Saudi Arabia	69,847
26.	South Africa	1,503,337
27.	Spain	985,159
28.	Syria	20,379
29.	Togo	25,325
30.	Uganda	10,471
31.	Uruguay	97,662
32.	Yemen	43,602
	Sub-Total:	$ 4,295,329

Total of All Nonpaying States: $74,466,423

Selected Bibliography

As of mid–1967, there was very little published secondary research on the United Nations peacekeeping effort in the Congo, and virtually no political analysis of the controversial operation. The present study has drawn almost exclusively from primary sources, including official U.N. records, government documents, and major U.S. and European newspapers. The documentary year-books of the Centre de Recherche et d'Information Socio-Politiques (CRISP) in Brussels have been especially helpful. Bibliographic sources were supplemented by extensive interviews in Europe, Asia, and Africa.

When the character of an entry in this selected bibliography is not evident from the title, a brief annotation has been added.

Alport, Lord. *The Sudden Assignment.* London: Hodder & Stoughton, 1965. The memoirs of the last High Commissioner to the Federation of Rhodesia and Nyasaland include a discussion of British and Federation policies toward Katanga secession.

Alexander, Major General H. T. *African Tightrope.* New York: Praeger, 1966. Ghana's Chief of Defense Staff from 1959 to 1961 deals at length with his experiences in the Congo and President Kwame Nkrumah's Congo policies.

Bell, M. J. V. *Army and Nation in Sub-Saharan Africa,* Adelphi Paper No. 21. London: Institute for Strategic Studies, 1965.

Bloomfield, Lincoln P. (ed.). *International Military Forces.* Boston: Little, Brown and Co., 1964. This symposium includes essays on the Congo by Brian E. Urquhart, Herbert Nicholas, Stanley Hoffman, Edward H. Bowman, and James E. Fanning.

Borri, Michel. *Nous ces affreux (dossier secret de l'ex-congo belge).* Paris: Editions Galic, 1962. A former French agent presents an informative and generally accurate account of the mercenaries in South Kasai and the French agents in Brazzaville.

Bowett, D. W. *United Nations Forces: A Legal Study.* New York: Praeger, 1964. A comprehensive summary of the legal problems of U.N. peacekeeping efforts, with emphasis on the Congo operation.

Boyd Andrew. *United Nations: Piety, Myth, and Truth.* 2d ed. revised. Baltimore: Penguin Books, 1964. This thoughtful political analysis of the United Nations contains an excellent essay on Rounds One and Two. (The author is a member of the editorial staff of *The Economist.*)

Brzezinski, Zbigniew (ed.). *Africa and the Communist World.* Stanford: Stanford University Press, 1963. An excellent review of recent Communist policies toward Africa, including the Congo.

Burns, Arthur Lee, and Nina Heathcote. *Peace-keeping by U.N. Forces: From Suez to the Congo.* New York: Praeger, 1963. A legal and political analysis focusing mainly on the Congo, through February, 1963.

Calder, Peter Ritchie. *Agony of the Congo.* London: Gollancz, 1961. The writer, who was in the Congo on a fact-finding mission for the World Health Organization, gives an account of the 1960 crisis.

Calvoccoressi, Peter. *World Order and New States.* New York: Praeger, 1962. Includes a chapter on U.N. peacekeeping with recommendations for enhancing the U.N. role.

Carter, Gwendolen M (ed.). *Five African States: Responses to Diversity.* Ithaca: Cornell University Press, 1963. One of the five essays deals with the Congo. The author presents a less than balanced view by attributing the separatist tendencies in Katanga and elsewhere in the Congo to an "exclusively white attitude."

Centre de Recherche et d'Information Socio-Politiques. *Congo: 1959 [1960, 1961, 1962, 1963, 1964].* Edited by J. Gérard-Libois and Benoit Verhaegen. Brussels: Les Dossiers du C.R.I.S.P., 1960–65.

Chomé, Jules. *Le Gouvernement congalais et l'O.N.U.* Brussels: Editions de Ramarques Congolaises, 1961. The author presents the views of the extreme left in Belgium.

Claude, Inis L., Jr. "The United Nations and the Use of Force," *International Conciliation,* No. 532 (March 1961), pp. 325–84. A review of the intentions of the drafters of the U.N. Charter on the use of force to maintain peace, and of the experience with U.N. forces.

Cleveland, Harlan. "The Future of the United States in the United Nations," *Annals of the American Academy,* Vol. 342 (July 1962), pp. 69–79. The issues of colonialism, nation-building, and peacekeeping are examined.

Cordier, Andrew, and Wilder Foote (eds.). *The Quest for Peace.* New York: Columbia University, 1965. The Dag Hammarskjold lectures on many aspects of U.N. activities, including a brief essay by Ralph J. Bunche on the Congo operation.

Cornevin, Robert. *Histoire du Congo (Leopoldville).* Paris: Berger-Levrault, 1963. A detailed and scholarly treatment of the Congo from the precolonial period until late 1963.

Dallin, Alexander. *The Soviet Union at the United Nations.* New York: Praeger, 1962. (Chapter 10 deals with the Congo.)

Davister, Pierre. *Katanga: enjeu du monde.* Brussels: Editions Europe-Afrique, 1960. A well-known Belgian journalist provides a largely objective eyewitness account of the events in Katanga.

Dinant, Georges. *L'O.N.U. face a la Crise congolaise.* Brussels: Editions Remarques Congolaises, 1961. A pro-Lumumba view of the Congo crisis and U.N. policies.

Dodd, Thomas J. "Congo: The Untold Story," *National Review*, Vol. 13 (August 28, 1962), pp. 136–44. The view of a U.S. senator sympathetic to Katanga.

Draper, S. I. A. D. "The Legal Limitations upon the Employment of Weapons by the United Nations Force in the Congo," *International and Comparative Law Quarterly*, Vol. 12 (April 1963), pp. 387–413.

Epstein, Howard M. (ed.). *Revolt in the Congo: 1960–64*. New York: Facts on File, Inc., 1961. A chronological record of events in the Congo drawn from newspaper dispatches.

Frank, Thomas M., and John Carey. "The Legal Aspects of the United Nations Action in the Congo." Working Paper for the Second Hammarskjold Forum, Association of the Bar of the City of New York, April 1962. Published in the Forum *Proceedings* (ed. Lyman M. Tondel), 1963. The Congo operation until September, 1962.

Ferkiss, Victor C. *Africa's Search for Identity*. New York: George Braziller, 1965. Discussion of attempts to reconcile traditional values and loyalties with modern economic and political demands. (One chapter is devoted to the Congo.)

Ganshof van der Meersch, W. J. *Fin de la souveraineté belge au Congo*. The Hague: Martinus Nijhoff, for Institut royal des relations internationales, 1963. Based on the report of the author who was sent to the Congo in May 1960 as Minister of General African Affairs. It contains detailed and valuable documentation on the armed forces, elections, and the negotiations which led to the formation of the Lumumba government.

Gérard-Libois, Jules. *Katanga Secession*. Madison: The University of Wisconsin Press, 1966. A thorough study of the secession of Katanga, based on many unpublished and confidential documents. Translation of original French edition published by Centre de Recherche et d'Information Socio-Politiques (Brussels), 1963.

Giles, Charles-André. *Kasa-vubu: au coeur du drame congolais*. Brussels: Editions Europe-Afrique, 1964. A flattering biography of Kasavubu.

Good, Robert C. "The Congo Crisis: A Study of Postcolonial Politics," in Laurence W. Martin (ed.), *Neutralism and Nonalignment*, pp. 34–63. New York: Praeger, 1962.

Gordon, King. *The United Nations in the Congo: A Quest for Peace*. New York: Carnegie Endowment for International Peace, 1962. The former chief Information Officer for the United Nations in the Congo gives an uncritical picture of events up to August, 1962.

Gullion, Edmund. "Crisis Management: Lessons from the Congo," *Crises and Concepts in International Affairs*, International Studies Association Proceedings (April, 1965), pp. 49–63. A positive appraisal of U.N. intervention by Washington's second ambassador to the Congo.

Halpern, Manfred. "The U.N. in the Congo," *Worldview*, Vol. 6, No. 10, (October 1963), pp. 4–8. This review essay is a positive appraisal of the U.N. effort.

Hempstone, Smith. *Rebels, Mercenaries, and Dividends: The Katanga Story*. New York: Praeger, 1962. A highly critical account of U.N. efforts to end Katanga secession.

Hoffman, Stanley. "In Search of a Thread: The UN in the Congo Labyrinth," *International Organization,* Vol. 16 (Spring 1962), pp. 331–61. The author contrasts the broad role assumed by Hammarskjold with the limitations of the United Nations.

Holmes, John. "The U.N. in the Congo," *International Journal,* Vol. 16 (Winter, 1960–61), pp. 1–16. The article analyzes the alienation of the more influential African states from the Secretary-General in the early Congo crisis.

Hoskyns, Catherine. *The Congo Since Independence: January 1960–December 1961.* London: Chatham House, Oxford University Press, 1965. A detailed political analysis of internal developments in the Congo, including U.N. activities.

Houart, Pierre. *La Pénétration communiste au Congo.* Brussels: Centre de documentation internationale, 1960. A commentary on the extent of Communist influence in the Congo during the period June–November, 1960.

Hovet, Thomas, Jr. *Africa in the United Nations.* Evanston: Northwestern University Press, 1963. An examination of the policies and tactics of African states at the United Nations.

———. *Bloc Politics in the United Nations.* Cambridge: Harvard University Press, 1960. A study on the formation of alliances at the United Nations, based on voting records.

Hymoff, Edward. *Stig Von Bayer, International Troubleshooter for Peace.* New York: James H. Heineman, 1965. A popular account of a Swedish U.N. officer in the Congo and Cyprus.

Institute for Defense Analyses. *National Armaments and International Force.* Report R–101. Washington: International Studies Division, Institute for Defense Analyses, July, 1963. Prepared for the Assistant Secretary for International Affairs, Department of Defense, this report includes an analysis of the Congo peacekeeping operation.

Institut Royal des Relations Internationales. "La Crise Congolaise, Janvier, 1959–15 Aout, 1960," *Chronique de Politique Etrangère* (Bruxelles), XIII, Nos. 4 to 6, July–Nov., 1960.

———. "Evolution de la Crise Congolaise, de Septembre, 1960 à Avril, 1961," *Chronique de Politique Etrangère* (Bruxelles), XIV, Nos. 5 to 6, Sept.–Nov., 1961.

———. "L'O.N.U. et le Congo, Avril 1961 à Octobre 1962," *Chronique de Politique Etrangère* (Bruxelles), XV, Nos. 4 to 6, Juillet–Novembre, 1962. These three special issues of the Chronique de Politique Etrangère contain valuable documents on the developments in the Congo and related events in Brussels and at the United Nations.

Jacobson, Harold K. "ONUC's Civilian Operations: State-Preserving and State-Building," *World Politics,* XVII (October, 1964), 75–107. An analysis of U.N. civilian activities in the Congo in their political context.

Janssens, Emile. *J'étais le général Janssens.* Brussels: Charles Dessart, 1961. the memoirs of the last Belgian commander of the *Force publique.*

Kanza, Thomas. *Congo 196–?* Brussels: Editions Remarques Congolaises, 1962. A Congolese intellectual criticizes Western policies and defends Lumumba as the authentic nationalist leader of the Congo.

Kitchen, Helen (ed.). *Congo Story.* New York: Walker and Co., 1967. Eighteen essays by scholars and statesmen, written from 1960 to 1966.

Kraft, Joseph. "The Untold Story of the U.N.'s Congo Army," *Harpers,* Vol. 221 (Nov., 1960), pp. 75–84. The article deals with the buildup of the UNF in July, 1960.

Lash, Joseph P. *Dag Hammarskjold: Custodian of the Brushfire Peace.* New York: Doubleday & Co., 1961. A thoughtful biography.

————. "Dag Hammarskjold's Conception of his Office," *International Organization,* Vol. 16, No. 3 (Summer, 1962), pp. 542–66.

Lawson, Richard. *Strange Soldiering.* London: Hodder & Stoughton, 1963. The experiences of a British officer who served with the Nigerian troops in the UNF.

Lefever, Ernest W. *Crisis in the Congo: a U.N. Force in Action.* Washington: The Brookings Institution, 1965. A study of the four-year operation, with emphasis on the U.S. role.

Lefever, Ernest W. and Wynfred, Joshua. *United Nations Peacekeeping in the Congo: 1960–1964: An Analysis of Political, Executive and Military Control.* Washington: Brookings Institution, 1966. 3 Volumes. A report prepared for the U.S. Arms Control and Disarmament Agency.

Legum, Colin. *Congo Disaster.* Baltimore: Penguin Books, 1961. A journalist's account of the first six months of Congolese independence.

Lemarchand, René. "The Limits of Self-Determination: The Case of the Katanga Secession," *The American Political Science Review,* Vol. 56 (1962), pp. 404–16.

————. *Political Awakening in the Congo.* Berkeley: University of California Press, 1964. An analysis of the factors underlying the Congo's political development

London, Kurt. *New Nations in a Divided World.* New York: Praeger, 1963. A collection of essays dealing with Communist policies towards the emerging nations of Africa and Asia.

Luard, Evan. *Peace and Opinion.* London: Oxford University Press, 1962. The author explores the potentialities of U.N. peacekeeping in general and U.N. military forces in particular.

Lumumba, Patrice. *Congo My Country.* London: Pall Mall Press, 1962. Lumumba's own analysis of the situation in the Congo, written in 1956–57.

McKay, Vernon (ed). *African Diplomacy: Studies in the Determinants of Foreign Policy.* New York: Praeger, 1966. One chapter by William J. Foltz deals with "military influences."

Merrian, Alan P. *Congo: Background of Conflict.* Evanston: Northwestern University Press, 1961. A study of Congolese attitudes and reactions to events before and during the first few months of independence.

Miller, Richard I. *Dag Hammarskjold and Crisis Diplomacy.* New York: Oceana Publications, 1961. Includes a chapter on Hammarskjold's policies in the Congo crisis.

Monheim, Francis. *Mobutu, l'homme seul.* Brussels: Editions Actuelles, 1962. A biography of General Mobutu by a personal friend; focuses on the 1960–61 period.

Mosely, Philip E. "Soviet Policy in the Developing Countries," *Foreign Affairs,* Vol. 43 (October, 1964), pp. 87–98. The writer applies the Soviet concept of a "national democracy" to Castro's Cuba and Lumumba's Congo.

Murray, G. S. "United Nations Peacekeeping and Problems of International Control," *International Journal,* Vol. 18 (Autumn, 1963), pp. 442–57. A survey of U.N. peacekeeping activities, focusing on the question of political control.

Nathanson, Nathaniel L. "Constitutional Crisis at the United Nations: The Price of Peacekeeping," *The University of Chicago Law Review,* Vol. 33, No. 2 (Winter, 1966), pp. 249–315. An analysis of peacekeeping operations, including the Congo effort.

Nehru and Africa—Extracts from Jawaharlal Nehru's Speeches on Africa, 1946–1963. New Delhi: Indian Council for Africa, 1964.

Nicholas, Herbert. "U.N. Peace Forces and the Changing Globe: The Lessons of Suez and Congo," *International Organization,* Vol. 17 (Spring, 1963), pp. 321–37.

O'Brien, Conor Cruise. *To Katanga and Back.* New York: Simon and Schuster, 1962. O'Brien's spirited account of his service as U.N. Representative in Katanga from May to December, 1961.

Okumu, Washington. *Lumumba's Congo: Roots of Conflict.* New York: Obolensky, 1963. A first-hand account by a Kenyan of the July–August, 1960 period. He suggests that the conflict between Hammarskjold and Lumumba was caused as much by Hammarskjold's failure to understand African politics as by Lumumba's erratic behavior.

Rikhye, I. J. *Preparation and Training of United Nations Peacekeeping Forces.* Adelphi Paper No. 9. London: Institute for Strategic Studies, 1964. The military adviser to the Secretary-General bases his comments primarily on the Congo experience in a paper prepared for an unofficial conference on U.N. Security Forces held in Oslo, February, 1964.

Roberts, John. *My Congo Adventure.* London: Jarrold, 1963. The experiences of a British mercenary in the Congo.

Rosner, Gabriella. *The United Nations Emergency Force.* New York: Columbia University Press, 1963. The study places UNEF in an historical perspective and covers its legal, political, and operational characteristics.

Russell, Ruth B. *United Nations Experience with Military Forces: Political and Legal Aspects.* Washington: Brookings Institution, 1964. Forty pages of this comprehensive political and legal analysis and interpretation are devoted to the Congo effort.

Schacter, Oscar. "Dag Hamarskjold and the Relation of Law to Politics," *The American Journal of International Law,* Vol. 56, Jan., 1962, pp. 1–8. A positive appraisal of Dag Hammarskjold's approach to international law and politics by the director of the U.N. General Legal Division.

―――. "Preventing the Internationalization of Internal Conflict: A Legal Analysis of the U.N. Congo Experience," *Proceedings of the American Society of International Law,* 1963.

Schuyler, Philippa. *Who Killed the Congo?* New York: Devin Adair, 1962. Critical of U.S. and U.N. policies for intensifying the Congo crisis, Miss

Schuyler emphasizes the Congo's need for Belgian administrators and experts.

Smith, Raymond. *The Fighting Irish in the Congo.* Dublin: Lilmac, 1962.

Stethem, Col. H. W. C. "Signal Squadron in the Congo," *Canadian Army Journal,* Vol. 17 (April, 1963), pp. 110–20.

Stoessinger, John G. *Financing the United Nations System.* Washington: Brookings Institution, 1964. Discusses the financing of the Congo and other peacekeeping operations.

Tondel, Lyman M., Jr. (ed.). *The Legal Aspects of the United Nations Action in the Congo.* Dobbs Ferry, N.Y.: Oceana Publications, 1963. The volume contains working papers by Thomas M. Frank and John Carey and comments by Frederick H. Boland, Ernest A. Gross, and Oscar Schachter.

Trinquier, Roger and others. *Notre Guerre au Katanga.* Paris: Editions de la pensée moderne, 1963. An eyewitness account of the fighting in Katanga written by French mercenaries. The book includes Col. Trinquier's brief experience with the Tshombe regime.

United Nations. *The United Nations and the Congo: Some Salient Facts,* 1963. Official U.N. "White Book" on the Congo operation.

U.S. Army. *Area Handbook for the Republic of the Congo (Leopoldville).* Special Operations Research Officer, American University. Washington: U.S. Government Printing Office, 1962.

U.S. Congress, House of Representatives, Foreign Affairs Committee, Africa Subcommittee. *Immediate and Future Problems in the Congo.* Hearing 88th Cong., 1st Sess., 1963.

U.S. Congress, House of Representatives, Foreign Affairs Committee. *U.N. Operations in the Congo.* Hearings. 87 Cong., 1st Sess., 1961.

U.S. Congress, House of Representatives, Foreign Affairs Committee. *United Nations Use of Peacekeeping Forces in the Middle East, the Congo and Cyprus.* 89th Cong., 2d Sess., 1966.

U.S. Department of State. *U.S. Participation in the U.N.* Reports by the President to the Congress, for the years 1960, 1961, 1962, 1963, and 1964.

Valahu, Mugur. *The Katanga Circus.* A Detailed Account of Three U.N. Wars. New York: Robert Speller & Sons 1964. Sympathetic to Katanga, the author questions the purpose and validity of the U.N. actions there.

Van Bilson, A. A. J. "Some Aspects of the Congo Problem," *International Affairs,* Vol. 38 (Jan., 1962), pp. 41–52. A discussion of the political events in the Congo that led to U.N. intervention.

Van den Haag, Ernest. "The Lesson of the Congo," *National Review,* Vol. 16 (September 8, 1964), pp. 771–73, 785. A negative view of the U.N. operation.

Van Langenhove, Fernand. *Le Role proéminent du Secretaire General dans l'Operations des Nations Unies au Congo.* Brussels: Institut Royal des Relations Internationales, 1964. A Belgian diplomat and scholar analyzes the enlarged role played by the Secretary-General in the Congo.

von Horn, Major General Carl. *Soldiering for Peace.* New York: David McKay Co., Inc., 1967. In this personal account of his service with the United Nations, von Horn devotes eight chapters, pages 140–252, to the Congo where he served as Force Commander from August to December, 1960.

Wainhouse, David W. *et al. International Peace Observation: A History and Forecast.* Baltimore: Johns Hopkins Press, 1966. This book is based upon a report prepared by the Washington Center of Foreign Policy Research of the Johns Hopkins University for the U.S. Arms Control and Disarmament Agency.

Welensky, Sir Roy. *Welensky's 4000 Days.* London: Collins, 1964. The former Prime Minister of the Federation of Rhodesia and Nyasaland discusses British and Rhodesian policies toward Katanga and the U.N. Congo effort.

Wigny, Pierre. "Belgium and the Congo," *International Affairs,* Vol. 37 (July, 1961). The former Belgian Minister of Foreign Affairs defends Belgian policies towards the Congo before and after Independence Day.

Young, Crawford. *Politics in the Congo.* Princeton: Princeton University Press, 1965. A political analysis of decolonization during the first four years of independence against the backdrop of colonial policies.

Index

Adoula, Cyrille, Prime Minister, Republic of the Congo: designated and endorsed as Prime Minister, 52; request for aid against Gizenga, 50–51; bilateral aid, 88; and Greene Plan, 70; U.S. view of, 82; and Soviet Union, 101–02 *passim;* position of Afro-Asian states, 101

Advisory Committee. *See* Congo Advisory Committee

Afro-Asian states: militants, 159–61 *passim;* moderates, 159–61 *passim;* neutralists, 160; Soviet policy, 105, 165; U.S. policy, 81; and U.N. authority in Congo, 161; impact on U.N. Mission, 168–71; position and role of, 157–71; troops, 157–59; man-month contributions, 158; troop withdrawal, 165; troop loyalty, 168, financial contributions, 169; and financing of the operation, 168–69; interests and contribution, 169–71; involvement in internal Congolese affairs, 169; and Katanga secession, 161, 166–68; attempt at Kasavubu-Lumumba reconciliation, 162–63

Airlift. *See* Logistical support, airlift and sealift

Alexander, Maj. Gen. H. T. (U.K.), Commander Ghanian contingent: ANC disarmament, 36n, 39, 65, 66n, 135n, 162n, 174–75, 195n

Alexander, Capt. William (USN), 89n

Alport, Lord, British High Commissioner to Federation of Rhodesia and Nyasaland, 126n, 127n

"American Plan," 88, 116

ANC. *See Armée Nationale Congolaise*

Argentina, 150

Armée Nationale Congolaise (ANC): indiscipline, 9, 64, 67; Africanization, 9; reorganization and training, 68–70; disarmament, 66–68, 71, 175; instabil-

ity and ineffectiveness, 9, 64, 214; -UNF relationship, 64–68, 195; Bukavu incident, 136, 231; Banana incident, 232–33; Kitona incident, 232–33; Matadi incident, 232–33; Belgian assistance, 145–46; North Katanga intrusion, 231–32; and February 21, 1961 Resolution, 21

Austria, 150

Ball, George W., U.S. Undersecretary of State, 82

Banana, naval facility near Kitona, 232–33

"Belgian factor," 138–40 *passim,* 148

Belgian Technical Mission (*Mistebel*), 135

Belgium: hopes for Congo, 131; premature granting of Congo independence, 6, 132–33; *Force Publique* mutiny, 7–8; troops and other personnel, withdrawal, 20, 139, 140; mercenaries from, 51, 141; Dayal's views toward, 138–39; troops in Katanga, 8; initial position toward Katanga, 133–35; support of Kasavubu-Mobutu regime, 136–37; relations with Leopoldville, 135–37; integration of Katanga, 144–45; and Rumpunch, 142; and Round Two, 144; and Round Three, 144; training of ANC, 145–46; bilateral aid, 146; Greene Plan, 69, 145; interests in Congo, 131; objectives and policy, 131–33 *passim,* 137; Round Table Conference (January, 1960), 132; *ultras,* 148; U.N. co-operation, 133–34; nonpayment, 146–47; impact on peacekeeping mission, 146–48; impact of mission on, 216; and Hammarskjold, 137–40; lack of decisive action, 219; Matadi intervention, 230; claims settlement, 147

Designed by Gerard A. Valerio
Composed in Baskerville by Monotype Composition Company
Printed on Perkins & Squier, RRR, offset by Universal Lithographers, Inc.
Bound by Maple Press, Inc. in GSB, S/535, #150, Cadet Blue